KROS

Englisch für Polizeibeamte

Englisch
für Polizeibeamte

Ein Lehrbuch

von

Marie-Luise Kros

Polizeischulrektorin

4., überarbeitete Auflage, 1990

RICHARD BOORBERG VERLAG STUTTGART · MÜNCHEN · HANNOVER

CIP-Titelaufnahme der Deutschen Bibliothek

Kros, Marie-Luise:

Englisch für Polizeibeamte : ein Lehrbuch / von Marie-Luise Kros. –
4., überarb. Aufl. – Stuttgart ; München ; Hannover :
Boorberg, 1990
   ISBN 3-415-01464-9

Satz und Druck: C. Maurer Druck, 7340 Geislingen (Steige)

Verarbeitung: Dollinger GmbH, Metzingen

© Richard Boorberg Verlag GmbH & Co, Stuttgart · München · Hannover, 1990

Vorwort

Immer bessere und schnellere Verkehrsmittel lassen die Entfernungen in der Welt schrumpfen und leichter überbrücken. So sprechen wir heute von unserem Land als einem typischen internationalen Durchreiseland. Dadurch trifft der Polizeibeamte immer häufiger in wechselnden Situationen wie z. B. Auskunft erteilen, Helfen, Einschreiten, auf englischsprechende Ausländer.

Da alle auszubildenden Polizeibeamten in den letzten Jahren über ein verbessertes Grundwissen in der englischen Sprache verfügen, kann heute auf ein Lehrbuch im klassischen Sinn in der Berufsausbildung der Polizei verzichtet werden. Dieses Buch erfüllt in seinen Dialogen und Sachtexten die Forderungen des Berufs.

Es soll nicht nur dem Wunsch entgegenkommen, Situationen polizeilichen Einschreitens im englischsprachigen Dialog darzustellen, sondern, wie dies im 2. Teil des Buches geschieht, im Sinne eines „Refresher-Course" systematisch Sprachstrukturen zu wiederholen und zu üben.

Die in jeder Fremdsprache notwendigen Strukturübungen sind so gewählt, daß sie anhand der vorgegebenen Texte durchgeführt werden.

Für die Arbeit mit dem Lehrbuch und für das Verständnis der Texte sind Vorkenntnisse erforderlich. Bei der Erstellung der Texte und Übungsbeispiele wurde auf größte Sorgfalt in bezug auf Berufsbezogenheit geachtet. So kann das vorliegende Buch sicherlich im Sinne eines typenspezifischen Unterrichts im Sprachunterricht Verwendung finden.

Durch die Verschiedenartigkeit der dargestellten Dialoge wird – über das „Englisch für Polizeibeamte" hinaus – vom Wortschatz und von den Sprachstrukturen her ein „Everyday-Spoken-English" vermittelt.

Part 1: Dialogues

beinhaltet eine Zusammenstellung von Situationen, denen ein Polizeibeamter in Ausübung seines Dienstes begegnen und die er nur mit der Fremdsprache Englisch bewältigen kann. Die Texte sind nach Themenkreisen zusammengefaßt.

Die „Exercises" sind nicht als methodische Aufbereitung des Textes anzusehen. Sie mögen gegebenenfalls als Anregung für unterrichtliche Übungen gelten. Denjenigen, die bei der Beschäftigung mit den Lektionen auf sich selbst gestellt sind und es nicht bloß beim Lesen bewenden lassen möchten, bieten sie sich als eine unterstützende Hilfe an.

Anhand der englischen Fragen kann der Leser sein Textverständnis überprüfen. Der zweite, meist deutsche Teil der Übungen, zielt auf die aktive Beherrschung von Sprachwendungen ab. Es handelt sich also hier weniger um Übersetzungsübungen als vielmehr darum, die im Text enthaltenen Wendungen zu gebrauchen und einzuüben.

Part 2: Useful Structures

bietet Übungen mit sich steigerndem Schwierigkeitsgrad an. Die Strukturen treten jeweils zunächst in einem Kontext auf und können dann anhand mehrerer Beispiele geübt werden, so daß sie sich verfestigen und einprägen.

Die Strukturübungen bauen auf Grammatikkenntnissen auf. Die Übungen zur Anwendung der grammatischen Zeiten setzen z. B. Kenntnisse darüber voraus, wie die Zeiten gebildet werden. Sollten für den Lernenden Schwierigkeiten bei den Strukturübungen auftauchen, so empfiehlt es sich, die entsprechenden Grammatikkapitel nachzuarbeiten.

Reading Texts

bietet kurze Lesetexte aus englischen Zeitschriften an. Die Inhalte weisen Bekanntes auf. Doch wird durch ihre Auswahl auf typisch Englisches hingewiesen. Die Texte geben Anregungen zu lebhaften Diskussionen und zur eingehenden Beschäftigung mit den in England vorhandenen Formen des Polizeiwesens.

Vocabulary

enthält zwar nicht das vollständige Vokabular jeder Lektion, bietet aber die für die Situation des jeweiligen Textes typischen Vokabeln.

Januar 1990   Marie-Luise Kros

Inhaltsverzeichnis

Seite

Vorwort 5

PART 1: DIALOGUES

I. Asking Directions 11
  1. Asking the Way (1) 11
  2. Asking the Way (2) 11
  3. Asking the Way (3) 12
  4. Asking the Way (4) 13
  5. Asking the Way (5) 14
  6. The Detour 15
  7. The Lost Motorist 16
  8. The Long Taxi Ride 18

II. Traffic Incidents 20
  1. The Witness 20
  2. A Breakdown (1) 21
  3. A Breakdown (2) 22
  4. The Lady Driver 23
  5. The Low Bridge 25
  6. An Accident (1) 27
  7. An Accident (2) 28
  8. An Accident (3) 29
  9. A Fatal Accident 30
 10. No Parking 31
 11. Traffic Check 32
 12. The Lorry that Stopped 33
 13. The Noisy Motorist 34
 14. The Empty Caravan 35

III. Crime 36
  1. The Robbed Woman 36
  2. Arresting a Thief 37
  3. The Burglary (1) 38
  4. The Burglary (2) 40
  5. The Burglary (3) 41
  6. The Stolen Car 43
  7. The Shoplifter 44
  8. The Letter Bomb 46
  9. The Kidnapped Boy (1) 48
 10. The Kidnapped Boy (2) 49
 11. The Water Inspector 51

12. The Au Pair Girl 52
13. The Football Fan 54
14. The Robbery (1) 55
15. The Robbery (2) 57
16. The Robbery (3) 59
17. The Drug Addict 61
18. The Bank Raid 62

IV. Asking for Help 64
  1. The Lost Child 64
  2. The Sick Man 64
  3. The Lost Hotel 65
  4. The World Tour 66
  5. The Cheap Theatre Tickets 68
  6. The Prowler 69
  7. The Spilt Beer 70
  8. The Wrong Room 72
  9. The Attempted Suicide 73
10. The Fire 74

PART 2: USEFUL STRUCTURES

  1. The Serious Crime *Indefinite Article: a – an; Irregular Plural* 77
  2. The New Car *s-Genitive – of-Genitive* 78
  3. A Pleasant Prospect *Personal Pronouns* 79
  4. The Observation *3rd Person Singular* 80
  5. The Injured Burglar (1) *Simple Present – Present Continuous* 81
  6. The Injured Burglar (2) *Simple Past – Past Continuous* 82
  7. The Fast Frenchman *"ago" (Interrogative and Negative Forms)* 83
  8. The Worried Man *Present Tense "to do" (Interrogative and Negative Forms)* . . . 84
  9. The Broken Lock *Past Tense "to do" (Interrogative and Negative Forms)* 85
10. Finding a Needle in a Haystack *Short Answers* 86
11. The Crafty Fox (1) *Short Answers* 88
12. The Crafty Fox (2) *Future* 89
13. Lost *Modes of expressing the Future* 91
14. Peace and Quiet *Future* 92
15. The Bare Truth *Question Tags* 94
16. More about a Piano *Comparison of Adjectives* 95
17. The Harder they Fall *not so . . . as, as . . . as* 97
18. The Naked Man *as well, also, too* 98
19. The Kind Lady *Reflexive Pronouns: myself, yourself, etc.* 99
20. The Caller *Conjunctions* 100
21. The Little Man *Adjectives and Prepositions* 101
22. The Car Chase *Substitution Exercises* 102
23. The Out-of-Date Burglar *Verbs and Prepositions* 103
24. The Pink Handbag *Past Tense – Past Perfect* 104
25. The Late Detective *Past Perfect Continuous* 106
26. If *If-clauses* 107

27. The Threat *Passive Voice: Present Tense* 109
28. The Antique Ring *Passive Voice: Present Perfect, Future* 110
29. The Burglary *some – any* 111
30. The Electric Drill *Gerund* 112
31. The Secondhand Car *Gerund* 113
32. The Crook *Polite Questions* 114
33. The Ladder *Questions beginning with "who", "what", "which", "where"* 115
34. The Coat *Relative Pronouns* 116
35. The Married Man (1) *Direct Speech – Indirect Speech* 117
36. The Married Man (2) *Direct Speech – Indirect Speech* 118
37. The Swindler *Direct Speech – Indirect Speech* 119
38. Decisions, Decisions! *Adjective/Adverb* 120

PART 3:   READING TEXTS

 1. Operational Police Structures 123
 2. The Role of the Chief Constable 124
 3. Basic Police Objectives 124
 4. Foot-Patrols 125
 5. Motor Cycles and Scooters 126
 6. Pedal Cycles 127
 7. Motor Cars and Police Vans 127
 8. Joan's the Village Bobby 128
 9. Social Violence 130
10. Police Developments 131
11. Police and Democracy 132
12. Traffic Policing and Self-Control 132

PART 4:   VOCABULARY

Dialogues 135
Useful Structures 145
Reading Texts 153

PART 1

DIALOGUES

I. Asking Directions

1. ASKING THE WAY (1)

A policeman is standing on the corner of a busy street. A man walks up to him and speaks to him in English.

Foreigner: Excuse me, officer, can you tell me the way to the railway station?

Policeman: I beg your pardon. Please, could you speak a bit slower?

Foreigner: Can you tell me the way to the railway station, please?

Policeman: Yes, of course. Go down this street to that bridge. You can see it from here. Can you see it?

Foreigner: Yes. I can see it. You mean that railway bridge?

Policeman: Turn left after you have passed that bridge. Go straight ahead till you come to the traffic lights.

Foreigner: How far are they from the bridge?

Policeman: About 150 metres, I think. Turn right at the traffic lights, and you will find the station on your left, just opposite the post-office.

Foreigner: Thank you very much, officer.

Policeman: You're welcome.

Exercises

1. Answer the following questions:
a) Where did the man want to go?
b) Where did he have to go first?
c) Which direction did he have to take after he had passed the bridge?
d) How far are the traffic lights from the bridge?
e) What is opposite the railway station?

2. Übertragen Sie die folgenden Sätze anhand des vorhergehenden Textes ins Englische:
a) Können Sie mir den Weg zum Bahnhof angeben (sagen)?
b) Könnten Sie bitte etwas langsamer sprechen?
c) Gehen Sie diese Straße hinunter!
d) Biegen Sie hinter der Brücke links ab!
e) Biegen Sie an der Verkehrsampel rechts ab!
f) Der Bahnhof ist direkt dem Postamt gegenüber.

2. ASKING THE WAY (2)

A policeman is standing on the pavement of a main road. A British car stops beside him, and the driver speaks to him in English.

Foreigner: Please, can you tell me how I can get to Düsseldorf?

Constable: Would you speak more slowly, please? Where do you want to go?

Foreigner: How can I get to Düsseldorf, constable?

Constable: Ah, to Düsseldorf. Yes, of course. Stay on this road, drive past the square on your right, and take the second turning on your left.

Foreigner: Second turning on the left, you said?

Constable: That's right. Go straight ahead for about 150 metres, and turn right. Follow the tram-lines. Drive on until you come to the traffic lights at a crossing. At that crossing you will see the first blue road sign for the Autobahn to Düsseldorf.

11

Foreigner: I think it's difficult to find the way. Here is a piece of paper and a pen. Would you be so kind as to make a sketch, please?

Constable: Yes, of course. Square on your right – second turning on the left – after 150 metres turn right – follow the tram-lines – traffic lights at a crossing and the blue road sign for the Autobahn to Düsseldorf.

Foreigner: Now it's easier to find the way. Thank you very much indeed.

Constable: Don't mention it. Good-bye, sir.

Exercises

1. Answer the following questions:
a) Where did the foreigner want to get to?
b) Which turning was it where the driver had to leave the road?
c) What kind of road sign was it the policeman directed the foreigner to?
d) What did the driver hand the policeman?
e) Why did he do this?

2. Übertragen Sie ins Englische:
a) Bitte, können Sie mir sagen, wie ich nach Düsseldorf komme?
b) Würden Sie bitte langsamer sprechen!
c) Bleiben Sie auf dieser Straße!
d) Fahren Sie geradeaus!
e) Fahren Sie weiter, bis Sie zu einer Kreuzung mit Verkehrsampeln kommen!
f) Es ist schwierig, den Weg zu finden.

3. ASKING THE WAY (3)

A policeman is standing outside the Town Hall. A man walks up to him and speaks to him in English.

Man: Good evening, officer, can you tell me the way to the theatre, please?

Policeman: Do you want to walk there?

Man: No, I've got my car with me.

Policeman: Oh yes, I see. Your car is facing in the right direction. The theatre is in Schillerstraße.

Man: Is it far?

Policeman: No, but it's difficult to get there by car because you are not allowed to turn left along Königsallee.

Man: That's this dual-carriageway that we're on now, isn't it?

Policeman: That's right. To get to the theatre, you drive along this street and take the second turning on the right, Christstraße.

Man: Second turning on the right?

Policeman: Yes. Then you take the first turning on the left – that's called Kant-straße. At the end of that street, you turn left.

Man: At the end, I turn left.

Policeman: That's it. You can't mistake that turning, because you will have come to the river.

Man: That's clear enough.

Policeman: You drive alongside the river, over the junction with this street – look, you can see the junction – it's the second set of traffic lights along Königsallee. The first set of lights is at Christstraße, where you turn right. The second set of lights is at Herderstraße, where you go across by the river.

Man: Yes, I see.

Policeman: After you have crossed this street, Schillerstraße is the first turning on your left. It's a one-way street and the theatre is on your left.

Man: Many thanks. Will I be able to park my car outside the theatre?

Policeman: You may be lucky, there may be a space at a parking meter. If there isn't, there is a multi-storey car park further along Schillerstraße on the left.

Man: That's fine. I can drop my wife and her mother at the theatre and then put the car in the car park.

Policeman: That's a good idea, the car will be safer in the car park than in the street.

Man: Many thanks for your help. Good-bye.

Exercises

1. Give directions to a motorist who wants to go from the Town Hall to
a) the theatre,
b) Kantstraße,
c) Schillerstraße.

2. Übertragen Sie ins Englische:
a) Möchten Sie zu Fuß gehen?
b) Ihr Auto hat die richtige Fahrt-richtung.
c) Sie fahren diese Straße entlang und nehmen die zweite Kreuzung rechts, Christstraße.
d) Am Ende der Straße biegen Sie links ab.
e) Es ist eine Einbahnstraße.
f) Dort könnte eine Parklücke an einer Parkuhr sein.
g) Da ist eine Hochgarage etwas weiter in der Schillerstraße.

4. ASKING THE WAY (4)

As a policeman is walking past the Town Hall, he is stopped by a man carrying a large suitcase.

Man: Excuse me, officer, which is the quickest way to the Park Hotel?

Policeman: It's some distance from here. It's on the south bank of the river, about three kilometres outside the town.

Man: Oh dear, it sounds a long way to walk.

Policeman: I think it's too far to carry a heavy suitcase. If I were you, I would go by bus.

Man: That's a good idea. Can you tell me what bus to catch?

Policeman: The only bus that goes to the hotel is the number seven.

Man: Where do I catch it?

Policeman: The nearest number seven bus stop is outside the railway station.

Man: Is that far?

Policeman: It's about a ten-minute walk. If you look along this street, you can see two sets of traffic lights. The railway station is a little way to the right at the first set of lights.

Man: Can I catch a bus to the station?

Policeman: Certainly. If you catch a number nine or eleven from the bus stop here, you can change buses at the railway station.

Man: So, I catch a nine or eleven at this stop and I change onto a number seven at the station. Is that right?

Policeman: That's right.

Man: Do I have to cross the road at the station?

Policeman: No. The bus you want goes from the bus stop on the same side of the road as the railway station.

Man: Fine. One last thing. Can you tell me what I have to ask for on the second bus?

Policeman: You have to get off the number seven bus at Gudrunstraße. Ask the conductor for Gudrunstraße and he will tell you when you get there.

Man: Thank you very much, you've been very helpful.

Policeman: That's all right.

Exercises

1 You are standing outside the Town Hall. A tourist asks you some questions. Answer his questions:
a) Where is the Park Hotel?
b) How many buses go to the hotel?
c) How do I get to the railway station on foot?
d) How can I get to the railway station by bus?
e) Where do I have to get off the number seven bus?
f) How long will it take me to walk to the railway station?

2. Übertragen Sie ins Englische:
a) Es ist eine ganz schöne (einige) Entfernung von hier aus.
b) An Ihrer Stelle würde ich mit dem Bus fahren.
c) Der einzige Bus, der zu dem Hotel fährt, ist die Linie 7.
d) Wenn Sie den Bus Nummer 9 oder 11 von der Haltestelle hier nehmen, können Sie am Bahnhof umsteigen.
e) Sie müssen aus dem Bus Nummer 7 an der Gudrunstraße aussteigen.
f) Fragen Sie den Schaffner, und er wird Ihnen Bescheid sagen, wenn Sie dort ankommen.

5. ASKING THE WAY (5)

A policeman is standing in the main square of a town. He sees two women studying a map a few yards away. One of the women walks towards him with the map in her hand. She speaks to him.

Woman: Good afternoon, officer, do you speak English?
Policeman: Yes, madam.
Woman: Oh good. Perhaps, you can help me. My friend and I want to go to this town.

She holds the map so that the policeman can see it, then she points to a town.

Woman: Is it far?
Policeman: No, it isn't far, it's the next town along the River Ruhr.
Woman: That's fine. How do we get there, please?
Policeman: Do you have a car?
Woman: No, we're on foot.
Policeman: Well, there are several ways you can go. It's too far to walk.
Woman: It doesn't look very far. It's only about an inch on this map.
Policeman: Yes, but that inch represents three miles.
Woman: Then it certainly is too far.
Policeman: You can go by bus, tram or train. Or, of course, you can take a taxi.
Woman: No, we can't afford a taxi. Which is the quickest of the other ways?
Policeman: The train is the quickest but the trains only run every hour and you have just missed one. The tram is the next quickest.
Woman: Does the tram take very long?
Policeman: No, and the service is very good. Where do you want to go exactly?
Woman: We're going to the opera. We have to be there by seven o'clock.
Policeman: You have plenty of time. If I were you, I would go by bus. The bus stops right outside the opera house. It's a long walk from the tram stop to the opera house.
Woman: That's a good idea. Where do we catch the bus?
Policeman: On the other side of the square. Look, you can see the bus stop near the statue.
Woman: Yes, I can see it. What number bus do we catch?

Policeman: There are two buses that go there. Both stop at the opera house. The numbers are forty-five and seventy-eight. The seventy-eight is the most direct, but there is not much difference between the two routes. Take whichever bus comes first.

Woman: I'm very grateful for your help.

Policeman: It's a pleasure. I hope you enjoy the opera.

Woman: I'm sure we will. Good-bye.

Policeman: Good-bye.

Exercises

1. Answer the following questions:

a) What was the woman carrying in her hand?

b) How far is the next town along the River Ruhr?

c) How often do the trains run there?

d) Which is the quickest method to travel – the train, the bus or the tram?

e) Which is the slowest?

f) Why did the policeman suggest that the women should go by bus?

g) Where can the women catch the bus?

h) How many bus routes go to the opera house?

i) Which bus route is the most direct?

2. Übertragen Sie ins Englische:

a) Haben Sie ein Auto?

b) Es gibt verschiedene Wege, dorthin zu kommen.

c) Es ist zu weit, um zu Fuß dorthin zu gehen.

d) Sie können mit dem Zug, mit der Straßenbahn oder mit dem Bus fahren.

e) Die (Verkehrs-) Verbindung ist gut.

f) An Ihrer Stelle würde ich mit dem Bus fahren.

g) Beide Busse halten am Opernhaus.

6. THE DETOUR

The crew of a police car see a British car coming towards them. They signal it to stop and one of the policemen gets out to speak to the driver.

Driver: I wasn't going very fast!

Policeman: That's not why I stopped you. You should not be on this road.

Driver: Why, what's the matter with it?

Policeman: It's closed to traffic.

Driver: Why is that?

Policeman: The railway bridge is being repaired.

Driver: Is there no chance of getting through?

Policeman: None whatever. The bridge goes over the railway and it is completely unusable.

Driver: Can I turn off somewhere ahead?

Policeman: There's nowhere you can turn off; there are no other roads this side of the railway.

Driver: So I've got to go back the way I came.

Policeman: I'm afraid so. Didn't you see the detour sign?

Driver: So that's what it meant! I wondered at the time what that sign said.

Policeman: It's a pity that you didn't take the trouble to find out what it meant before you drove this far.

Driver: I was in a hurry.

Policeman: Yes, but you have wasted more time by driving all this way for nothing than if you had stopped and asked.

Driver: I suppose so. Do I have to go right back to that sign before I can turn off this road?

Policeman: Where are you trying to get to?

Driver: I am going to Herne.

Policeman: In that case you need not go back that far because you can just go back six kilometres and then turn to your right. The road is rather narrow and winding but it will save you having to go all the way back to the main road. It's a typical country lane so you will have to drive carefully.

Driver: Thanks very much. Do you happen to know where St. Pius' Church is?

Policeman: Yes, it's on the far side of the town.

Driver: It would be! I'm late enough already.

Policeman: What time are you supposed to be there?

Driver: Three o'clock. What time is it now, please?

Policeman: It's nearly half past two.

Driver: Do you think I'll get to the church on time?

Policeman: I very much doubt it. I would advise you to go back to the main road. Then, if you stay on that road, you will see the church on the right after you have driven through the centre of the town.

Driver: Is it quicker to go that way?

Policeman: It is a little further in distance but it will be easier to find the church and it will be safer than driving too quickly on the country road.

Driver: Thanks very much. I'll do as you say and go via the main road. Will I be very late do you think?

Policeman: You won't be there by three o'clock. What are you going there for?

Driver: A wedding.

Policeman: Well, if the bride is very late, you might just make it in time!

Driver: You don't know the bride. She'll be on time. She's never late.

Policeman: Then I'm afraid you'll miss the wedding.

Driver: I shan't miss it, but there will be a lot of worried people at the church.

Policeman: Why?

Driver: I'm the bridegroom!

Exercises

1. Answer the following questions:
   a) Why is the road closed to traffic?
   b) How far is it back to the country lane?
   c) Where is the driver going?
   d) At what time is he supposed to be at the church?
   e) How much time has he to get there?
   f) Why is he going to the church?
   g) Which way did the policeman advise the driver to go?
   h) Why will the driver not miss the wedding?

2. Übertragen Sie ins Englische:
   a) Die Eisenbahnbrücke wird repariert.
   b) Sahen sie das Umleitungsschild nicht?
   c) In diesem Fall brauchen Sie nicht so weit zurückzufahren.
   d) Es ist eine typische Landstraße, und Sie werden sorgfältig fahren müssen.
   e) Sie (die Kirche) liegt an der anderen Seite der Stadt.
   f) Ich würde Ihnen raten, auf die Hauptstraße zurückzufahren.
   g) Wenn Sie auf dieser Straße bleiben, werden Sie rechts die Kirche sehen.

7. THE LOST MOTORIST

A policeman sees a car driving along a city street. It is dark but the car has only its parking lights switched on. The policeman stops the car und sees that it is British.

Policeman: Pull over to the kerb, please.

Driver: Certainly, officer. I'm very pleased to see you.

Policeman: I beg your pardon.

Driver: I'm very pleased that you stopped me, I'm lost . . . I've been driving around this town for nearly half an hour.

Policeman: Where are you trying to get to?

Driver: I'm looking for the way to Bonn.

Policeman: You should take the autobahn – it's by far the quickest way.

Driver: I know. I was on the autobahn but I wanted to stop for dinner. So when I saw the sign for this town I turned off the motorway. Now I can't get back on it.

Policeman: You're going the wrong way.

Driver: I thought I was, I've completely lost my sense of direction.

Policeman: The autobahn is that way. You must go through the city centre.

Driver: I'll turn round and go back the way I've come.

Policeman: You can't do that. You are not allowed to make 'U' turns on this road. It's forbidden.

Driver: What shall I do then?

Policeman: You will have to go to the next roundabout and take this road in the opposite direction.

Driver: Is it far?

Policeman: No, only about a hundred metres.

Driver: That's all right then.

Policeman: When you get to the end of this road you will come to a 'T' junction.

Driver: Yes, I remember it.

Policeman: When you get there, you turn left.

Driver: Right.

Policeman: No . . . left!

Driver: I'm sorry, officer . . . I meant to say that I understood.

Policeman: I see. Well, you turn left and then continue for about three kilometres until you see the blue signs for the autobahn . . .

Driver: Then I can just follow them . . .

Policeman: Yes.

Driver: So it's down the road and then left.

Policeman: That's right . . . left.

Driver: That's clear enough.

Policeman: Be careful when you see autobahn signs. There are two sets of signs, one for going north and the other for going south.

Driver: Which do I want?

Policeman: Bonn is to the south of here.

Driver: Of course, I should have remembered that.

Policeman: You can tell that your are on the right road . . . you will pass a large block of offices with an illuminated sign on the top.

Driver: Does it say Mercedes?

Policeman: Yes, have you already seen it?

Driver: Yes, we had our dinner in a restaurant just opposite that building.

Policeman: That's easy then. You must know the way back there.

Driver: Oh no, I don't, I've been about four times round the city centre since we had dinner.

Policeman: If you follow the directions I've just given you, you will find it easily enough.

Driver: Thanks, I'll get cracking then. We're very late as it is; it will be midnight before we reach Bonn.

Policeman: Nearer one o'clock I think. Before you go, I want to tell you why I stopped you.

Driver: Oh, I thought you stopped us because you knew that we were lost.

Policeman: No, I stopped you because you were breaking the law.

Driver: Was I? I didn't realise that.

Policeman: You were driving with only your parking lights on.

Driver: Isn't that all right?

Policeman: No, you should use your headlights.

Driver: I'm terribly sorry, in Britain you don't have to have headlights on if there is street lighting.

Policeman: Well, you have to in Germany.

Driver: Thank you for telling me. Are you going to fine me?

Policeman: No, that won't be necessary, provided that you switch your lights on when you drive off.

Driver: I certainly will. I'm very grateful to you.

Policeman: That's all right . . . good night, sir. – Safe journey.

Driver: Many thanks – good night.

Exercises

1. Answer the following questions:
   a) Why did the policeman stop the car?
   b) Why was the driver pleased to see the policeman?
   c) Where is the driver going?
   d) Why did he leave the autobahn?
   e) In which direction was he told to turn at the 'T' junction?
   f) How could he tell that he was on the right road?

2. Übertragen Sie ins Englische:
   a) Fahren Sie an die Straßenseite.
   b) Sie sollten die Autobahn nehmen – das ist der schnellste Weg.
   c) Es ist nicht gestattet, auf dieser Straße zu wenden.
   d) Sie müssen zum nächsten Kreisverkehr fahren und diese Straße in entgegengesetzter Richtung nehmen.
   e) Sie fahren links ab und fahren etwa drei Kilometer geradeaus, bis Sie die blauen Verkehrszeichen für die Autobahn sehen.
   f) Sie fuhren nur mit Standlicht.
   g) Sie müssen mit Abblendlicht fahren.

8. THE LONG TAXI RIDE

A policeman sees an argument taking place near a stationary taxi. As he gets near to them, he hears that a man is speaking in English to a taxi driver who appears not to understand what the man is saying.

Man: Ah, here's a policeman. He'll be able to resolve this. Officer, could you help me, please?

Policeman: What is the trouble, sir?

Man: This taxi driver is trying to overcharge me.

Policeman: What makes you think that?

Man: I arrived at the railway station and hired this taxi.

Policeman: Where did you ask to go?

Man: To the Town Hall.

Policeman: Well, you are at the Town Hall. It's the building behind you.

Man: Yes, I know. But the driver took a roundabout way to get here.

Policeman: How do you know that?

Man: I've been here before. I visit this town every year on business. The journey from the railway station normally takes only half the time it took today and the fare is less than half what this driver is asking.

Policeman: I see. Can you tell me which way you came?

Man: Not exactly, but I can tell you some of the places that we passed.

Policeman: What were they?

Man: Well, when I've come here before, I've always passed the museum.

Policeman: That's right. That is the most direct route from the railway station to the Town Hall.

Man: Right. Well, today this driver came via the planetarium, the opera house, the university and a sports stadium.

Policeman: You must have been round the town!

Man: That's what I thought. There can't be much of the town that we didn't pass through.

Policeman: Not very much, perhaps.

Man: Now I'm being charged over double what I'm normally asked for the journey from the railway station and I'm not going to pay.

Policeman: I see.

Man: It's a very nice town but I didn't ask for a tour of it and I don't see why I should pay for one.

Policeman: Let me have a word with the taxi driver for a moment, sir.

The policeman has a short conversation in German with the taxi driver, then he speaks again in English.

Policeman: The taxi driver says that you asked him to show you the town. He came here a longer way round so that you could see as much of the town as possible.

Man: He is a liar. All I said to him were two German words – ,Rathaus, bitte'.

Policeman: Are you sure that you said only two words?

Man: I'm certain. I can't speak German so I have to use a phrase book. Here is the book in my pocket.

Policeman: That seems clear enough. Just a moment please.

He speaks again to the taxi driver.

Policeman: Well, the driver says that there must have been a misunder-standing . . .

Man: That's one way of putting it!

Policeman: He says that he is willing to take half of what he asked you for. Is that reasonable?

Man: I suppose so. It's a little more than last year, but prices have gone up any-way, I suppose.

Policeman: Yes, they have. I think that if you pay him what he now asks, that is about the right amount for a journey from the railway station to here by the most direct route.

Man: Thank you very much. I'll pay him then. I'm most grateful for your help. I'll tell you one thing though –

Policeman: What is that?

Man: I'm not going to give him a tip!

Exercises

1. Answer the following questions:
a) Where did the man hire the taxi?
b) Where did he ask to go to?
c) How often does the man visit this town?
d) What building does the most direct route pass?
e) What other buildings did this driver pass today?
f) Why did the taxi driver take the longer way round?
g) What were the two German words spoken by the man to the taxi driver?
h) How was the man so certain that he had said only two words?

2. Übertragen Sie ins Englische:
a) Wohin wollten Sie fahren?
b) Können Sie mir sagen, auf welchem Weg Sie hierher kamen?
c) Lassen Sie mich einen Augenblick mit dem Taxifahrer sprechen.
d) Der Fahrer sagt, daß ein Mißverständnis vorgelegen haben muß.
e) Er sagt, daß er die Hälfte von dem nehmen will, was er (vorher) verlangte.
f) Das ist ungefähr die richtige Summe für eine Fahrt auf dem kürzesten Weg vom Bahnhof nach hier.

II. Traffic Incidents

1. THE WITNESS

A policeman is dealing with a serious traffic accident. A car has collided with a tree and the driver is dead. The policeman sees a British car parked a little way from the scene of the accident. The policeman goes over to this car and speaks to the driver.

Policeman: Did you see this accident, sir?

Man: Yes, I saw it. It has shaken me up very badly.

Policeman: I would like you to tell me all about it.

Man: I will be pleased to tell you what I can. It all happened very quickly and there's not much to tell.

Policeman: Which direction was the car travelling?

Man: You mean the car that crashed?

Policeman: Yes, that's right.

Man: It was going towards the city centre.

Policeman: And where were you?

Man: I was coming from the city centre, so I was travelling in the opposite direction to the other car.

Policeman: Was any other car involved in the accident?

Man: No, only the car that hit the tree. There was nothing else near it when the accident happened.

Policeman: I see. Now can you tell me exactly what happened?

Man: Yes. I saw the other car coming towards me. Then suddenly it swerved across the road in front of me and hit the tree on my side of the road.

Policeman: Why did it swerve?

Man: I don't know. There was no reason for it to swerve at all.

Policeman: Was there anything on the road?

Man: Nothing at all. Perhaps my wife can help you. She saw it, too.

Policeman: I would like to speak to your wife, please.

Man: Mary, tell the policeman what you saw.

Woman: The driver of the other car collapsed, I think.

Policeman: What did you see?

Woman: Well, the car was coming towards us quite normally.

Policeman: Yes. Then what happened?

Woman: The driver suddenly slumped forward over the steering-wheel. Then the car went out of control and swerved across the road.

Policeman: So you think the driver of the car that crashed was unconscious or dead before the car hit the tree?

Woman: I'm sure he was.

Man: I'm afraid I didn't notice the driver. I was too busy trying to avoid the car itself.

Policeman: Thank you very much, sir, and you, madam. You have been a very great help.

Man: I'm glad we were able to help, officer.

Policeman: Before you leave, I would like to have your name and your address while you are in Germany.

Man: Do you think we will be needed again, officer?

Policeman: It may be necessary, but we will not trouble you unnecessarily.

Woman: My husband and I will do everything we can.

Policeman: Thank you very much.

Exercises

1. Answer the following questions:

a) Where was the British car when the policeman arrived?

b) How did the policeman ask the British driver to tell him what happened?

c) Why did the British driver say that there was not much for him to tell?

d) In what direction was the British car travelling?

e) How many cars were involved in the accident?

g) Why did the British driver not notice the driver of the other car?

2. Übertragen Sie ins Englische:

a) Haben Sie diesen Unfall gesehen?

b) In welche Richtung fuhr das Auto?

c) War ein weiteres Fahrzeug in den Unfall verwickelt?

d) Erzählen Sie mir genau, was geschehen ist!

e) Wir werden Sie nicht unnötigerweise belästigen.

2. A BREAKDOWN (1)

A police officer is driving a police car along a motorway when he sees a car standing in the emergency lane. There is a red warning triangle on the road behind the car. The policeman notices that the car has an English number plate. A man is looking at the engine of the car. The police car stops and the policeman speaks to the Motorist.

Policeman: Hallo! What's the matter with your car?

Motorist: I'm not sure.

Policeman: What happened?

Motorist: I was driving along quite normally, then, suddenly, the engine overheated and stopped.

Policeman: Have you checked your fan belt?

Motorist: Yes. That was the first thing I thought of. The fan belt is all right.

Policeman: What about the radiator. Is there enough water in it?

Motorist: I haven't checked it. I'll have a look now.

Policeman: Be very careful. If the water in the radiator is boiling, it is dangerous to take off the radiator cap.

Motorist: Thanks for reminding me. I'll cover it with a cloth and take the cap off slowly. Here's a cloth, now . . . if I turn the radiator cap very slowly . . . that's it.

Policeman: The engine is certainly very hot!

Motorist: Yes, but there's plenty of water in the radiator. There must be something seriously wrong with the engine. I will have to get someone to repair it.

Policeman: I think that we should call for a breakdown truck.

Motorist: I think so, too, but it's difficult for a foreigner to phone.

Policeman: I'll do it for you. Stay here and I'll order the breakdown truck by radio. It'll be here within a few minutes.

Motorist: Thank you.

The policeman goes to his car and calls for a break-down truck by radio. Some minutes later one arrives. The policeman tells the attendant to take the car to the nearest garage.

Policeman (to the motorist): He'll tow your car to the nearest garage. Get in please. I will explain to the mechanic what has happened and I'm sure he will be able to fix the car for you.

Motorist: Many thanks for your help.

Exercises

1. A tourist's car has broken down. He tells you that the engine has over-heated. You try to help him:

a) Ask the tourist if he has a red warning triangle in his car.

b) Tell him to place his red warning triangle on the road behind his car.

c) Ask him to check if there is enough water in the radiator.

d) Tell him to take off the radiator cap slowly.

e) Ask him if he wants you to call a breakdown truck.

f) Tell him that you are going to radio for a mechanic to repair his car.

2. Übertragen Sie ins Englische:

a) Was ist mit Ihrem Auto los?

b) Haben Sie nach dem Keilriemen gesehen?

c) Was ist mit dem Kühler? Hat er genug Wasser?

d) Seien Sie sehr vorsichtig. Wenn das Wasser im Kühler kocht, ist es sehr gefährlich, den Verschluß zu öffnen.

e) Ich denke, wir sollten einen Abschleppwagen rufen.

f) Bleiben Sie hier, und ich werde den Abschleppwagen über Funk rufen.

g) Er wird Ihren Wagen zur nächsten Werkstatt bringen.

h) Ich werde dem Monteur erklären, was geschehen ist, und ich bin sicher, er wird das Auto wieder für Sie herrichten können.

3. A BREAKDOWN (2)

It is late afternoon in a busy town. The traffic rush-hour has begun and there are long queues of motor vehicles as people try to go home from work. In one street the traffic is at a complete standstill. When a policeman goes to find the cause of the hold-up, he sees a car with its bonnet up blocking a narrow street. The owner of the car is standing beside, looking at the engine.

Policeman: What's the trouble?

Man: I don't know. It suddenly stopped.

Policeman: Is it the engine?

Man: Yes, I was driving along and the engine suddenly cut out. I can't start it again.

Policeman: Look, you are completely blocking this street. It's much too narrow for your car to stay here. We will have to move it off the road.

Man: Yes, of course. I'm sorry, I didn't realise that I was causing so much trouble.

Policeman: There's a forecourt just ahead. It's not a heavy car. We can push it onto the forecourt.

Man: Fine. Just a minute, I'll wind the window down so that I can steer.

Policeman: Is the handbrake off?

Man: Yes.

Policeman: Is it out of gear?

Man: It's an automatic. I'll put it into neutral.

Policeman: Right, let's push it.

The man, assisted by the policeman and some bystanders pushes the car onto an open space off the road.

Policeman: That's better. Now we can have a look at your car. Did the engine stop suddenly or slowly?

Man: It stopped suddenly. I can't understand it. There's plenty of petrol in the tank.

Policeman: If the engine stopped suddenly, I doubt if it's the fuel system that's wrong. I expect it's an electrical fault.

Man: Do you think so?

Policeman: Yes. If it's a fuel blockage, the engine usually stops slowly. If it's an electrical fault, it stops quickly.

Man: I'd better check to see whether there's any electric current. I'll take one of the sparking plugs out. I've got a plug spanner in my tool kit in the boot.

The man removes one of the sparking plugs and lays it on the cylinder block.

Man: If I try to start the engine, will you watch the sparking plug to see whether there is a spark, please?

Policeman: Certainly.

The man switches on the ignition and presses the starter button. The starter motor turns the engine but there is no spark.

Policeman: There is no spark at all. It looks as though there is no high tension current.

Man: Oh dear. I wonder what is wrong.

Policeman: It could be the coil. It may have burnt out. It might simply be a fuse.

Man: It looks as though I ought to call a mechanic. Is there a garage near here?

Policeman: There are several garages in this area, but I'm not sure whether any of them deal with British cars. This is a Jaguar, isn't it?

Man: Yes. I suppose there aren't many Jaguar agents in German towns. Hang on, I have a book in the car that lists garages and the makes of car they deal with.

Policeman: If you can tell me the name of a garage that deals with Jaguars, I will help you to call them.

Man: Thank you very much. Now, where's the book . . . Here it is . . . It says that the Central Garage is a Jaguar agent.

Policeman: That's lucky! It's not very far away. It's quite a big garage. I'm sure they will be able to repair your car.

Man: That's fine. Thank goodness the car broke down where it did. It usually breaks down miles from the nearest town!

Exercises

1. Answer the following questions:
a) When did this incident happen?
b) Why did the policeman think that the car had an electrical fault?
c) How did the man check that it was an electrical fault?
d) What is the name of the garage that the man is going to call?
e) Why must he go to this garage?

2. Übertragen Sie ins Englische:
a) Sie blockieren die Straße total. Wir müssen Ihr Auto aus dem Weg räumen.
b) Es ist kein schweres Auto, wir können es an den freien Platz schieben.
c) Ist die Handbremse gelöst?
d) Ist es (das Auto) auf Leerlauf geschaltet?
e) Setzte der Motor plötzlich oder langsam aus?
f) Wenn die Kraftstoffzuleitung verstopft ist, setzt der Motor gewöhnlich langsam aus. Wenn es sich um einen elektrischen Defekt handelt, setzt er plötzlich (schnell) aus.
g) Es gibt verschiedene Autoreparaturwerkstätten in dieser Gegend, aber ich bin nicht sicher, ob einige davon mit britischen Wagen zu tun haben.
h) Wenn Sie mir den Namen der Werkstatt nennen, die mit Jaguars zu tun hat, werde ich Ihnen helfen, sie anzurufen.

4. THE LADY DRIVER

A policeman sees two cars that have been involved in a collision. They are both facing the same way. The front car is an Audi which is damaged at the rear. The car behind it is an Austin bearing British registration plates. The front of the Austin is badly dented. The policeman speaks to the driver of the British car:

Policeman: Is this your car?

Man: Yes, it is.

Policeman: Where is the driver of the car in front?

Man: I don't know. She got out of her car and ran back up the road.

23

Policeman: She has probably gone to call the police.

Man: Possibly.

Policeman: How did you come to collide with the car in front of you?

Man: Look, to save any misunderstanding, I did not collide with that car.

Policeman: But the back of that car is still touching the front of your car and both are damaged.

Man: I know that – and I'm bloody furious about it!

Policeman: If your car didn't collide with that one, how did they both come to be damaged?

Man: The stupid woman who was driving that car reversed into me – that's how.

Policeman: What? . . . I find that very hard to believe.

Man: I could hardly believe it myself when it happened, but that's what she did.

Policeman: I think you'd better tell me all about it.

Man: With pleasure, I was driving along quite normally when I came up behind this car.

Policeman: This red Audi?

Man: That's right. I could see that it was being driven by a woman and she was obviously about to do something stupid.

Policeman: How could you tell that?

Man: She kept putting her brakes on and off – I could tell that from her brake lights.

Policeman: Anything else?

Man: Yes, she kept continually looking out of the window to her right – she wasn't looking where she was going at all.

Policeman: What did you do?

Man: I slowed down and stayed a reasonable distance behind her until I could overtake.

Policeman: Then what happened?

Man: She suddenly jammed on her brakes and stopped dead.

Policeman: Were you able to stop in time?

Man: Yes, just about – you see I'd been expecting something, so I was able to stop about three yards behind her.

Policeman: What happened then?

Man: Of all the silly things – she just reversed into me.

Policeman: And collided with the front of your car?

Man: Yes. Then she jumped out of her car, shouted something to me in German and ran off.

Policeman: It all sounds a bit improbable to me – are you sure that's what happened?

Man: Sure? Of course I'm sure – I know it looks like an ordinary collision, but believe me, it happened just as I've told you.

Policeman: Right, I'll see if I can find a witness who can substantiate your story.

Man: I'd be very grateful if you would!

Policeman: Wait here until I return. I won't be long.

Man: Just a minute, here she comes!

Policeman: The driver of the other car?

Man: Yes, that's her – she's got a kiddy with her now. She was on her own when the accident happened.

Policeman: Good. Now we can get her side of the story.

Man: Excuse me, madam, do you speak English?

Woman: A little, why do you ask?

Man: Would you mind explaining to this police officer what happened?

Woman: Not at all. I am sorry that I had to leave so quickly.

Man: Never mind that. Just tell this policeman what happened.

Policeman: This man says that you reversed into his car.

Woman: Yes, that's right. You see I was looking for an address where I had to collect my daughter from a party. My husband took her there and I had to fetch her home. I was rather late. That's why I ran off so quickly.

Policeman: Why did you drive backwards?

Woman: Because I went past the house, of course!

Policeman: But didn't you see the car behind you?

Woman: No. I had no idea that it was there. It is his fault – he should have hooted to warn me that he had crept up behind me!

Policeman: That's one way of looking at it, I suppose. I think that a court would take the view that you should not have driven backwards like that!

Exercises

1. Answer the following questions:
a) How many cars were involved in this incident?
b) What was the make of the car driven by the man?
c) What was the cause of the collision?
d) How did the man know that the woman was going to do something stupid?
e) Why did the woman run off so quickly after the collision?
f) Who was with the woman when she returned to the scene of the accident?

2. Übertragen Sie ins Englische:
a) Wie kam es dazu, daß Sie mit dem Wagen vor Ihnen kollidierten?
b) Konnten Sie rechtzeitig halten?
c) All das klingt mir ein bißchen unwahrscheinlich.

d) Ich will sehen, ob ich einen Zeugen finden kann, der Ihre Aussage bestätigen kann.
e) Dieser Mann sagt, daß Sie sein Auto beim Zurücksetzen angefahren haben.

5. THE LOW BRIDGE

A policeman is sent to a narrow road where the traffic is held up by a tall lorry which has become wedged under a low bridge. The policeman sees that the lorry carries British identification markings and he speaks to the lorry driver in English.

Policeman: What are you doing here?

Driver: Well, I'll tell you one thing, I'm not trying to steal the bridge!

Policeman: This is not a joking matter. You have blocked the road and caused a serious traffic jam.

Driver: All right. I'm sorry, but I'm fed up. Everything has gone wrong today. I've had nothing but trouble ever since I set out from France this morning.

Policeman: What sort of trouble?

Driver: I got held up by customs officers because I'd mislaid some of the documents. It took me an hour to find them. Then I had engine trouble and that took over an hour to fix. Now this.

Policeman: Why did you come along this road?

Driver: I was trying to make a short cut to make up some of the time I lost this morning.

Policeman: Didn't you see the signs back there showing the height of this bridge!

Driver: No. I must have missed them.

Policeman: Well, surely you could see that this bridge was too low for your lorry to get under?

Driver: I knew it would be a close thing, but I thought that I could just make it.

Policeman: Well, you didn't, and I suppose you can't reverse out?

Driver: No, I'm afraid of pulling part of the bridge with me.

Policeman: You're probably right. This is a railway bridge and it could cause a serious accident if you damaged it.

Driver: What shall I do?

Policeman: Your lorry doesn't look much too high, only a few centimetres . . .

Driver: Another inch on the height of the bridge and I would have just got under, I think.

Policeman: Yes. If you can lower the height of your lorry a little and keep to the centre of the arch, you will be able to get through.

Driver: How do I lower the height of my lorry?

Policeman: You will have to let some air out of the tyres.

Driver: That's a good idea, I shouldn't have to let much out to bring the height down enough to get through.

Policeman: You get on with it while I clear the traffic in front of your lorry. Wait for me to signal to you before you try to move the lorry. Understand?

Driver: I understand.

A short while later, the driver has released air from the tyres of the lorry which is no longer touching the bridge.

Policeman: That's better. You can get through now. Drive very slowly, in a straight line and keep to the centre of the road until you are completely clear of the bridge on the other side. Watch me and I will signal to you when to start.

Driver: Thanks very much.

Policeman: That's all right. When you get to the other side of the bridge stop in the lay-by because I want to talk to you.

Driver: What about?

Policeman: I want to tell you where you can have your tyres blown up and we have to discuss the matter of your not seeing the low bridge warning signs!

Exercises

1. Answer the following questions:

a) What happened to the lorry?

b) Why was the lorry driver held up by customs officers?

c) How long was he held up by engine trouble?

d) Why did the lorry driver drive along that road?

e) What sort of bridge is the lorry wedged beneath?

f) How did the driver lower the height of his lorry?

2. Übertragen Sie ins Englische:

a) Sie haben die Straße blockiert und eine erhebliche Verkehrsstauung verursacht.

b) Sahen Sie die Verkehrszeichen dort hinten nicht, die die Höhe der Brücke angeben?

c) Sicherlich konnten Sie sehen, daß diese Brücke für Ihren LKW zu niedrig war, um darunter durchzufahren.

d) Wenn Sie die Höhe Ihres LKWs ein wenig verringern könnten und sich in der Mitte des Bogens halten, werden Sie hindurchkommen können.

e) Sie müssen etwas Luft aus den Reifen lassen.

f) Warten Sie auf mich, damit ich Ihnen Zeichen geben kann, ehe Sie versuchen, den Wagen zu fahren.

g) Wenn Sie auf die andere Seite der Brücke gelangt sind, halten Sie auf dem Seitenstreifen, weil ich mit Ihnen sprechen möchte.

6. AN ACCIDENT (1)

A police officer is driving his patrol car along a street. He sees that an English car has had an accident. He stops and speaks to the driver of the car.

Policeman: What happened, sir?

Driver: I swerved to miss a dog and hit this lamppost.

Policeman: Which way were you driving?

Driver: I was driving towards the city.

Policeman: Where did the dog come from?

Driver: He ran from my right, across the road in front of my car.

Policeman: Did you hit the dog?

Driver: No, I missed it.

Policeman: Are you injured?

Driver: No, I'm all right, thank you.

Policeman: Were you alone in your car?

Driver: Yes.

Policeman: Is your car drivable?

Driver: Yes, but it's badly damaged. One of the headlamps is broken, the wing is dented and the bumper is twisted.

Policeman: Please move your car to that lay-by. Park it there, then wait for me and I will come and take some particulars from you.

The driver reverses his car away from the lamppost. He then drives it to the lay-by.

Policeman: Now, sir, what is your full name, please?

Driver: Arthur Walter Smith.

Policeman: What is your address?

Driver: I haven't an address in Germany. I'm on a touring holiday.

Policeman: May I see your passport, please?

Driver: Here you are.

Policeman: Thank you. Now I would like to see your driving licence and insurance.

Driver: Here's my driving licence and my insurance certificate.

Policeman: Thank you. Yes, these documents are in order. Here, you may have them back now.

Driver: Will that be all then?

Policeman: Yes. I'll inform the local authority about the damaged lamppost. I suggest that you inform your insurance company about the accident.

Driver: I will. Thank you for dealing with it so quickly.

Exercises

1. An English car has collided with a lamppost. You have to find out how the accident happened.

a) Ask the driver wich way he was driving.
b) Ask him when the accident happened.
c) Ask him if he is injured?
d) Ask him if his car is damaged.
e) Ask him his name.
f) Ask him to show you his driving licence.

2. Übertragen Sie ins Englische:

a) Was ist geschehen?
b) In welche Richtung fuhren Sie?
c) Sind Sie verletzt?
d) Ist Ihr Fahrzeug fahrtüchtig?
e) Bitte fahren Sie Ihr Auto auf den Seitenstreifen.
f) Warten Sie auf mich, ich komme und nehme Ihre Personalien auf.
g) Ich werde die Ordnungsbehörde über den beschädigten Laternenpfahl informieren.
h) Ich schlage vor, daß Sie Ihre Versicherung von diesem Unfall in Kenntnis setzen.

7. AN ACCIDENT (2)

A police officer is walking along a main road. He sees a crowd of people near the traffic lights and the traffic is beginning to pile up. He pushes his way through the crowd and sees that two men are arguing loudly near two cars, one of which has run into the other.

Police Officer: What has happened?

First man: This fool ran into the back of my car.

Second man: He stopped too quickly. He should have kept going.

Police Officer: Please, don't both talk at once. I can only understand you if you speak one at a time. Now, sir, will you tell me what happened?

First man: I was driving towards the traffic lights. They changed from green to amber as I reached them, so I stopped. The other car ran into the back of mine.

Police Officer: I see. Now, will you please tell me what happened?

Second man: I was driving behind him when he suddenly braked. He had plenty of time to get across the junction before the lights changed to red. Anyway, he stopped quickly and I didn't stop quickly enough and so I ran into the back of him.

Police Officer: You are blocking the road here, will you both move your cars across the junction. Stop over there and wait for me.

Both of the cars are driven across the junction. The policeman walks over and speaks to the drivers.

Police Officer: May I see your driving licence and insurance, please?

First man: Certainly, here they are.

Police Officer (after he has checked them): These are correct. Thank you, you may have them back now.

First man: Thank you.

Police Officer (speaking to the second man): Show me your driving licence and insurance, please.

Second man: Here you are.

Police Officer: Thank you . . . Yes, they are all right. . . . Here you are, thank you. – Now, gentlemen, as the damage of your cars is less than 1 000 DM, you must simply exchange your names and addresses and then you may go.

First man: Here is my card. I have written the name of my insurance company on the back.

Second man: Thank you. I have written my particulars on this piece of paper.

Police Officer: All right then. Now you may go. Please drive carefully!

Exercises

1. Answer the following questions:

a) Why was there a crowd of people near the traffic lights?
b) Why did the first man suddenly brake?
c) How did the accident happen?
d) What did the policeman tell the drivers to do in order to clear the road?
e) Which documents did the policeman want to see from both the drivers?
f) What was the policeman's order after he had checked the documents?

2. Übertragen Sie ins Englische:

a) Bitte sprechen Sie nicht beide zu gleicher Zeit. Ich verstehe nur, wenn Sie einzeln sprechen.
b) Sie versperren die Straße.
c) Bitte, fahren Sie Ihren Wagen über die Kreuzung hinweg.
d) Darf ich Ihre Fahrerlaubnis und Ihren Versicherungsschein sehen?
e) Der Schaden an den Fahrzeugen liegt unter 1 000 DM.

f) Sie müssen Ihre Namen und Ihre Ad-
ressen austauschen, und dann
können Sie weiterfahren.

8. AN ACCIDENT (3)

An essential point of German Traffic Laws
is this: At an uncontrolled or unsigned road
junction or crossing, the vehicle approaching from the right has right of way. In Great
Britain this is not so. There, vehicles on
major roads always have priority over
vehicles on minor roads.
Another difficulty for British drivers in
Germany is caused by the fact that in
Britain all the traffic drives on the lefthand
side of the road and the steering-wheel is on
the right-hand side of British cars.
An accident has occurred because a British
driver failed to allow a German car "right
of way" at an unsigned junction.
When a police car arrives at the scene, the
two policemen in it see that the British car
has swerved onto a verge, while the German car is still on the road.

Policeman: Is anyone injured?
German Driver: No, I was on my own
and I am all right.
British Driver: Yes, look my wife is hurt.
Policeman: What is the matter with her?
British Driver: She's fainted and I think
her arm is broken.
Policeman: Let me see ... Yes, you're
right. I will make her injured arm as comfortable as I can ... There, that should be
all right. The ambulance should not be
long. My colleague is calling one now.

The second policeman calls an ambulance
using the radio in his car. Then he goes to
the German driver.
The first policeman speaks to the British
driver.

Policeman: An ambulance will soon be
here. How is your wife now?

British Driver: She is conscious now but
her arm is causing great pain.
Policeman: Try to keep her still until the
ambulance arrives.

A few minutes later an ambulance arrives
at the scene. The injured woman is taken to
the nearest hospital. While one policeman
is dealing with the German driver, the
other policeman speaks to the British
driver.

Policeman: You are British, aren't you?
British Driver: I am.
Policeman: May I see your driving licence
and certificate of insurance?
British Driver: Here you are.
Policeman: Thank you. Would you please
tell me now how this accident happened?
British Driver: Well, it was a straight
road I was driving along. Suddenly the
other car came out of the side street on
my right and I crashed into it. I am very
sorry, but as it was only a narrow street
he came from, and I am not used to looking out for traffic coming from the right,
I failed to give way at that junction. I am
very sorry – it was my fault.
Policeman: I see. May I hand you this
form concerning traffic accidents involving foreign nationals? Let's look at the
damage to your car and then fill in this
form. I think I must report you for this.

When the formalities are over, the Englishman apologizes to the German driver and,
as their cars are drivable, they both drive
away.

Exercises

1. Answer the following questions:
a) What essential point of German
   Traffic Laws is mentioned?
b) In what way is the law different in
   Great Britain?
c) Why did this accident happen?

d) Where was the British car when the police arrived?

e) What injury had the British driver's wife received?

f) How was an ambulance called and by whom?

g) Where was the injured woman taken?

h) What did the policeman hand to the British driver?

2. Übertragen Sie ins Englische:

a) Ist jemand verletzt?

b) Der Krankenwagen wird bald hier sein.

c) Sie sind Engländer, nicht wahr?

d) Würden Sie mir nun bitte erzählen, wie der Unfall geschah!

e) Füllen Sie bitte dieses Formblatt aus!

f) Ich muß gegen Sie Anzeige erstatten.

9. A FATAL ACCIDENT

Two policemen are called to the scene of an accident in which a British car has run into the back of a lorry. When they arrive, the policemen see that the front of the car has gone a long way under the rear part of the lorry. The driver of the car is seriously injured and is trapped in the wreckage of his car.

Several people are trying to get him out. A young woman speaks to one of the policemen.

Woman: My husband is badly hurt. Can you do something quickly?

Policeman: We will do what we can. Is that your husband in the car?

Woman: Yes.

Policeman: We have already called an ambulance, it shouldn't be long.

Woman: Will he be all right?

Policeman: I don't know. We'll get him to hospital as soon as possible. What happened?

Woman: My husband was driving along quite slowly. He had started to overtake that lorry when it suddenly stopped dead. Our car ran straight into the back of it.

Policeman: What is your name, please?

Woman: Mrs. Cameron. My husband John and I are on holiday. We were going to tour the Rhine valley.

Policeman: Are you injured, Mrs. Cameron?

Woman: No, I was lucky. I had my seat belt on and my side of the car wasn't damaged. I'm sure it was because I was wearing my seat belt that I wasn't thrown forward against the windscreen.

As they are talking, a man stops his car nearby and walks towards them. When he hears that they are speaking English, he also speaks in that language.

Man: I am a doctor. Can I assist you in any way?

Policeman: Yes. My colleague is trying to release this lady's husband who is trapped in that car. Can you give him an anaesthetic to ease his pain?

Doctor: I'll see what I can do.

The doctor goes to the wrecked car. He returns after a few minutes.

Woman: How is my husband, doctor?

Doctor: I'm sorry, there is nothing I can do for him.

Woman: He can't be dead?

Doctor: I'm afraid he is. He was killed instantly when the collision occurred.

Woman: Oh, my God!

Doctor: You are suffering from shock. I will give you a sedative.

Policeman: I will take you to our police station. There ist nothing that you can do here. Come along, we will do our best to help you.

Exercises

1. Answer the following questions:
a) Why did the car collide with the lorry?
b) When did Mr. Cameron die?
c) What did the policeman ask the doctor to do?
d) What is the doctor going to give to Mrs. Cameron?
e) Where is the policeman going to take Mrs. Cameron?

2. Übertragen Sie ins Englische:
a) Wir haben schon einen Krankenwagen gerufen; es wird nicht lange dauern.
b) Wir werden ihn so schnell wie möglich ins Krankenhaus bringen.
c) Sind Sie verletzt?
d) Es tut mir leid, ich kann für ihn nichts mehr tun. Er wurde sofort bei dem Zusammenstoß getötet.
e) Sie stehen unter Schockeinwirkung. Ich gebe Ihnen ein Beruhigungsmittel.

10. NO PARKING

A policeman, as he is walking his beat, has noticed a car parked close to a pedestrian crossing. The distance between the car and the crossing is less than five metres, so that it is difficult for pedestrians to see the traffic coming from the left and for car drivers to see the pedestrians.
The car has a British number-plate.
As the motorist returns to his car, the constable speaks to him.

Policeman: Good afternoon. I think you are British, aren't you?

Motorist: That's right. Good afternoon, officer.

Policeman: Do you speak German, sir?

Motorist: Oh, no. Only a few words.

Policeman: And you are the driver of this car, aren't you?

Motorist: Yes, I am.

Policeman: Did you leave your car in this position?

Motorist: Yes, I did.

Policeman: As you can see, sir, you have left your car close to a pedestrian crossing; the distance is only two metres. To leave your vehicle at a distance of less than five metres from a pedestrian crossing is an offence.

Motorist: Well, look here, officer, I didn't mean any harm. I'm sorry. May I tell you that in Great Britain there is a row of studs at a distance of about forty-five feet from the actual pedestrian crossing. You're not allowed to park between the studs and the pedestrian crossing itself.
I am very sorry that I didn't know your road regulations.

Policeman: I see. In our country you're not allowed to park a vehicle at a distance of less than five metres from a pedestrian crossing.
Would you please show me your driving licence and certificate of insurance?

Motorist: Here you are.

Policeman: Yes, sir, your driving licence and certificate of insurance are both in order. Here you are.

Motorist: Thank you.

Policeman: This time I'll let you off with a warning. But if your car is found again in such a place where a vehicle should not be parked, you may be fined five marks.
Please move on now so that the crossing will be safe again.
Anyway, have a nice time in Germany.

Motorist: Thank you for your information, officer.

Policeman: Good-bye, sir.

Motorist: Good-bye, officer. Thank you very much.

Exercises

1. Answer the following questions:

a) Where was the car parked?

b) How did the policeman know that it was a British car?

c) What was the difficulty for pedestrians using the crossing?

d) What is the difference between British and German road regulations for cars parked near a pedestrian crossing?

e) What documents did the policeman want to see?

f) Did the policeman fine the motorist?

2. Übertragen Sie ins Englische:

a) Sie sind der Fahrer dieses Wagens, nicht wahr?

b) Haben Sie das Auto so abgestellt?

c) Der Abstand beträgt nur zwei Meter.

d) Würden Sie mir bitte Ihren Führerschein und Versicherungsschein zeigen!

e) Diesmal will ich es bei einer mündlichen Belehrung bewenden lassen.

11. TRAFFIC CHECK

The time is 11 o'clock on a Saturday night, on one of the main roads in a town. A group of policemen have come to carry out a traffic check.

The officer who stops the approaching traffic is dressed in a light-reflecting coat, cap and a belt with flashing lights. He is holding a 'stop' sign in his right hand. Among the approaching cars there is a British one.

Policeman: Please drive your car into that lay-by, sir.

Motorist: Why, what's going on?

Policeman: We are just checking vehicles. I will come and speak to you when you have driven your car into the lay-by.

Motorist: All right.

Policeman: Now, sir. My name is Tillmann. May I see your driving licence, registration book and certificate of insurance, please?

Motorist: Here you are.

Policeman: Thank you.
(Going to the front of the car): Now will you switch on your headlights, please! – Right. – Put your lights on main beam! – That's it. – And now will you dip your headlights, please. – Thank you. Would you switch them off. –
(Going to the back part of the car): Now will you apply your brakes, please.
(Turning to the motorist): Your brake lights are not coming on.

Motorist: Well, I can't imagine why. They were all right when I set out.

Policeman: Well, turn on your ignition and then apply your brakes, please. – I see. Your brake lights are all right. Now, I have noticed that your breath smells of alcohol. Have you been drinking?

Motorist: Yes, I had a glass of wine with dinner tonight.

Policeman: Just one glass of wine? Well, you still have to take the breathalyzer test. – Take this tube, and blow into this bag in one breath, please, thank you. Yes, you are lucky, sir. The resultat is negative. Here are your documents back. You may continue on your way. But drive carefully, sir. And good night.

Motorist: Good night, officer.

Exercises

1. Answer the following questions:

a) What were the policemen doing?

b) How did they check the vehicles?

c) Was there anything wrong with the Englishman's car?

d) Had the driver been drinking?

e) What was the result of the breathalyzer test?

2. Übertragen Sie ins Englische:
a) Wir kontrollieren Fahrzeuge.
b) Fahren Sie Ihr Auto auf den Seiten-streifen!
c) Darf ich Ihren Führerschein, Kraft-fahrzeugschein und Versicherungs-schein sehen?
d) Schalten Sie die Scheinwerfer ein! – Fernlicht, bitte! – Abblendlicht, bitte! – Betätigen Sie die Bremse!
e) Haben Sie Alkohol getrunken?
f) Sie müssen den Alco-Test machen!
g) Das Ergebnis ist negativ.
h) Sie können weiterfahren.

12. THE LORRY THAT STOPPED

The crew of a motorway patrol car see a TIR lorry stop at the side of a motorway. The lorry has British markings and one of the policemen speaks to the driver in English.

Policeman: Why have you stopped? Have you broken down?

Driver: No, I have got something in my eye and I can't see properly.

Policeman: Show me, please. Oh yes, I see what you mean. Your eye is watering badly.

Driver: It's very sore. I was driving with my window open. I think a piece of grit must have gone in my eye.

Policeman: Would you like me to look at it to see if I can help?

Driver: That's very kind of you.

Policeman: Here, stand so that the light falls on it . . . now keep still. Where is the pain, at the top or bottom of your eye?

Driver: The top.

Policeman: I'll just pull the eyelid up . . . Ah yes, I can see it. There is a small piece of grit under your eyelid. I will pick it off with the corner of my handkerchief . . . that's it.

Driver: That feels better. Well done.

Policeman: Good. Now I would like to check your documents, please.

Driver: What do you want to see?

Policeman: I'll start with your personal documents – passport, driving licence and log sheet.

Driver: Here they are.

Policeman: Thank you. What is your full name, please?

Driver: William Walters.

Policeman: Your documents show William Arthur Walters. Is that right?

Driver: Yes, Arthur is my middle name, but I don't normally use it.

Policeman: I see from the records on your log sheet that you have been driving for three hours since you last had a break. Is that right?

Driver: Yes, I'm going to stop in the next town for a meal.

Policeman: May I now see the documents for your lorry – the insurance certificate and carnet de passage.

Driver: Here you are.

Policeman: This is a Leyland lorry and its registration mark is PAL.625.L. Is that correct?

Driver: Yes. The lorry belongs to my firm in Nottingham, Bailes Transport Com-pany.

Policeman: Good. These are all right. Finally, may I see the TIR carnet and the transit document for your load?

Driver: Yes, certainly. This is the carnet and this is my movement certificate.

Policeman: Thank you. What are you carrying?

Driver: Record players and hi-fi equip-ment.

Policeman: Where did you enter Germany?

Driver: At Aachen.

Policeman: What is your destination?

Driver: Munich.

Policeman: Right, thank you. Here are your documents, they are all in order.

Driver: Good. Is that all? May I go now?

Policeman: Yes. As you are probably aware, it is illegal to stop on a motorway except in cases of breakdown or other emergency.

Driver: But something in my eye was an emergency.

Policeman: Yes, that's what I was going to say. Under these circumstances, I am not going to take any action about your stopping as I am satisfied that it was a genuine emergency and so you may go.

Driver: Thank you and my extra thanks for getting the grit out of my eye. It feels quite normal now.

Policeman: That's quite all right – drive carefully!

Exercises

1. Answer the following questions:

a) Why did the driver of the lorry stop?
b) Where was the piece of grit?
c) How did the policeman get it out?
d) What was the driver's full name?
e) When did he last have a break?
f) Where did the lorry enter Germany?
g) What was the lorry carrying?
h) Where was the lorry going?

2. Übertragen Sie ins Englische:

a) Warum halten Sie? Haben Sie eine Panne?
b) Nun möchte ich gern Ihre Papiere kontrollieren.
c) Ich will mit Ihren persönlichen Ausweisen anfangen – Reisepaß, Führerschein, Fahrtenbuch.
d) Ich sehe aus den Aufzeichnungen Ihres Fahrtenbuches, daß Sie seit der letzten Pause drei Stunden lang gefahren sind.
e) Darf ich nun die Unterlagen für Ihren LKW einsehen – Versicherungsschein und Zollpassierscheinheft.

f) Zum Schluß möchte ich gern die Papiere für Ihre Ladung sehen.
g) Was befördern Sie?
h) Wo kamen Sie über die Grenze (nach Deutschland)?
i) Wie heißt der Bestimmungsort?
j) Es ist nicht erlaubt, auf der Autobahn zu halten außer bei Pannen und dringenden Notlagen.

13. THE NOISY MOTORIST

A policeman is walking along a residential street one evening when he hears the continuous sound of a car horn coming from the next street. He goes to find out who is making this noise and sees a man sitting in a car outside a block of flats.

Police Officer: Please take your hand off the horn button.

Man: What? I can't hear you.

Police Officer: Stop that noise!

Man: Oh, I see. There. I've stopped!

Police Officer: Thank you. Why were you making that noise?

Man: I was trying to speak with my girl friend.

Police Officer: I don't understand.

Man: Well, I will explain. She lives on the top floor of these flats and I don't want to climb up all those stairs just to ask her to come out with me.

Police Officer: Why not?

Man: She might not want to come and I will have wasted all that energy climbing those stairs.

Police Officer: You are not allowed to sound your horn like that.

Man: Why not?

Police Officer: Because it will annoy other people.

Man: Oh dear, I forgot about that. I'm sorry, I won't do it again.

Police Officer: Very well. I will let you off with a warning this time, but if you do it again I shall report you. You may only sound your horn when there is danger. Do you understand?

Man: Yes. Thank you very much. I will go up the stairs and knock on her door. Perhaps if she sees that I have taken the trouble to do that, she will come out with me!

Police Officer: Good night.

Exercises

1. Answer the following questions:
a) What did the policeman hear?
b) Why was the motorist making that noise?
c) Where did his girl friend live?
d) Why is one not allowed to sound a car horn for this purpose?
e) When may a car horn be sounded?
f) What did the young man do in the end?

2. Übertragen Sie ins Englische:
a) Hören Sie auf, solchen Lärm zu machen!
b) Es ist Ihnen nicht gestattet, die Hupe hierfür zu betätigen.
c) Es wird andere Leute stören.
d) Sie dürfen die Hupe nur bei Gefahr betätigen.
e) Diesmal will ich es bei einer mündlichen Belehrung bewenden lassen.

14. THE EMPTY CARAVAN

A British car is towing a caravan along a German motorway when it is stopped by a police car. The driver of the police car goes to talk to the British driver:

Man: I'm sorry, I didn't mean to do anything wrong.

Policeman: I beg your pardon?

Man: I didn't know that I was doing anything wrong.

Policeman: Well, I want to speak to you about something.

Man: Is it because I inadvertently disobeyed one of your traffic signs? There are some of them that I don't understand.

Policeman: Then you should learn to understand them. It's very dangerous to drive if you don't know what all the warning signs mean.

Man: Yes, I know. I nearly had an accident in Bavaria last year because I misunderstood a sign. I was driving along a narrow road when I saw a sign beside the road and I thought that it was just the name of the next village.

Policeman: What did it say?

Man: 'Gefahr!'

Policeman: That means 'danger!'

Man: Yes, I discovered that when I nearly drove over the side of a mountain – half the road had been swept away by an avalanche!

Policeman: That should have taught you a lesson!

Man: It did. I now know what 'Gefahr' means.

Policeman: That's not quite what I meant. Now, I have stopped you to . . .

Man: Could you hang on just a moment while I tell my wife that everything is all right. She'll think that I'm in trouble when she sees you.

Policeman: I don't think she will – she's not here.

Man: Of course she is. She's in the caravan getting the dinner ready. – That's funny, the caravan is empty.

Policeman: Did you stop at a lay-by about forty miles back along the autobahn?

Man: Yes, but only for a moment. I drove off the motorway to clean my windscreen, then I drove on again.

Policeman: And was your wife in the caravan at that time?

Man: Of course, why?

Policeman: Apparently she got out to get some water when you stopped.

Man: Oh no! I didn't . . . I couldn't have . . .

Policeman: You left her behind.

Man: Oh my God!

Policeman: She telephoned the police and I was asked to stop you and to tell you where she is.

Man: I must go back and pick her up.

Policeman: You can't turn round on the autobahn – you will have to go another five miles to the next exit and then take the south-bound autobahn back towards Stuttgart.

Man: Right. Thank you so much for all the trouble that you've taken, I'm very grateful.

Policeman: I must also remind you that it is illegal to carry a passenger in your caravan while it is being towed.

Man: I'm sorry, I didn't know that. I won't do it again.

Policeman: Very well, but one last thing . . .

Man: Yes!

Policeman: Your wife asks that you turn off the gas under the potatoes. They are probably overcooked already!

Exercises

1. Answer the following questions:
a) What was the British car towing?
b) In which direction was it travelling?
c) For what reason did the British driver think that he had been stopped?
d) Where did he nearly have an accident last year?
e) Which sign did he misunderstand?

f) Where did he stop to clean his windscreen?
g) Why did his wife leave the caravan?

2. Übertragen Sie ins Englische:
a) Es ist sehr gefährlich zu fahren, wenn Sie nicht wissen, was all die Warnschilder bedeuten.
b) Ich habe Sie angehalten, weil . . .
c) Hielten Sie auf einem Rastplatz an der Autobahn, der ungefähr 40 Meilen von hier entfernt ist?
d) War Ihre Frau zu dieser Zeit in dem Wohnwagen?
e) Sie rief die Polizei an, und ich wurde gebeten Sie anzuhalten, um Ihnen zu sagen, wo sie ist.
f) Sie dürfen auf der Autobahn nicht wenden – Sie müssen bis zur nächsten Abfahrt weitere 5 Meilen fahren und dann auf die nach Süden verlaufende Autobahn zurück in Richtung Stuttgart.
g) Ich muß Sie auch daran erinnern, daß es nicht erlaubt ist, Personen während der Fahrt im Wohnwagen mitzuführen.

III. Crime

1. THE ROBBED WOMAN

A woman runs into a police station and speaks to the police officer on duty.

Woman: Please help me!

Police Officer: What's the matter?

Woman: A man just robbed me of my handbag.

Police Officer: Are you hurt?

Woman: Yes, he hit me over the head with a cosh.

Police Officer: Let me see your head. Yes, you have a bump coming up there but it is not bleeding. Would you like to sit down here?

Woman: Thank you.

Police Officer: I will arrange for an ambulance to take you to hospital in a few moments. I think that you should have an X-ray.

Woman: I will go to the hospital if you think I should.

Police Officer: Good. Now tell me what happened, please.

Woman: I was walking along a side street just along the main road from here. A man ran up behind me, coshed me and grabbed my handbag.

Police Officer: Then what happened?

Woman: He jumped into a car and drove off.

Police Officer: Did you get the number of the car?

Woman: I'm afraid not. I was too dazed and only got the last three figures. They were nine, one, seven.

Police Officer: What sort of car was it?

Woman: A Volkswagen beetle.

Police Officer: What colour was it?

Woman: Dark red.

Police Officer: Can you tell me anything else that would help to identify this car?

Woman: Only that it had a spotlight on the roof.

Police Officer: Can you describe the man?

Woman: He was about twenty, I think. He had dark hair, rather long and wavy.

Police Officer: Anything else?

Woman: Yes. He was about six feet tall and was wearing fawn trousers and a dark brown anorak.

Police Officer: Could you identify this man?

Woman: Yes, I'm sure I could.

Police Officer: Will you identify the man if we catch him?

Woman: I certainly will.

Police Officer: Thank you. If you will wait here a little while, I will give this information to our patrol cars by radio. Oh, by the way, what was in your handbag?

Woman: About two hundred marks and my passport. Oh, and my make-up, of course.

Police Officer: Thank you. Just wait there a moment. I will soon be back.

Exercises

1. Answer the following questions:

a) Why did the woman run into the police station?

b) Was she hurt?

c) What did the police officer do to help the woman?

d) What details of the car did she remember?

e) What did she know about the man?

f) What was in the handbag?

2. Übertragen Sie ins Englische:

a) Möchten Sie sich setzen?

b) Ich werde dafür sorgen (arrangieren), daß ein Krankenwagen Sie zum Krankenhaus bringt.

c) Sie sollten sich röntgen lassen.

d) Erzählen Sie mir, was geschah.

e) Was für ein Auto war es?

f) Können Sie den Mann beschreiben?

2. ARRESTING A THIEF

In the main railway station of an industrial town, a man, badly dressed and unshaven, has entered the booking hall. This poorly-dressed man is carrying a suitcase of very fine leather. He goes straight to the left-luggage lockers where he looks for an empty locker. A detective who has gone to the station to make special enquiries, has seen the strange looking man and speaks to him:

Detective: What are you doing there? I'm a police officer.

Man: I am just looking at these left-luggage lockers.

Detective: Do you want to leave your suitcase here?

Man: No, no, officer. My train leaves in a few minutes.

Detective: Have you got a ticket?

Man: Yes, officer. I told you, my train leaves in a few minutes.

Detective: Show me your ticket, please.

Man (searching in his pockets): I can't find my ticket. Perhaps I've lost it.

Detective: All right, don't look for your ticket now. What have you got in this case?

Man: Well, I've just got my personal belongings.

Detective: I see. And what are they?

Man: Well, underclothes, socks, shoes, things like that.

Detective: I see. Well, would you mind showing me, please? Open the case. (He looks at the contents of the case). Yes, I can see your shoes and your underclothes. But here, what about this bag?

Man: Ah, I forgot to tell you about this. This is my wife's jewellery. She asked me to look after it for her.

Detective: And your wife has this number of necklaces and rings?

Man: Yes, she likes jewellery.

Detective: What is your full name, please?

Man: Why do you want to know my name? I'm in a hurry.

Detective: Have you got any means of identification?

Man: Sorry, no, I haven't.

Detective: Well, I am not satisfied with your story and I am arresting you. Further enquiries will be made into this at the police station. This may very well be stolen jewellery. Come with me.

Man: You're making a great mistake, officer. I warn you.

Detective: I am taking you to the police station.

Exercises

1. Answer the following questions:
a) What was strange about the poorly-dressed man?
b) Did he show the detective a ticket for the train?
c) What was in the suitcase?
d) What did the man say about the jewellery?
e) What did the detective do with the man?

2. Übertragen Sie ins Englische:
a) Was tun Sie hier?
b) Haben Sie eine Fahrkarte?
c) Was haben Sie in diesem Koffer?
d) Können Sie sich ausweisen?
e) Weitere Untersuchungen hierüber werden auf der Polizeiwache angestellt werden.

3. THE BURGLARY (1)

A police officer receives a radio call to go to a flat where there has been a burglary. When he arrives at the flat, the policeman is met by a woman who speaks to him in English.

Policeman: Did you call the police?

Woman: Yes, thank you for coming so quickly.

Policeman: What's happened?

Woman: Someone broke into my flat while I was out shopping.

Policeman: When did you discover this?

Woman: When I came home about ten minutes ago.

Policeman: How long were you out?

Woman: Only about an hour.

Policeman: I must have a look round your flat to make sure that there is no one still here, hiding until the coast is clear.

Woman: I would be very grateful if you would make a thorough search. I would hate to think that there was still a man hidden somewhere in my flat. I get very nervous when my husband is away.

Policeman: I will make quite certain that there is no one here.

Woman: Shall I come with you? This has been a terrible shock.

Policeman: I will check the kitchen first. If there is nothing there that I need for fingerprint examination, you can stay there and make yourself a cup to tea.

Woman: That's a good idea. Perhaps you will have a cup of tea as well.

The policeman searches the flat and en-sures that there is no one hidden in any of the rooms or cupboards. Then he rejoins the woman in the kitchen.

Policeman: I've searched everywhere. The burglar has gone.

Woman: I'm very glad. Can I start clear-ing up the mess now?

Policeman: Not yet. I want to examine each room for clues. There may be some fingerprints or footprints.

Woman: If there are any marks, they must be those of the man who broke in. I dusted everywhere only this morning.

Policeman: I'll have a look then. There is one thing that I cannot understand at the moment.

Woman: What's that?

Policeman: I can't see how the thief broke in. I haven't found a point of entry yet. The door hasn't been forced and although there are some open windows, you are on the third floor and there is no way of climbing up.

Woman: I've no idea how he could have got in.

Policeman: Are you sure that you locked the door when you went out shopping?

Woman: I'm positive that I did.

Policeman: Was the door still locked when you came home?

Woman: Yes, I had to use my key to get in. You see it's a self-locking door. All you have to do when you go out is to slam the door and it is automatically locked.

Policeman: That's very strange. Undoubtedly someone has been in here because someone has searched all your rooms, but I just can't work out how. Was anyone in the flat when you left?

Woman: No. I was on my own. I picked up my shopping basket and walked to the shops and came back an hour later.

Policeman: Who has a key to your front door?

Woman: Only my husband and myself. I haven't given a key to the children. I was afraid that they might lose it at school.

Policeman: How do they get into the flat when you are out?

Woman: They use the key under the mat.

Policeman: The what?

Woman: Oh, I never thought to tell you. We keep a spare front door key under the mat outside the front door.

Policeman: Show me, please.

Woman: Look, here is the mat. You just lift up the corner and the key is . . . oh dear, it's gone.

Policeman: Now we know how the burglar got in.

Exercises

1. Answer the following questions:
a) Who called the police?
b) How long was the woman away from her home?
c) Why did the policeman search the flat?
d) What did the woman do while the policeman searched the flat?
e) On which floor is the flat?
f) Where did the woman leave a key?

2. Übertragen Sie ins Englische:
a) Haben Sie die Polizei gerufen (riefen Sie)?
b) Wann haben Sie dies entdeckt (entdeckten Sie dies)?
c) Ich will sicherstellen, daß niemand hier ist.
d) Ich möchte jedes Zimmer nach Spuren durchsuchen. Es könnten dort Fingerabdrücke oder Fußspuren sein.
e) Ich kann nicht verstehen, wie der Dieb eingebrochen ist.
f) Sind Sie sicher, daß die Tür verschlossen war, während Sie zum Einkaufen waren?
g) War die Tür noch verschlossen, als Sie nach Hause kamen?

4. THE BURGLARY (2)

A policeman is dealing with a case of burglary. Entry was gained into a flat by a thief who used a key left by the householder under the doormat outside her front door.

Policeman: Now that we know that the thief used your key and still has it in his possession, you must have the lock on your front door changed straight away.

Woman: Is that necessary?

Policeman: It's necessary. He may come back and steal some more of your belongings.

Woman: Oh my God, that would be awful. Once is enough.

Policeman: Will you now come to each room with me and tell me what has been disturbed, please.

Woman: We can start here, in the living room. He has been to the sideboard and he's pulled all the drawers out and emptied them on the floor.

Policeman: Has anything else been touched?

Woman: Yes, that big bottle on top of the sideboard. That's empty now, but it used to be half full of coins. My children use it as a money box.

Policeman: Right, let me have a close look at it. It looks as though there may be a fingermark on it. I'll put it to one side for examination later.

Woman: There's nothing else that I can see here that has been moved.

Policeman: All right, let's look in the largest of the bedrooms.

Woman: He's made a dreadful mess here. He's pulled all the stuff out of the top of the wardrobe and he's scattered all my clothes on the floor.

Policeman: Have you any idea what is missing?

Woman: I'm not sure. I had some small pieces of jewellery in a music box. That must be here somewhere. Here it is.

Policeman: Don't touch it. Let me look at it first.

Woman: It's empty. That's terrible. I've lost all my little bits and pieces. They weren't very valuable but some of them were given to me by my grandmother.

Policeman: Later on, I'll ask you to describe all the pieces of jewellery for me. Can you think of anything else that may have been taken?

Woman: Not in here, unless some of my husband's clothes have been stolen. My husband will be able to tell you that.

Policeman: When will he be home?

Woman: The day after tomorrow. I can tell you that something has been taken from the room next door.

Policeman: What is that?

Woman: A transistor radio. It was given to my eldest son by his uncle last Christmas.

Policeman: Can you describe it?

Woman: It was quite small.

Policeman: Do you know what make it is?

Woman: I believe it is a Sony, it's certainly one of the Japanese makes.

Policeman: Have you a guarantee card or receipt that might have the serial number of the radio?

Woman: I can probably look for it tonight when I clear up.

Policeman: Will you do that, please. I shall be getting in touch with you because I want you to list everything that has been stolen and describe as much of it as you can.

Woman: I'll do it tonight.

Policeman: I may also have to take your fingerprints to eliminate any marks that you may have left. In that way, I shall be able to make sure that I have the thief's prints.

Woman: I understand. Will I be all right here on my own after you have gone?

Policeman: Oh yes. You can lock your door from the inside so that a key won't turn the lock from the outside. If you telephone now, you should be able to get a man to come and put another lock on your door.

Woman: I feel very nervous about being on my own now.

Policeman: Perhaps you should get a dog. A watchdog can be very useful for deterring housebreakers.

Woman: Dog? . . . But we've got one. I'd forgotten all about him in the excitement. Where is he?

Policeman: Well, he's not in the flat.

Woman: There's only one answer. He's been stolen.

Exercises

1. Answer the following questions:

a) Why must the lock be changed on the front door of the flat?

b) Where did the policeman find a fingerprint?

c) What was stolen from the largest bedroom?

d) When will the woman's husband be returning home?

e) Who owned the transistor radio that was stolen?

f) What was the last thing that the women realized had been stolen?

2. Übertragen Sie ins Englische:

a) Wollen Sie bitte jetzt mit mir in jedes Zimmer kommen und mir sagen, was in Unordnung gebracht worden ist.

b) Es sieht aus, als ob dort Fingerabdrükke sein könnten.

c) Berühren Sie sie (die Spieluhrschachtel) nicht. Lassen Sie mich erst sehen.

d) Später werde ich Sie bitten, mir alle Schmuckstücke zu beschreiben.

e) Wissen Sie, welches Fabrikat es ist?

f) Haben Sie einen Garantieschein oder eine Quittung, auf der die Seriennummer des Radios eingetragen ist?

g) Ich bitte Sie, jeden Gegenstand, der gestohlen worden ist, aufzuschreiben und soweit wie möglich zu beschreiben.

5. THE BURGLARY (3)

A woman walks into a police station and speaks to the uniformed officer on duty.

Woman: I received a telephone call to come here today. My name is Mrs. Howard.

Policeman: Good morning Mrs. Howard. One of our detectives wishes to see you. I'll let him know that you're here. Will you take a seat for a moment, please.

The policeman leaves the room and returns after a few minutes, accompanied by a detective.

Detective: Hallo, Mrs. Howard. Thank you for coming so promptly. We believe that we have some of your property that was stolen.

Woman: Have you caught the man who broke into my flat?

Detective: It's too early to say that. We have a man here that we suspect of being the burglar. He has some property in his possession that we would like you to see.

Woman: I do hope that it is mine. Losing all my jewellery and trinkets was a great shock.

Detective: Come along with me to my office and I will show you what we have.

The detective shows Mrs. Howard to his office. He then produces a white suitcase, which he opens to show Mrs. Howard the contents.

Detective: I would like you to look closely at the articles that are in this suitcase to see if you can identify any of them.

Woman: I can tell you that this is my suitcase.

Detective: How can you be sure?

Woman: I recognize that piece of string tied to the handle. It's part of the label that I put on the case when I flew out here from England.

Detective: You didn't mention a suitcase when you gave us a list of the property stolen from your flat.

Woman: No, I hadn't missed it. It was kept in one of the large cupboards in the hall. I hardly ever go to that cupboard and so I didn't notice that it had gone.

Detective: I see. Well, that's a hopeful sign that we have the right man. Have a look at these pieces of jewellery. Do you recognize them?

Woman: Oh yes. That is my necklace that my husband bought me for my birthday two years ago. That's the brooch that my mother gave me.
Oh yes, here's my gold bracelet . . . and my ring . . . and look! . . . this is my son's transistor radio. He will be pleased to get it back.

Detective: Can you tell me whether this is all your property?

Woman: Yes, it is. Everything that was taken from the flat is here, and I am quite certain that it all belongs to me or my family.

Detective: Good. I'm very pleased. It means that we have caught a thief who has been causing us a lot of trouble for a long time.

Woman: It's marvellous to get all my things back.

Detective: You haven't got quite everything back yet.

Woman: Yes I have, it's all here!

Detective: Not quite all. When we went to search the thief's house, we had a great deal of difficulty in dealing with a dog that tried to bite us. I have a feeling that it may be your dog. You told us that one had been stolen from your apartment.

Woman: Is it a large poodle, a black one?

Detective: It is.

Woman: That's wonderful. I shall be so glad to have him back. He's such a good watchdog.

Detective: He would be a better watchdog if he kept burglars out of your home and didn't bite policemen when they try to rescue him.

Exercises

1. Answer the following questions:
a) Why did the woman go to the police station?
b) Where did the detective take her?
c) What did the detective show to Mrs. Howard?
d) Who bought the necklace for Mrs. Howard? When was it given to her?
e) How did Mrs. Howard recognize her suitcase?
f) What did Mrs. Howard's dog look like?

2. Übertragen Sie ins Englische:
a) Einer unserer Kriminalbeamten möchte Sie sprechen.
b) Wir glauben, etwas von Ihrem Eigentum zu haben, das gestohlen wurde.
c) Ich wünsche, daß Sie sich die Gegenstände, die in diesem Koffer sind, genau ansehen.
d) Sie haben keinen Koffer erwähnt, als Sie uns die Liste gaben.
e) Schauen Sie sich diese Schmuckstücke an. Erkennen Sie sie wieder?

6. THE STOLEN CAR

Two police officers in a patrol car see a beige Opel Rekord car being driven out of a car park beside the autobahn. They notice that the driver accelerates very quickly onto the autobahn so that another car has to brake quickly to avoid it. The policemen quickly follow the suspect car onto the autobahn and soon manage to stop it. They get out of the patrol car and question the driver of the Opel, a young man who replies in English.

1st Policeman: What nationality are you?

Driver: I'm American.

1st Policeman: That was a dangerous piece of driving, wasn't it?

Driver: Yes, I'm sorry. I was in a hurry to get on the road again.

2nd Policeman: You could have easily caused an accident. You have risked your life and the lives of others. – May I see your driving licence, registration book and certificate of insurance?

Driver: I have got only my driving licence and my passport.

2nd Policeman: Are you the owner of this car?

Driver: No, no, officer. It's my friend's car! But he doesn't know that I have taken it. I wanted to visit a girl friend near Waltrop. He is not supposed to know that – you know what I mean, officer?

2nd Policeman: Well, what is your friend's name and address?

Driver: Do you really want to know that? – Okay, his name is Klaus Bäcker, und he lives in Dortmund.

2nd Policeman: Klaus Bäcker, you said, Dortmund . . .? Can you be more precise?

Driver: 3 Goethestraße.

2nd Policeman: Thank you very much. One moment, please. My colleague will speak to you now.

He goes to the patrol car.

1st Policeman: It's your friend's car, you said?

Driver: Yes, officer, my friend's.

1st Policeman: Did you often travel with him in this car?

Driver: Yes, of course.

1st Policeman: Have you any idea how many kilometres the car has done?

Driver: Sorry, I've never looked.

1st Policeman: And do you know what's in the glove compartment?

Driver: Sorry, I can't remember.

1st Policeman: Can you tell me anything about what there is in the boot?

Driver: Sorry, it's only my friend's car.

2nd Policeman (who has just returned): We shall be wanting a further statement from you. Your friend Klaus Bäcker doesn't exist. There is no Klaus Bäcker at 3 Goethestraße, Dortmund.

Driver: I am not going to say any more. You're trying to frighten me.

2nd Policeman: You are under arrest now. Will you please come with us? We have only to wait for another patrol car; our colleagues will take care of the vehicle. – We will take you to the autobahn police station Recklinghausen, where further enquiries will be made.

Exercises

1. Answer the following questions:
a) Why did the police officers wish to stop the car?
b) What excuse did the American give for his dangerous driving?
c) What name and address did he give for his friend?
d) Where was the American going?
e) What parts of the car did the policeman mention in his questions?
f) What did the American do when he was told that Klaus Bäcker did not exist?
g) Where did the policeman take the American?

2. Übertragen Sie ins Englische:
a) Sie haben Ihr eigenes Leben und das anderer aufs Spiel gesetzt.
b) Sind Sie der Eigentümer dieses Wagens?
c) Mein Kollege wird mit Ihnen sprechen.
d) Wir wünschen noch weitere Aussagen von Ihnen.
e) Kommen Sie mit uns. Sie sind verhaftet!

7. THE SHOPLIFTER

A policeman is walking through a shopping centre when he sees two women outside a large store. One of them is holding the arm of the other, who is trying to pull herself free. The policeman recognizes one of the women as a store detective.

Woman: Can you speak English?

Policeman: Yes.

Woman: Then tell this stupid woman to let go of my arm.

Store Detective: I also speak English. I want you to come back to the store.

Woman: Why should I?

Store Detective: Because you have taken some things from the store without paying for them.

Woman: That's nonsense. You're accusing me of being a thief. I've never stolen anything in my life.

Policeman: If you are innocent, then you have nothing to fear from going back into the store so that we can investigate this matter.

Woman: Why can't we sort it out here?

Policeman: It's too public. We can't talk properly with this crowd around us. Come along, we'll go with this lady to the manager's office.

Woman: I don't mind coming with you but I'm not doing anything that she tells me to. I'm always willing to help the police.

Policeman: Good. Let's go then.

The policeman goes with the woman and the store detective to the store manager's office.

Policeman (speaking to the store detective): Is your English good enough to be able to explain what happened in English?

Store Detective: Of course. The facts are very simple. This woman took some bottles of perfume and cosmetics from the counter and put them in her handbag.

Policeman: Did you actually see her do this?

Store Detective: I saw her quite clearly. I had been watching her for some time. One of the assistants had pointed her out to me. She thought that she looked suspicious and, after about ten minutes, so did I.

Policeman: What happened after she put the cosmetics in her handbag?

Store Detective: She picked up a small bottle of cheap toilet water und paid for it.

Policeman: Are you sure that she didn't pay for the other items?

Store Detective: I'm quite sure that she didn't. I checked with the counter assistant immediately afterwards. She told me that this woman had handed her just the one article and paid for that only.

Policeman: Then what happened?

Store Detective: She left the store and I followed her. I stopped her outside and then you came along.

Policeman: I see. (He turns to the Englishwoman). You have heard what the store detective said. What do you want to say about this?

Woman: There's nothing to say. She is telling a pack of lies.

Policeman: Did you buy some toilet water?

Woman: Yes, and I have a receipt for it.

Policeman: Where is it?

Woman: In my handbag.

Policeman: Will you show it to me, please?

Woman: No, I won't.

Policeman: Why not?

Store Detective: Because she knows that you'll see the rest of the stuff that she didn't pay for!

Woman: If she doesn't shut her mouth, I'll shut it for her!

Policeman: All right, that's enough. Show me the things that you bought in this store and any receipts that you have.

Woman: Do I have to?

Policeman: Yes, I insist.

Woman: Very well then.

The woman opens her handbag and tries to prevent the policeman from seeing its contents. As she takes out a bottle of toilet water, the policeman notices several other bottles in the handbag.

Woman: Here you are. Here's what I bought . . . and here's the receipt to show that I paid for it.

Policeman: What about all the other bottles in your handbag?

Woman: I bought them a long time ago in another shop.

Policeman: Show them to me, please.

Woman: Must I? . . . Very well . . . here, take my bag and help yourself.

Policeman: Thank you.

He empties the contents of the handbag onto a table.

Store Detective: There you are. She has the perfume and all the other cosmetics exactly as I described them.

Policeman: Can you be sure that these came from this store?

Store Detective: Yes, from the price labels . . . look, every one has one of this store's labels on it.

Woman: All right, don't sound so smug about it. I'll pay for it all then we can forget about it.

Store Detective: It's too late for that.

Woman: Then keep it, I don't care. I don't like that brand of make-up anyway.

Policeman: You should have thought of that before you took it. I am arresting you for theft.

Exercises

1. Answer the following questions:

a) Where did the policeman take the woman?
b) What did the woman take from the counter?
c) Where did she put the articles?
d) Why was the store detective watching the woman?
e) How many articles did the woman pay for?
f) What did the policeman notice as the woman took a bottle of toilet water from her handbag?
g) Why was the store detective sure that the perfume and cosmetics came from this store?

2. Übertragen Sie ins Englische:

a) Wenn Sie unschuldig sind, haben Sie nichts zu befürchten.
b) Wir können nicht vernünftig sprechen, wenn alle diese Leute um uns herumstehen.
c) Ist Ihr Englisch gut genug, um auf Englisch erklären zu können, was geschah?
d) Was geschah, nachdem sie die Kosmetika in ihre Handtasche steckte?
e) Sind Sie sicher, daß sie für die anderen Gegenstände nicht zahlte?
f) Sie haben gehört, was die Kaufhausdetektivin sagte; was möchten Sie dazu sagen?
g) Zeigen Sie mir die Dinge, die Sie in diesem Kaufhaus gekauft haben und die Quittungen, die Sie haben.
h) Daran hätten Sie denken sollen, bevor Sie es nahmen! Ich verhafte Sie wegen Diebstahls.

8. THE LETTER BOMB

A British businessman has called the police to his office.

Man: I'm grateful to you for coming. I hope that I have not wasted your time.

Policeman: You telephoned to say you thought that you had received a bomb through the post. Is that right?

Man: Yes, that's right. I'm not sure that it is a bomb, but I thought that I had better be on the safe side. Better safe than sorry.

Policeman: That's right. Where is the package?

Man: I've put it in a storeroom out of harm's way.

Policeman: What made you suspect that it was a bomb?

Man: I read an article in a newspaper that described some of the letter bombs that have been delivered to other firms.

Policeman: Is there any reason why a bomb should be sent to your firm?

Man: No other than the fact that this is a Jewish company.

Policeman: Will you take me to see the suspicious package, please?

Man: Certainly. If you will follow me, I'll lead the way.

The man takes the policeman to a storeroom and points to a package on a table.

Man: There it is.

Policeman: Thank you. I'll take a look at it . . . Yes, it's about the right size. I see that it was posted in Amsterdam. Do you know anyone in Holland who might send you a package like this?

Man: There isn't anyone. All our customers are in Germany and Switzerland.

Policeman: It is a very distinctive small parcel, wrapped in brown paper and sealed with adhesive tape. I can't see a return address.

Man: There isn't one. That's one of the things that made me wonder whether it could contain explosive.

Policeman: It certainly looks suspicious.

Man: Are you going to open it?

Policeman: No, that's a job for an expert.

Man: Is it as dangerous as that?

Policeman: It's very dangerous to tamper with any suspected bomb. The slightest disturbance of the detonator will set a bomb off.

Man: You are fairly certain that this is a bomb then.

Policeman: I'm not sure but I'm not going to take any chances. I will make a report about this. What is your full name, please?

Man: George Martin.

Policeman: But this package is addressed to Mr. J. Goldstone. Who is he?

Man: He is the senior manager here. I am in charge of security.

Policeman: I would like Mr. Goldstone to see the suspect package.

Man: Must you? He's a very busy man.

Policeman: The police are also very busy. Will you ask Mr. Goldstone to come here, please.

Man: Very well.

He leaves the room and returns after a few minutes with Mr. Goldstone.

Policeman: Are you Mr. J. Goldstone?

Mr. Goldstone: Yes.

Policeman: Will you look at this small parcel. Do you recognise the handwriting on the label?

Mr. Goldstone: Just a moment, let me put my glasses on ... now, let me see ... ah yes ... I know that writing.

Policeman: Whose is it?

Mr. Goldstone: It's my brother's. He's on holiday. He's on one of those coach tours which visit all the capitals in Europe in two weeks. He was going to send me some cigars from Amsterdam.

Policeman: Are you sure?

Mr. Goldstone: I'm absolutely certain. Here you are ... a small box of Dutch cigars ... you must have one for yourself after all the trouble we have caused you!

Exercises

1. Answer the following questions:

a) Why did the man call the police?

b) Where was the package?

c) Where was the package posted?

d) Why did the policeman not open it?

e) Who was Mr. J. Goldstone?

f) Why did Mr. Goldstone recognise the handwriting?

g) What was in the package?

h) Why was the package posted in Amsterdam?

2. Übertragen Sie ins Englische:

a) Sie riefen an, um zu sagen, daß Sie per Post eine Bombe bekommen haben.

b) Was veranlaßt Sie zu befürchten, daß es eine Bombe ist?

c) Gibt es einen Grund, daß an Ihre Firma eine Bombe geschickt werden sollte?

d) Wollen Sie mich bitte zu dem verdächtigen Päckchen führen?

e) Nein, das ist Aufgabe eines Sachkundigen.

f) Erkennen Sie die Handschrift auf dem Schildchen?

9. THE KIDNAPPED BOY (1)

A detective has been called to the house of a British diplomat, Sir Henry Miller.

Detective: Good evening, sir. I am Detective Prey.

Sir Henry: My name is Miller, Sir Henry Miller. I am most grateful to you for coming so quickly.

Detective: What has happened?

Sir Henry: My son has been kidnapped.

Detective: When did it happen?

Sir Henry: About half an hour ago.

Detective: Where?

Sir Henry: Near the park.

Detective: What happened?

Sir Henry: My son Simon was taken by his nanny to the park to play. She takes him every afternoon if the weather is fine.

Detective: I see, and what happened this afternoon?

Sir Henry: As she was coming out of the park at about a quarter to four, two men grabbed Simon and drove off with him. Miss Dixon, the nanny, ran back here and told my butler, who told me and I called you.

Detective: Why didn't Miss Dixon telephone the police straight away?

Sir Henry: Because she's a stupid girl and she panicked. I suppose it would have been difficult for her anyway – she speaks very little German. She has been here only two months.

Detective: How old is Simon?

Sir Henry: He's just over six.

Detective: Have you had a ransom demand yet?

Sir Henry: No, but doubtless I shall hear something soon.

Detective: Where is Miss Dixon now?

Sir Henry: She's in her room. She is very upset.

Detective: That's understandable, but I will have to talk to her.

Sir Henry: I'll send for her, but I'm afraid she will be able to tell you very little about what happened.

Detective: She may be able to tell me something about the men that took Simon, or the car that they used.

Sir Henry: I have already asked her about them.

Detective: Can she help?

Sir Henry: Not much I'm afraid. All she could remember was that the car was a large white Mercedes driven by a woman and the two men were wearing dark suits.

Detective: Did she take the number of the car?

Sir Henry: Naturally I asked her that. She said that she was too shocked to be able to take any notice of details like the number of the car. She ist not a very intelligent young woman. I really don't know why I hired her.

Detective: Can't you think of any reason why anyone would take your son?

Sir Henry: Isn't it always the same reason – money?

Detective: No, not always. There are other motives for kidnapping.

Sir Henry: Do you think that it might be political?

Detective: I don't know. Could it be?

Sir Henry: I suppose it's a possibility.

Detective: Can you think of any political group that would want to make demands on you?

Sir Henry: Not at the moment. I think it's far more likely that this is the work of some of your local criminals who hope to extort money from me.

Detective: We shall soon know when you hear from the kidnappers.

Sir Henry: How do you think they will contact me?

Detective: I think you are likely to receive a telephone call in the first instance.

Sir Henry: I hope that it's soon. Just waiting for something to happen is dreadful.

Detective: Can I see the young lady now, please?

Sir Henry: Of course. Do you mind if I stay in the room while you question her?

Detective: Certainly not, but I would like you to remain in the background and let me ask the questions.

Sir Henry: Of course, thank you.

Exercises

1. Answer the following questions:

a) When was Simon kidnapped?

b) Where did it happen?

c) How many men took part in the kidnapping?

d) How were they dressed?

e) What sort of car was used?

f) Who was driving the car?

2. Übertragen Sie ins Englische:

a) Warum hat Fräulein Dixon nicht sofort die Polizei angerufen?

b) Haben Sie schon eine Lösegeldforderung erhalten?

c) Hat sie die Nummer des Autos aufgenommen?

d) Können Sie sich einen Grund dafür denken, daß jemand Ihren Sohn mitgenommen hat?

e) Können Sie sich eine politische Gruppe vorstellen, die Forderungen an Sie richten will?

f) Ich glaube, Sie werden wahrscheinlich zunächst einen Telefonanruf bekommen.

g) Ich möchte, daß Sie im Hintergrund bleiben und mich die Fragen stellen lassen.

10. THE KIDNAPPED BOY (2)

A detective is investigating a case in which the son of a diplomat, Sir Henry Miller, has been abducted. He is about to question the nanny who was with the child when he was kidnapped.

Sir Henry: Come in, please, Miss Dixon. This gentleman is a police officer and he wants to ask you some questions.

Miss Dixon: I'm dreadfully sorry about all this, Sir Henry.

Sir Henry: It's all right. It wasn't your fault. You mustn't blame yourself for what happened.

Detective: I just want to ask you a few questions about the people who took Simon.

Miss Dixon: I can't tell you very much. It all happened so quickly.

Detective: You took Simon to the park, is that right?

Miss Dixon: Yes. It was a lovely afternoon and we stayed there from 2 o'clock until about a quarter to four.

Detective: What happened when you left the park?

Miss Dixon: There were two men standing just outside the park gate.

Detective: What did they look like?

Miss Dixon: They were ordinary looking men wearing dark suits.

Detective: Did they say anything to you?

Miss Dixon: No, not a word. They just got hold of Simon and pulled him into the back of a car.

Detective: What sort of car?

Miss Dixon: I'm not sure. I think it might have been a Mercedes.

Detective: What colour?

Miss Dixon: White.

Detective: Did you notice anything else about it?

49

Miss Dixon: No, I'm afraid not.

Detective: Did you notice the colour of the upholstery when the door was open?

Miss Dixon: Let me think ... yes ... it was red, bright red.

Detective: Good. Now, are you quite sure that you heard nothing said by either man?

Miss Dixon: No, I don't think so ... Well, not really anything very important.

Detective: You must let me decide what is important. Did you hear anything said?

Miss Dixon: Just one word.

Detective: What was it?

Miss Dixon: As the second man got into the car, and just before he shut the door, he said 'right'.

Detective: Are you sure?

Miss Dixon: Yes, I'm positive.

Detective: The English word 'right' – not a German word?

Miss Dixon: That's right.

Sir Henry: You didn't tell me that ...

Detective: Just a moment, Sir Henry, please allow me to handle this.

Sir Henry: I'm sorry. Do carry on, please.

Detective: Didn't it strike you as strange that the man spoke in English?

Miss Dixon: Not at the time ... everyone around me speaks English ... I didn't realize until now that it was unusual.

Detective: Who was driving the car?

Miss Dixon: A blonde woman.

Detective: Can you describe her?

Miss Dixon: Not very clearly as I only saw her from behind.

Detective: Tell me about her.

Miss Dixon: She looked very elegant with an expensive hair style and what looked like sapphire ear-rings.

Sir Henry: What did you say? Did you say sapphire ear-rings?

Miss Dixon: Yes, that's right.

Sir Henry: One large sapphire surrounded by small white diamonds?

Miss Dixon: Yes, that's it exactly!

Sir Henry: Oh my God!

Detective: Do you know this woman?

Sir Henry: I know her very well. She's my wife!

Detective: Your wife? Why should she help to kidnap your son?

Sir Henry: We are separated and I am going to divorce her. When she left me about six months ago, I refused to let her take Simon, so she has taken him by force.

Detective: Have you a court order placing the boy in your custody?

Sir Henry: Not yet. My lawyers are working on it.

Detective: If you are quite certain that it was your wife who took Simon, then this does not seem to be a police matter.

Sir Henry: I'm quite sure it was my wife, so I need not trouble you any further. This is now a family matter and I will deal with it. Thank you so much for your help. The truth would have taken much longer to emerge without your assistance.

Exercises

1. Answer the following questions:
   a) At what time did Miss Dixon go to the park?
   b) How long did she stay there?
   c) When did she leave?
   d) What colour was the interior of the car?
   e) What word did Miss Dixon hear one of the kidnappers say?
   f) Describe the ear-rings worn by the woman driving the car.
   g) Who did Sir Henry Miller think the driver was?

2. Übertragen Sie ins Englische:

a) Ich möchte Ihnen nur einige Fragen in bezug auf die Leute stellen, die Simon mitgenommen haben.
b) Sagten Sie etwas zu Ihnen?
c) Sahen Sie die Farbe der Polster, als die Tür offen war.
d) Sie müssen mich entscheiden lassen, was wichtig ist. Hörten Sie, daß etwas gesagt wurde?
e) Kommt es Ihnen nicht eigentümlich vor, daß der Mann Englisch sprach?
f) Wer fuhr das Auto?
g) Können Sie sie beschreiben?
h) Wenn Sie ganz sicher sind, daß es Ihre Frau war, die Simon mitgenommen hat, so scheint dies keine Angelegenheit mehr für die Polizei zu sein.

11. THE WATER INSPECTOR

The detective goes to the house of an elderly lady who has been robbed.

Lady: Please, come in. Do you speak English?

Detective: Yes, can you speak German?

Lady: Only a little, I'm afraid. Although I've lived in Germany for ten years, I've never been able to learn your language. I suppose I'm too old to learn.

Detective: It's all right, I don't mind speaking English.

Lady: Thank you so much.

Detective: I understand that you have been robbed.

Lady: Yes, that's right.

Detective: When did it occur?

Lady: This morning, at about eleven o'clock.

Detective: Why did you wait four hours before you phoned the police?

Lady: I didn't telephone you . . . that was my daughter-in-law.

Detective: Does she live here?

Lady: Oh no, I live on my own. I used to live here with my husband but he passed away about a year ago and so I live by myself.

Detective: But your daughter-in-law rang?

Lady: Yes, that's right. You see, I didn't know what to do when I found out that I had been robbed so I phoned my daughter-in-law.

Detective: I see. She then rang the police.

Lady: No. She telephoned my son, but he wasn't in his office, so she left a message for him to ring her. When he came in, he rang her and she told him what had happened.

Detective: And he told his wife to call the police.

Lady: That's right.

Detective: Good. Now perhaps you will tell me what happened . . .

Lady: Certainly. A man rang my doorbell and I answered the door.

Detective: What did he look like?

Lady: He was just on ordinary looking man. I should say he was quite young – about forty perhaps.

Detective: What did he say?

Lady: I'm not quite sure. As I said, I'm not very good at German. I think he said that he had come to test the water pressure. I'm sure it was something to do with water.

Detective: Why are you so sure?

Lady: Because he asked me to go into kitchen to turn on the cold water tap.

Detective: Did you do that?

Lady: Yes, and the water ran out as usual.

Detective: Then what happened?

Lady: I came back here and told him that the water was all right.

Detective: What did he say then?

Lady: He thanked me and left.

Detective: When did you notice that something was missing?

Lady: About a quarter of an hour later when I went to look for my purse.

Detective: Where was your purse before it was stolen?

Lady: Just there on top of the sideboard.

Detective: Has anyone else been here today?

Lady: No, only the man about the water and you.

Detective: How much money did you have in your purse?

Lady: I'm not absolutely sure, but I think I had about eight hundred marks.

Detective: What?

Lady: It might have been a little more, but I don't think so.

Detective: Why do you keep so much money in your purse?

Lady: I thought it was safe here. I've never had anything taken before.

Detective: You should never walk around with large sums of cash in your purse.

Lady: Will you be able to get my money back?

Detective: I doubt it. It will take time to catch this man.

Lady: But surely the water company will know where he is, won't they?

Detective: He wasn't a genuine workman. He was a thief who poses as one to get into houses.

Lady: Do you mean to say he wasn't a proper water inspector?

Detective: I'm sure he wasn't.

Lady: Oh dear, my son will be cross. He's told me so many times not to let strangers into the house.

Detective: Then why did you let him in? Had you seen him before?

Lady: No, but he was a water inspector – he told me so. I never thought of him as a stranger! Surely there's nothing strange about people like postmen, policemen and meter readers, is there?

Detective: I'm not sure about genuine ones, but fake water inspectors are very strange indeed and must never be let into your house!

Exercises

1. Answer the following questions:
a) How long has the lady lived in Germany?
b) When did the theft occur?
c) Who did the lady telephone?
d) Who called the police?
e) What did the man ask the lady to do?
f) Where was the purse before it was stolen?
g) How much money was in the purse?

2. Übertragen Sie ins Englische:
a) Es macht mir nichts aus, Englisch zu sprechen.
b) Ich höre, daß Sie beraubt worden sind.
c) Warum warteten Sie vier Stunden lang, bevor Sie die Polizei anriefen?
d) Nun wollen Sie mir bitte erzählen, was geschah.
e) Wann stellten Sie fest, daß Sie etwas vermißten?
f) Wo war die Geldbörse, bevor sie gestohlen wurde?
g) War heute sonst noch jemand hier?
h) Wieviel Geld war in Ihrer Geldbörse?

12. THE AU PAIR GIRL

A detective is investigating a burglary in a large house. He is about to question the English au pair girl.

Detective: Do you know that there was a burglary here last night?

Girl: Yes. I was the first one up this morning, so it was me that saw the mess first.

Detective: What time was that?

Girl: About half past seven.

Detective: Do you always get up at that time?

Girl: Yes. I have to get the breakfast ready. I squeeze some oranges to make the orange juice and prepare the coffee for eight o'clock.

Detective: I see. What time did you go to bed last night?

Girl: About ten o'clock, but I lay awake reading until nearly midnight.

Detective: Did you hear anything during the night?

Girl: Oh no. I sleep very soundly.

Detective: The thieves got in through the back door, your room is just above there; are you sure that you didn't hear anything at all?

Girl: No, I don't think so. I thought I heard someone at about half past twelve, but then I knew there couldn't be anyone so I went to sleep.

Detective: I beg your pardon – what did you say?

Girl: I thought I heard someone – but I was wrong.

Detective: What made you think that you heard someone?

Girl: I thought I heard a key in the door.

Detective: After midnight?

Girl: Yes.

Detective: What did you do?

Girl: Do?

Detective: Yes.

Girl: Nothing. I just waited and when nothing happened, I went to sleep.

Detective: You waited . . . is that right?

Girl: Yes.

Detective: What were you waiting for?

Girl: Waiting for? . . . why . . . nothing.

Detective: You're blushing. I don't think that you are being completely truthful with me.

Girl: I don't know what you mean.

Detective: I think you do. Now tell me what you were waiting for.

Girl: If I tell you, will you promise not to tell Frau Koch?

Detective: That depends on what you tell me. Now . . . I want the truth! What were you waiting for?

Girl: I thought that it might be my boy friend.

Detective: What boy friend?

Girl: Maarten de Vries.

Detective: Has he got a key to the back door of this house?

Girl: Yes, I gave him one.

Detective: Why?

Girl: He asked for it.

Detective: But why did you give him one?

Girl: Why do you think? So that he could come and see me.

Detective: How long has this been going on?

Girl: Three weeks tomorrow.

Detective: When did you give him the key?

Girl: Only yesterday. Before that he used to whistle below my window on the nights that he could come, and I would let him in. I was always afraid that Frau Koch would hear us, so Maarten suggested that I have a copy made of the door key.

Detective: Where does Maarten live?

Girl: I don't know. Why do you want to know? You can't think that Maarten would steal anything?

Detective: Well, if I can find him, I can ask him. If he is innocent then there is no harm in telling me where to find him. Are you sure that he told you his correct name – De Vries?

Girl: He didn't tell me. I found out for myself.

Detective: How?

Girl: His passport dropped out of his pocket when he was here the night before last. I still have it. I was going to give it back to him last night if he had come.

Detective: Let us go and get the passport. It will give me great pleasure to hand it back to Maarten de Vries, then I can ask him a few questions at the same time!

Exercises

1. Answer the following questions:

a) Who discovered the burglary?
b) What time did the girl go to bed?
c) At what time did the girl think that she heard the noise of the key in the door?
d) Why did the detective think that the girl was not being completely truthful?
e) Who was this girl waiting for?
f) When did she give him the key to the door?
g) How did the girl find out the name of her boy friend?

2. Übertragen Sie ins Englische:

a) Wissen Sie, daß hier in der vergangenen Nacht ein Einbruch stattgefunden hat?
b) Hörten Sie in der vergangenen Nacht irgend etwas?
c) Ich glaube nicht, daß Sie mir gegenüber ganz aufrichtig sind.
d) Erzählen Sie mir, worauf Sie warteten!
e) Hat er einen Schlüssel zu der Hintertür dieses Hauses?
f) Wann gaben Sie ihm einen Schlüssel?
g) Wo wohnt Maarten?
h) Sind Sie sicher, daß er Ihnen seinen tatsächlichen Namen genannt hat?

13. THE FOOTBALL FAN

A policeman is on duty near a football stadium shortly before the kick-off of an international football match. He sees five boys fighting with another boy who has been knocked to the ground. As the policeman approaches the five boys run away leaving the boy lying on the ground.

Boy: Are you a copper?

Policeman: I'm a policeman, yes.

Boy: Thank Christ, you turned up. They would have killed me.

Policeman: I doubt that. Get up. I want to talk to you.

Boy: What about?

Policeman: Why were you fighting?

Boy: I wasn't fighting. I was minding my own business when they set about me.

Policeman: Why did they do that?

Boy: How do I know?

Policeman: There must have been a reason.

Boy: Well, I don't know what it was.

Policeman: Tell me what happened.

Boy: I was walking to the match . . .

Policeman: On your own?

Boy: No, with two of my mates.

Policeman: What happened?

Boy: We saw those German supporters so we shouted a few things to them.

Policeman: What did you shout?

Boy: I don't remember.

Policeman: I don't suppose you shouted anything very pleasant. What happened then?

Boy: They turned round and came after us so we all ran away, but I fell over and they caught me.

Policeman: And that was when I came along, was it?

Boy: Yes. Thanks very much. Can I go now, sir?

Policeman: Not for a moment. What's your name?

Boy: Arthur... Arthur Watson.

Policeman: How old are you?

Boy: Sixteen.

Policeman: I don't believe you. Show me your passport.

Boy: All right. I'm fourteen.

Policeman: Where's your passport?

Boy: My dad's got it.

Policeman: Where is your father?

Boy: I don't know. He went into a pub to have a few beers before the match, so I went with my mates.

Policeman: How are you going to find your father to go home?

Boy: I'm going to meet him in the football ground. I've got my own ticket.

Policeman: Show me.

Boy: It's in my pocket... here, hang on, I can't find it.

Policeman: Search all your pockets.

Boy: I have... it's not in any of them. One of those Germans must have nicked it.

Policeman: Pardon?

Boy: Nicked it... stolen it. I've been robbed.

Policeman: You may have lost it... when did you last have it?

Boy: I can't remember... What can I do? How can I get into the match?

Policeman: You can't get in without a ticket. You will have to come with me.

Boy: But my father's got my train ticket to go home.

Policeman: We'll get the announcer at the stadium to tell your father to collect you from the police station. If you are well-behaved, you may be able to see the match on television.

Boy: Fancy coming all this way just to see it on telly...

Policeman: You should have kept out of trouble...

Boy: It wasn't my fault... how was I to know that those German boys would understand what I shouted at them in English!

Exercises

1. Answer the following questions:
a) Where did this incident occur?
b) How many boys were fighting?
c) What age is the boy?
d) Where is his passport?
e) Where did his father go?
f) Why can't the boy go to the football match?
g) How will the policeman tell the boy's father where to collect the boy?

2. Übertragen Sie ins Englische:
a) Steh auf, ich möchte mit dir sprechen.
b) Weshalb hast du dich (habt ihr euch) geprügelt?
c) Es muß einen Grund gegeben haben.
d) Wie alt bist du?
e) Ich glaube dir nicht, zeig mir deinen Reisepaß.
f) Wo ist dein Reisepaß?
g) Durchsuch all deine Taschen.
h) Du könntest ihn verloren haben, wann hast du ihn zuletzt gehabt?
i) Wir werden zum Stadionsprecher gehen, um deinem Vater mitzuteilen, daß er dich von der Polizeistation abholt.
j) Du hättest dich aus dem Streit heraushalten sollen.

14. THE ROBBERY (1)

A police car is sent to deal with an emergency call from a telephone box on a quiet road just outside a large town. When it arrives at the kiosk, it is met by a young man who has a large gash on his forehead.

Man: We've been held up and robbed!

Policeman: When?

Man: About half an hour ago.

Policeman: Why did it take so long to call us?

Man: It happened about a mile and a half down the road. This is the nearest phone.

Policeman: That's a nasty gash on your head. You will have to go to hospital.

Man: It's not too bad. My boss is much worse off than me.

Policeman: Where is he?

Man: He's still in the car.

Policeman: Where is the car?

Man: It's still where we got held up and robbed.

Policeman: We had better go there straight away. We can talk in the car on the way.

Man: I'm not sure that there's much I can tell you. It all happened very quickly.

Policeman: Don't worry, we'll sort it out. Here's my colleague with the first aid box . . . let him put a piece of sticking plaster on your forehead.

Man: Thank you . . .

Policeman: Good, now get into the car. Mr. . . .

Man: Phelps . . . Richard Phelps

Policeman: Get in, Mr. Phelps.

The man gets into the police car, which sets off towards the scene of the robbery.

Policeman: Did the men who robbed you drive off in a car?

Man: Yes, a white Mercedes.

Policeman: Can you remember its number?

Man: I've written it down on this cigarette packet.

Policeman: Good, let me have it and I'll circulate it on the radio.

Man: Here you are.

Policeman: Thanks. How many men were there?

Man: I saw four.

Policeman: Was there anything distinctive about them?
We will get down to details later.

Man: They all wore stockings over their faces.

Policeman: What about their clothes?

Man: Two of them were wearing black windcheaters . . . that's about all I can tell you.

Policeman: That will do for now. Which way did they drive off?

Man: Towards the town.

Policeman: Right. I'll put that out over the air.

The policeman uses the radio to circulate the information that he has obtained from the man.

Policeman: Right, that's done. I've also asked for an ambulance to meet us at the scene of the robbery.

Man: Thank you, I'm sure that Herr Schnabel will need one.

Policeman: He's your employer?

Man: Yes. He runs a large business about twenty kilometres up the road . . . just before you get to the village.

Policeman: Yes, I know it well.

Man: He takes a lot of cash and so once a week he drives to the bank in town to deposit it.

Policeman: And I suppose he does it at the same time on the same day every week.

Man: That's right. He's a stickler for doing everything at exactly the right time.

Policeman: That would be a great help to the men who robbed him. They've probably been watching him for weeks until they had worked out a foolproof plan.

Man: I don't suppose Herr Schnabel thought of that.

Policeman: I'm afraid a lot of people don't. Here we are – this is the place, isn't it?

Man: Yes. Here's Herr Schnabel sitting in his car.

Policeman: And I suppose the other car was used to ram yours, was it?

Man: That's right. That's how they stopped us. Our car was so badly damaged that it was not fit to be driven.

Policeman: I see. Just sit where you are for a moment, please, Mr. Phelps.

The police car stops near two cars and the policemen deal with Herr Schnabel, who is put in an ambulance. Later the policeman speaks to Mr. Phelps once more.

Policeman: Right. Herr Schnabel will be taken good care of at the hospital. Are you sure that you ought not to go with him?

Man: I don't know. I have a splitting headache!

Policeman: I'm not surprised. You're lucky that you weren't killed . . . You must have received a blow with something heavy.

Man: I was hit with an iron bar.

Policeman: Why don't you go to the hospital and we'll send a detective to see you there.

Man: Perhaps I'd better . . . I'm beginning to feel dizzy.

Policeman: That will probably be shock . . . come along, I'll help you to the ambulance.

Man: Are you sure there is nothing for me to do here?

Policeman: The fingerprint experts and photographers will be here soon. There's nothing for you to do. You concentrate on trying to remember all you can about the men who attacked you.

Exercises

1. Answer the following questions:
a) Who made the emergency call to the police?
b) Why did he call the police?
c) What had happened to his forehead?
d) How did the robbers leave the scene of the robbery?
e) How often did Herr Schnabel drive to the bank?
f) How did the robbers stop Herr Schnabel's car?
g) What was Mr. Phelps hit with?

2. Übertragen Sie ins Englische:
a) Warum hat es so lange gedauert, uns anzurufen?
b) Das ist eine böse Schnittwunde an Ihrem Kopf, Sie müssen ins Krankenhaus.
c) Wir sollten besser sofort dorthin fahren. Wir können unterwegs im Auto sprechen.
d) Hier ist mein Kollege mit der Erste-Hilfe-Ausrüstung; lassen Sie ihn ein Pflaster auf Ihre Stirn kleben.
e) Fuhren die Männer, die Sie beraubten, in einem Auto davon?
f) Gab es etwas Charakteristisches bei ihnen?
g) Ich bin nicht überrascht; Sie können froh sein, daß Sie nicht getötet wurden. Sie müssen einen Schlag mit einem schweren Gegenstand bekommen haben.

15. THE ROBBERY (2)

A young man is in hospital having been in a car which was rammed by robbers earlier in the day. He is being interviewed by a detective.

Detective: Mr. Richard Phelps?

Man: That's me.

Detective: I'm Detective Horst Krause. I want to talk to you about the robbery that took place earlier today.

Man: I don't think I'm going to be much help – I can't remember very much about what happened.

Detective: Don't worry. I'll just ask a few questions and you answer to the best of your ability. When did the robbery happen?

Man: At exactly half past ten.

Detective: Good . . . I know where it happened . . . Who was driving the car you were in?

Man: Herr Schnabel . . . I work for him.

Detective: Right. Now then . . . at half past ten Herr Schnabel was driving his car towards the town . . . what happened?

Man: There was a grey Peugeot parked just off the road in a cart-track.

Detective: How many men were in the car?

Man: I'm not sure, I couldn't see because of a hedge, but I think there were two.

Detective: What happened then?

Man: As we drew level with the Peugeot, it shot forward and rammed our car.

Detective: And you stopped?

Man: We had to. The force of the car ramming us knocked our car into the bank at the side of the road.

Detective: What did the men do then?

Man: One man came to my side of the car and the other one attacked Herr Schnabel.

Detective: What did they look like?

Man: They were both about the same height . . . as I told the policeman earlier, they were wearing stockings over their heads.

Detective: How tall were they?

Man: About my height . . . five feet eight.

Detective: What did they do?

Man: They pulled open the doors of our car, pulled us out and hit us.

Detective: What with?

Man: Iron bars . . . I caught a glancing blow on my forehead and one on my arm. Herr Schnabel wasn't so lucky. He was hit on the head and knocked unconscious.

Detective: Did you remain conscious?

Man: Oh yes. I was dazed, but I saw everything that happened.

Detective: What did the men do after they struck you?

Man: One of them grabbed the briefcase from the back seat of the car.

Detective: Then?

Man: They got into the white Mercedes and drove off.

Detective: How many men were in the Mercedes?

Man: Only the driver.

Detective: So, two men attacked you and there was one man in the Mercedes – that makes three.

Man: Yes, that's right.

Detective: But you told the police officer at the scene that you saw four men. Where was the fourth man?

Man: I'm not sure.

Detective: Were there three or four men?

Man: Only three . . . I must have been confused when I said earlier that there were four.

Detective: I see.

Man: Have you traced the getaway car? I gave the number to the police.

Detective: Oh yes, we've found it. It was stolen from Düsseldorf and abandoned here in town shortly after the robbery.

Man: How is Herr Schnabel?

Detective: He is very badly hurt.

Man: Oh my God . . . that's terrible.

Detective: Yes, isn't it . . . but that's what happens when someone hits you with an iron bar.

Man: I was very lucky.

Detective: Yes, weren't you! I'm a little puzzled about your injuries . . .

Man: What's wrong with them?

Detective: Well . . . the cut on your head . . . although it bled a lot . . . it's not very deep . . . are you sure you were hit with an iron bar?

Man: Yes, of course I'm sure.

Detective: But you have only a bruise . . . Herr Schnabel's arms were broken . . .

Man: I suppose the man that hit me must have had less strength than the one who hit Herr Schnabel.

Detective: Yes, that's probably it. Can I ask you about the previous times that you've done the same journey with Herr Schnabel.

Man: What about them?

Detective: Have the trips always taken place at the same time as today?

Man: Yes, every week it was the same.

Detective: Have you ever noticed anyone following you on these trips?

Man: No, I can't say that I have.

Detective: How long have you worked for Herr Schnabel?

Man: About six months . . . it's an exchange visit . . . one of his German workers has gone to Britain for the same period.

Detective: When are you due to return to Britain?

Man: At the end of this week.

Detective: So this would have been your last trip with the money to the bank?

Man: Yes . . . I hadn't realized that . . . that was bad luck.

Detective: Yes, wasn't it . . . especially for Herr Schnabel!

Exercises

1. Answer the following questions:

a) When did the robbery happen?
b) Where was the grey Peugeot parked?
c) What did the Peugeot do?
d) What happened to Herr Schnabel?
e) From where was the white Mercedes stolen?
f) How long has Mr. Phelps worked for Herr Schnabel?
g) When is he due to return to Britain?

2. Übertragen Sie ins Englische:

a) Ich möchte mit Ihnen über den Raubüberfall sprechen, der heute stattgefunden hat.
b) Machen Sie sich keine Sorgen, ich will nur ein paar Fragen stellen und Sie beantworten sie so gut wie möglich.
c) Wie viele Männer waren in dem Auto?
d) Wie sahen sie aus?
e) Wie groß waren sie?
f) Blieben Sie bei Bewußtsein?
g) Es (das Auto) wurde in Düsseldorf gestohlen und in dieser Stadt kurz nach dem Raubüberfall abgestellt.
h) Haben Sie jemals jemanden gesehen, der Sie auf dieser Fahrt verfolgte?

16. THE ROBBERY (3)

A young man is being questioned by a detective about a robbery which occurred earlier in the day.

Detective: I want to make sure that I have the facts clear in my mind. Correct me if I go wrong, will you please?

Man: Certainly.

Detective: Two men hit you and Herr Schnabel with iron bars and one of them took the briefcase containing a week's takings from Herr Schnabel's firm . . . right?

Man: That's right.

Detective: And you said that this journey has always taken place on the same day and at the same time of day.

Man: That's all quite correct.

Detective: Are you quite sure that you've told me all you know?

Man: What else can I tell you?

Detective: How many times have you made this journey to the bank?

Man: Every week for the six months I've been working for Herr Schnabel.

Detective: Many times . . . and always the same route?

Man: Yes.

Detective: So you know the road very well?

Man: Of course.

Detective: Then why did you walk a mile and a half back along the road to a telephone box when there is a farm house with a telephone only two hundred metres further along the road?

Man: I'd forgotten about the farm house . . . I was confused . . . I'd just been hit on the head.

Detective: Yes, that blow on the head. You said that you were hit with an iron bar?

Man: That's right.

Detective: But the doctor found a small splinter of wood in the cut on your forehead.

Man: Perhaps I was hit with a piece of wood then . . . it certainly hurt.

Detective: I'm sure it did, but not as much as the fractured skull and broken arms that Herr Schnabel suffered.

Man: Are you sure he won't die?

Detective: You are very anxious about him.

Man: I am . . . I like him. He's been very good to me.

Detective: But his wife says that you and he were always quarrelling!

Man: She's exaggerating.

Detective: And the quarrels were about some of the friends that you have made.

Man: Herr Schnabel is an old-fashioned reactionary . . . he doesn't like my friends – they are too modern for him.

Detective: You've been asked several times if today's journey was at the same time as usual . . . each time you've said that it was.

Man: That's right.

Detective: I'm going to ask you once more . . . is that true?

Man: Are you calling me a liar?

Detective: In this case I am . . . Herr Schnabel normally leaves home at half past nine, but today he left later than usual, at ten o'clock, because his wife is ill and he stayed to help her.

Man: Well, I didn't think half an hour was important.

Detective: Perhaps it isn't normally, but today it was.

Man: Why was it so important today?

Detective: Because the farmer who uses the cart-track, where the Peugeot waited, went along it at twenty past ten this morning.

Man: Well?

Detective: The Peugeot wasn't there then, yet it was in position when you came along ten minutes later.

Man: So?

Detective: The villains who staged this robbery knew exactly when your car would be coming . . .

Man: They must have followed us on previous occasions.

Detective: In that case they would have expected you at ten o'clock – not half past. No, someone told them when to expect your car.

Man: It wasn't me!

Detective: Are you sure? You made a telephone call this morning – shortly after Herr Schnabel told you that he would be leaving half an hour late. Who did you call?

Man: A friend.

Detective: Who?

Man: I can't tell you.

Detective: Why not?

Man: You know why . . . I can't grass on my friends.

Detective: So you organised the robbery this morning.

Man: I didn't organise it . . . I just passed on information . . . I didn't rob anyone.

Detective: You hated Herr Schnabel and you used this method to get at him . . . to have him killed.

Man: No! I didn't want him to be badly hurt.

Detective: How much of the stolen money was to be your share?

Man: A quarter.

Detective: I think the time has come for you to tell me all about this . . . I must first caution you that what you say may be given in evidence . . .

Exercises

1. Answer the following questions:
a) How many times had Mr. Phelps made the journey to the bank?
b) What reason did Mr. Phelps give for walking to a telephone box and not to the farm house?
c) What did the doctor find in the cut on Mr. Phelps' forehead?
d) Why did Mr. Phelps and Herr Schnabel quarrel?
e) Why did Herr Schnabel leave home later than usual?
f) At what time did the farmer go along the cart track?
g) Was the Peugeot there at that time?

h) When did Mr. Phelps make a telephone call that morning?
i) Who did he telephone?
j) How much of the stolen money was to be Mr. Phelps' share?
k) Who hit Mr. Phelps with a piece of wood? Why did he do this?

2. Übertragen Sie ins Englische:
a) Wie oft haben Sie diese Fahrt zur Bank gemacht?
b) Ich werde Sie noch einmal fragen: Ist das wahr?
c) Die Schurken, die diesen Raubüberfall inszeniert haben, wußten genau, wann Ihr Auto kommen würde.

17. THE DRUG ADDICT

A police officer sees a young man lying on the steps of a block of offices. The young man is dirty and has long, unkempt hair. He looks pale and thin and rather helpless. Thinking that the young man is ill, the policeman walks over to him and speaks to him.

Policeman: Are you all right?

Young man: Yes. I'm tired, that's all.

Policeman: You are British, aren't you?

Young man: Yes, I'm from London.

Policeman: What are you doing here?

Young man: I'm travelling around.

Policeman: How did you get here?

Young man: I hitch-hiked. Why are you asking me so many questions?

Policeman: Come with me. I want to find out more about you.

As the young man gets up, he takes a cigarette packet from his pocket and throws it into the gutter.

Policeman: Why have you thrown that away?

Young man: It's empty, why do you think?

Policeman: Pick it up and give it to me.

Young man: Here you are. I tell you that it's empty.

The policeman opens the packet. There are no cigarettes in it, but he sees that it contains a small piece of crumpled silver paper. He unwraps the silver paper and finds that it contains a piece of brown substance.

Policeman: This looks like cannabis!

Young man: It is. I'd forgotten that it was there.

Policeman: It is an offence to possess cannabis. I am going to arrest you.

Young man: Oh God! Do you have to make a fuss over a little piece of hemp?

Policeman: Yes. It's a serious matter to have dangerous drugs in your possession. Show me your arms.

The young man rolls back his sleeves. His arms are covered with red needle marks.

Young man: I haven't got any hard drugs on me. It's days since I last had a fix.

Policeman: What drugs have you been taking?

Young man: Anything I can get. Mostly heroin mixed with cocaine if I can get them. I swear I haven't any on me now. Look, here are my syringe and needles.

Policeman: All right, come with me.

Young man: Will I be sent back home?

Policeman: Perhaps. How old are you?

Young man: Eighteen. My parents think that I'm working in Germany.

Policeman: It is not for me to decide what happens to you. I am going to take you to the police station now.

Exercises

1. Answer the following questions:

a) Why did the police officer speak to the young man?
b) Where did the young man throw the cigarette packet?
c) What was in the cigarette packet?
d) What did the police officer see on the young man's arm?
e) What drugs are mostly taken by the young man when he can get them?
f) What did the young man give to the police officer?

2. Übertragen Sie ins Englische:

a) Was tun Sie hier?
b) Warum haben Sie das weggeworfen?
c) Es ist strafbar (eine Übertretung), Marihuana zu besitzen.
d) Es ist eine ernste Angelegenheit, im Besitz gefährlicher Drogen zu sein.
e) Welche Drogen haben Sie genommen?
f) Wie alt sind Sie?

18. THE BANK RAID

There has been an armed robbery at a bank in the centre of a large town. An English tourist happened to be there at the time when the robbery took place. The tourist is being questioned about the robbery by a police officer.

Policeman: I understand that you were in the bank this morning.

Tourist: That's right. I went there to cash some traveller's cheques.

Policeman: What time did you go into the bank?

Tourist: About eleven o'clock. I went in through the main door and started to walk to the counter. Then I heard the door crash open behind me and someone shouted something in German.

Policeman: Do you know what was said?

Tourist: I'm afraid not . . . it started with 'Achtung' . . . and that's the only word I recognized.

Policeman: All right. What happened then?

Tourist: I looked round and saw three masked men behind me.

Policeman: What did they do?

Tourist: One stayed by the door and the other two went towards the counter.

Policeman: What did you do?

Tourist: Stood where I was. I was absolutely rooted to the spot with fear. I just prayed that no one would be killed.

Policeman: Can you describe the men?

Tourist: It's very difficult because they were wearing nylon stockings over their faces.

Policeman: Let's take one man at the time. You say that one of them stayed by the door. What did he look like?

Tourist: He was a big man.

Policeman: How tall was he?

Tourist: I would say . . . about your height. Yes, about six feet tall.

Policeman: How was he dressed?

Tourist: I can't honestly say. I was too aware of the gun he was carrying.

Policeman: What sort of gun was it?

Tourist: A sawn-off shotgun. It was a double-barrelled gun cut down to about eighteen inches in length. The end of the butt had been sawn off as well.

Policeman: That's very clear. Now tell me about the other two men.

Tourist: They were about five feet eight inches tall, both wearing dark clothes and with stockings over their heads.

Policeman: What did they do?

Tourist: One of them had a sack. He took it to the counter and gave it to the cashier. He said something to her but I don't know what.

Policeman: What did the third man do?

Tourist: He just stood there and pointed a pistol at the cashier.

Policeman: What sort of pistol?

Tourist: It's difficult to say. It was an automatic and not a revolver, that I know. As to what sort of automatic pistol it was, that's not so easy. It could have been a Luger.

Policeman: Did the man with the sack have a gun?

Tourist: Yes, he did. When the cashier didn't take the sack immediately, he fired one shot into the air. It was a small calibre automatic. You can soon find out what sort of gun it was because the cartridge case was ejected when he fired that round of ammunition into the ceiling. The cartridge case must still be on the floor and the bullet must be lodged in the ceiling.

Policeman: We've found them, thank you. Is there anything else that you can remember that will help us?

Tourist: I don't think so . . . oh yes, just one small point. The tall man with the shotgun . . .

Policeman: Yes? What about him?

Tourist: The other two men wore gloves but he didn't. I remember noticing that he had something tattooed on the back of his left hand.

Policeman: Could you see what it was?

Tourist: I couldn't be sure, but I think it was some kind of bird.

Policeman: Thank you, you've been very helpful. One last thing; what did you do when the three men left the bank?

Tourist: I breathed a big sigh of relief and thanked God that my prayer was answered – no one was killed.

Exercises

1. Answer the following questions:
a) Where is the bank that was robbed?
b) Why was the tourist in the bank?
c) At what time did the robbery occur?
d) How were the robbers disguised?
e) How many guns did the robbers have? What sort of guns were they?
f) Which man had a tattoo on his hand?

2. Übertragen Sie ins Englische:
a) Ich höre, Sie waren heute morgen in der Bank.
b) Um wieviel Uhr gingen Sie in die Bank?
c) Können Sie die Männer beschreiben?
d) Wie sah er aus? Wie war er gekleidet?
e) Gibt es sonst noch etwas, woran Sie sich erinnern können, das uns helfen könnte?
f) Schönen Dank, Sie haben uns sehr geholfen (waren sehr hilfreich).

IV. Asking for Help

1. THE LOST CHILD

This dialogue takes place at a police station. An unhappy woman comes in. She is crying. She speaks to the police officer.

Woman: Please help me. I have lost my little boy. He is only four.
Policeman: When did you last see him?
Woman: About half an hour ago.
Policeman: Where did you lose him?
Woman: It was in the market place.
Policeman: What does he look like?
Woman: He has fair hair and blue eyes.
Policeman: What is he wearing?
Woman: He is wearing blue, short trousers and a yellow shirt. His jacket is beige and his socks are white.
Policeman: What is his full name?
Woman: His name is Robert Smith. We call him Bob.

Policeman: You are very lucky. Your little boy is sitting in the canteen eating an ice-cream.
Woman: Thank God for that!
Policeman: A cab driver found him wandering near the market, so he put him in his taxi and brought him to the police station.
Woman: Is he all right?
Policeman: Yes, he is all right. He was a bit frightened at first, but the ice-cream has calmed him.

Exercises

1. Answer the following questions:
a) Who came into the police station?
b) What was the lady's trouble?
c) Where did she lose her little boy?
d) What colour were his hair and eyes?
e) What was he wearing?
f) Who had brought the boy to the police station?

2. Übertragen Sie ins Englische:
a) Wann haben Sie ihn zuletzt gesehen (sahen Sie ihn)?
b) Wo haben Sie ihn verloren?
c) Wie sieht er aus?
d) Wie ist er angezogen? (Was trägt er?)
e) Er trägt eine blaue, kurze Hose und ein gelbes Hemd.
f) Wie heißt er?

2. THE SICK MAN

A police constable is walking his beat. Suddenly he notices a man sitting on the kerb. The man looks ill, so the police constable turns to him and speaks to him.

Police Constable: What is the matter, sir?
Sick man: It's my heart. I've had heart attacks before.
Police Constable: Can I help you, sir? Shall I undo your tie for you?
Sick man: Yes, please. – That's better.
Police Constable: Do you want to go to a hospital?

Sick man: Yes, please.
Police Constable: Did anyone see what happened?
Witness: Yes, I saw it, officer. He was just walking along. Suddenly he seemed to stagger and then he sat down on the kerb.
Police Constable: Would you mind waiting with him, sir. I am going to call for an ambulance.
Witness: All right, officer.

The police constable now goes to a telephone-box. He calls for an ambulance. Then he returns to the scene and he speaks to the sick man again.

Police Constable: Now, sir, what is your full name, please?
Sick man: John Henry Wilson.
Police Constable: And what is your full postal address?
Sick man: 46 Dortmund-Schüren, Marsbruchstr. 10.
Police Constable: Would you like me to inform anyone about this?
Sick man: Yes, please, my wife, Irene.
Police Constable: That's Mrs. Irene Wilson of the same address, is it?
Sick man: That's right.
Police Constable (to the witness): Now, sir, what is your full name and address?
Witness: My name is Peter Schmidt, 46 Dortmund, Münsterstraße 29.
Police Constable: Thank you very much for your assistance, sir.
Witness: Not at all.

After some minutes the ambulance arrives. The police constable tells the attendants about the sick man's illness. They take him to the hospital.
Finally the police constable arranges for a message to inform the sick man's wife about what has happened.

Exercises

1. Answer the following questions:

a) Where was the man sitting?
b) What happened and why?
c) What did the witness tell the policeman about the man?
d) What did the police constable do to help the man?
e) Who did the man want to inform about his sickness?
f) Where did the policeman go to call for an ambulance?

2. Übertragen Sie ins Englische:
a) Darf ich Ihnen helfen?
b) Möchten Sie zum Krankenhaus?
c) Macht es Ihnen etwas aus, bei ihm zu warten?
d) Ich werde einen Krankenwagen rufen.
e) Wie lautet Ihre Adresse?
f) Möchten Sie, daß ich jemanden hierüber informiere?

3. THE LOST HOTEL

Late one evening, a man and a woman walk into the police station. They both look very worried. As soon as they start speaking, the police officer who is on duty in the station realizes that they are foreigners.

Man: Please can you help us. We have lost our hotel.
Police Officer: You've what?
Man: We've lost our hotel. We booked a room in a hotel earlier this evening and now we can't find the hotel.
Police Officer: What was the name of the hotel?
Man: That's the trouble. We don't know the name. We can't understand German and the name of the hotel is German.
Police Officer: Can you remember anything about the hotel at all?
Man: I'm sorry. I can't remember what it looked like.

65

Woman: I remember seeing that it had orange curtains and white doors. The receptionist was a fair-haired woman of about thirty and she was wearing a light brown dress.

Man: That doesn't help you very much, I'm afraid.

Police Officer: I can't identify the hotel from what you have told me.
Can you tell me how you got to the hotel?

Man: We came to the railway station at about six o'clock.

Police Officer: What did you do then?

Man: We walked out of the main entrance of the station, then we turned right and walked about a hundred metres.

Police Officer: Did you pass the Odeon Cinema?

Woman: Yes, we did. We turned left just after we'd passed the cinema.

Police Officer: How far did you walk then?

Man: Not very far, the hotel was only about fifty metres along that road.

Police Officer: Most probably it is the Hotel Münchener Hof.

Man: That sounds like it.

Police Officer: Didn't they give you a key?

Man: No, they didn't.

Woman: Yes, they did! The receptionist gave it to me. Here it is in my handbag. You were quite right, officer. The name on the key tag is Hotel Münchener Hof.

Exercises

1. Answer the following questions:
a) Why did the man and woman look worried?
b) Why could they not remember the name of the hotel?
c) How did the woman describe the hotel receptionist?
d) When did the man and the woman arrive at the railway station?

e) What did they pass on their way from the railway station to the hotel?
f) Where did they find the name of the hotel?

2. Übertragen Sie ins Englische:
a) Können Sie sich an irgend etwas von dem Hotel erinnern?
b) Können Sie mir sagen, wie Sie zu dem Hotel gelangten?
c) Sind Sie am „Odeon" vorbeigekommen?
d) Höchstwahrscheinlich ist es das Hotel Münchener Hof.
e) Gab man Ihnen einen Schlüssel?

4. THE WORLD TOUR

Late one night, a policeman sees a young man lying in the doorway of a shop. He speaks to the man and receives a reply in English.

Man: Hallo... you woke me up. I was fast asleep.

Policeman: Are you all right?

Man: Yes, thanks.

Policeman: Why are you lying in that doorway?

Man: It was the best place I could find to spend the night.

Policeman: I see. Get up, please.

Man: Must I? I've only just got comfortable.

Policeman: Stand up!

Man: Hold on, don't get mad – I can't stand up quickly... my legs are stiff... Ow!... I've got cramp.

Policeman: I'm not surprised. Now, show me your passport, please.

Man: Certainly. It's here in my rucksack.

Policeman: Where are you from?

Man: My home is in Ontario.

Policeman: You're Canadian then?

Man: That's right . . . here's my passport.

Policeman: I see from the stamps in your passport that you've visited a large number of countries recently.

Man: I'm on a tour of the world.

Policeman: How are you travelling?

Man: Mostly by hitch-hiking.

Policeman: When did you enter Germany?

Man: Tuesday morning.

Policeman: Where are you going now?

Man: To sleep, if I get the chance!

Policeman: Please don't try to be funny – just answer my questions!

Man: Okay, whatever you say! I'll tell you anything you want to know.

Policeman: Where are you making for?

Man: Nowhere in particular. I want to get to Switzerland if I can, but I'm not too worried if I miss it and go straight to Italy.

Policeman: Why are you sleeping here in this doorway?

Man: I was tired. I got a lift on a truck that stopped here, and as it was so late, I decided to sleep rough. I've had to do that many times before.

Policeman: Why don't you go to a hotel for the night?

Man: It's too expensive.

Policeman: There's a hostel on the other side of the town – that's very cheap.

Man: How far is it?

Policeman: Three kilometres. About half an hour's walk.

Man: Christ, that's a long way.

Policeman: It's not that far. Anyway, you can't sleep here.

Man: Can you give me a lift to the hostel?

Policeman: No, I cannot. My job is to patrol the streets here, not to provide a taxi service.

Man: Can't I sleep at the police station?

Policeman: No, we only accommodate people who have committed crimes.

Man: I can smash a window if you like, then you can lock me up.

Policeman: I wouldn't do that if I were you. You are likely to find that you will be locked up for longer than you wish!

Man: I definitely can't sleep here?

Policeman: No, you may not.

Man: Oh well, I suppose I'd better go to the hostel. Which way is it, please?

Policeman: You go straight along this road as far as you can.

Man: How far is that?

Policeman: About three kilometres.

Man: That's a hell of a way.

Policeman: When you reach the end of this road you turn to the right and the hostel is on the right hand side of the road.

Man: I guess I'd better start walking then.

Policeman: That would be a very good idea. Good night.

Man: Good night. The Indian police let me sleep out at night, I don't see why you can't.

Policeman: Because this isn't India and I'm not an Indian policeman! Good night!

Exercises

1. Answer the following questions:

a) Where was the young man sleeping?
b) Why could he not stand up quickly?
c) Which country does the man want to go to next?
d) Why did the man not go to a hotel?
e) How far is the hotel?
f) When did the man enter Germany?

2. Übertragen Sie ins Englische:

a) Geht es Ihnen gut?
b) Stehen Sie bitte auf!
c) Zeigen Sie mir bitte Ihren Reisepaß!
d) Woher kommen Sie?

e) Wann sind Sie nach Deutschland gekommen?
f) Wohin fahren Sie jetzt?
g) Warum übernachten Sie nicht in einem Hotel?
h) Meine Aufgabe ist es, die Straße zu überwachen, nicht aber ein Taxi zu besorgen.

5. THE CHEAP THEATRE TICKETS

A policeman is called to a theatre where a concert is to be held that evening. When he arrives, the policeman is met by the theatre manager and two angry Americans, a man and his wife.

Man: Look here, officer, there's been some sort of mistake. The manager won't let us in. He keeps shouting at us but we can't understand a goddam word he says.

Policeman: Perhaps I can help. The theatre is completely sold out. There are no seats available.

Man: But we have tickets.

Policeman: Will you show them to me, please?

Man: Sure, here they are.

Policeman: Where did you get these tickets?

Man: We had a hell of a job getting any tickets at all. We tried to get them through our hotel, but they couldn't help us.

Policeman: It's a very popular concert and there have been no tickets for sale at the theatre for several weeks. People are asking very high prices for spare tickets.

Man: I know that. I was offered a couple of tickets at ten times the regular price, but I wasn't having any of that. I'm not a sucker.

Policeman: Yet you bought these tickets.

Man: Sure I did. They were only five times the price on the ticket. They're twenty mark tickets.

Policeman: Yes, but where did you buy them?

Man: In a bar last night.

Policeman: Do you know the name of the man who sold them to you?

Man: Yes, he introduced himself to us. What was his name, Kathy? Do you remember?

Woman: His first name was Hans ... Hans Schmidt, I think.

Policeman: I see. Do you know where he lives?

Man: No, I have no idea.

Policeman: Do you know anything else about him other than his name? Can you describe him?

Man: No, I don't know anything about him. He was just a nice, average sort of a guy.

Policeman: He wasn't a very honest man.

Man: What do you mean?

Policeman: These tickets are not for the concert tonight. I take it that you cannot read German?

Man: No, this is our first time in Germany. We're only here for two days, then we go on to France for two days and so on. We're going to do the whole of Europe in twenty days.

Policeman: The man that you met in the bar has swindled you.

Man: But the tickets are for this theatre. Look, it says so on the tickets.

Policeman: Yes, the tickets are for this theatre but not for the concert this evening. The man who tricked you has used genuine tickets for this theatre, but he has altered the date. These tickets are for a modern play that is being performed here next week.

Man: Oh, my God, then the tickets are forgeries. What can I do?

Policeman: Very little, I'm afraid, other than to be more careful in future where you buy theatre tickets.

Exercises

1. Answer the following questions:
a) Where did this incident take place?
b) How much did the American pay for the two tickets that he bought?
c) What has been altered on the tickets?
d) How long are the Americans staying in Europe?
e) Who sold the forged tickets to the Americans?
f) What is being performed at the theatre next week?

2. Übertragen Sie ins Englische:
a) Vielleicht kann ich helfen.
b) Wo haben Sie sie (die Eintrittskarten) gekauft?
c) Kennen Sie den Namen des Mannes?
d) Wissen Sie, wo er wohnt?
e) Wissen Sie sonst etwas über ihn?
f) Der Mann, den Sie in der Bar getroffen haben, hat Sie betrogen.

6. THE PROWLER

At about eleven o'clock one night, a police car is sent to a bungalow in a residential suburb of a large town. One of the policemen in the car rings the doorbell and the door is opened by a young woman.

Woman: Are you the police?

Policeman: Yes, are you the lady who called us?

Woman: Yes, there was a prowler in my garden.

Policeman: When was this?

Woman: About a quarter of an hour ago.

Policeman: My colleague will have a look round to see if there are any traces of him. Can I come in? It's very chilly. You'll catch cold standing here in your dressing gown.

Woman: Are you sure that you're a policeman?

Policeman: Yes – surely you recognize my uniform?

Woman: Not really. I haven't been in Germany very long.

Policeman: Look, here's my identification card. My name is Winkler.

Woman: Oh yes, that's all right then. Come in. You must forgive me for being nervous, but that man in my garden frightened me.

Policeman: I understand. Tell me, what happened.

Woman: There's not very much to tell. I was in my bedroom.

Policeman: Is that at the back of the house?

Woman: It's not a house, it's a bungalow and my bedroom faces the garden at the side.

Policeman: I see. What happened?

Woman: I was getting undressed to go to bed when I heard a noise.

Policeman: What sort of noise?

Woman: It sounded like someone walking through the shrubs in the garden.

Policeman: What did you do then?

Woman: I stopped and listened.

Policeman: Did you hear anything else?

Woman: Yes, there was a scraping noise just outside my bedroom window.

Policeman: What did you do then?

Woman: I put my dressing gown on quickly and went to the window and looked out.

Policeman: Did you see anyone?

Woman: Yes. There was a man with his face pressed against the glass.

Policeman: Were the shutters of your bedroom window closed?

Woman: No, but the curtains were drawn . . . well, nearly drawn . . . there was a narrow gap between them and the man was looking through that.

Policeman: Why didn't you lower the shutter?

Woman: I don't like them. We don't have them where I come from and they give me a closed-in feeling . . . I suffer from claustrophobia.

Policeman: It sounds as though you'd better close them for the rest of tonight and try to get used to them.

Woman: I suppose so. Who was the man do you think?

Policeman: I don't know, but I expect it was a Peeping Tom. Do you often undress with the light on and the curtains partly open?

Woman: Of course not – what do you think I am?

Policeman: I'm sorry. I didn't mean to be insulting but your bedroom light would be conspicuous and would attract the attention of a man who likes peeping through windows.

Woman: I see. I shall have to be more careful in future.

Policeman: That would be wise. Can you describe the prowler that you saw tonight?

Woman: No, I'm afraid not, but one thing I can tell you – he is very wet!

Policeman: How on earth do you know that?

Woman: After I went to the window, he ran away and I heard him crash through the shrubbery and then fall into the fish pond.
It's a large pond and very deep.

Policeman: Right. We'll be on the lookout for him. It's so cold outside he must be wishing that he'd stayed at home tonight.

Woman: Yes. It might even cool his desire to stare at women through bedroom windows.

Exercises

1. Answer the following questions:

a) At what time was the police car sent to the bungalow?
b) Who rang the door bell?
c) Why had the woman called the police?
d) Where is her bedroom?
e) What did the woman hear?
f) Why did she have the shutters open?
g) What did the prowler fall into?

2. Übertragen Sie ins Englische:

a) Sind Sie die Dame, die uns anrief?
b) Mein Kollege wird sich umsehen, ob es irgendwelche Spuren von ihm gibt.
c) Waren die Fensterläden Ihres Schlafzimmers geschlossen?
d) Warum ließen Sie die Fensterläden nicht herunter?
e) Entschuldigung, ich wollte nicht beleidigend sein.
f) Können Sie den Mann beschreiben, den Sie heute abend sahen?
g) Wir werden uns nach ihm umsehen.

7. THE SPILT BEER

Late one evening a police car has been sent to a bar in the centre of a city. The proprietor of the bar takes the policemen to two men sitting at a table in the corner of the bar.

Man: You're too late.

Policeman: Too late for what?

Man: Too late to catch the bloke that hit my mate Sid.

Policeman: What's the matter with your friend?

Man: He's been punched in the face.

Policeman: Yes, I can see that his face is swollen. He will have a black eye in the morning. It also looks as though he's had too much to drink!

Man: He's had a right skinful all right. He kept saying that German beer was weaker than English beer. I tried to tell him that it wasn't but he wouldn't listen to me.

Policeman: What happened to him?

Man: What do you mean?

Policeman: How did he get punched in the face?

Man: He went up to the counter to get some more beer and on the way back someone bumped into him and knocked one of the glasses of beer out of his hand and spilt all the beer on the floor.

Policeman: What happened then?

Man: He brought the other glass here and put it on the table.

Policeman: Then what did he do?

Man: He went to get an apology from the man who bumped into him.

Policeman: Can he speak German?

Man: Not a word. He was so drunk he could hardly speak his own language, let alone German!

Policeman: How did he expect to ask for an apology if he can't speak German?

Man: God knows. I tried to tell him not to, but he wouldn't listen to me.

Policeman: So he went up to the man who'd spilt his beer and then what happened?

Man: Ah . . . that's where he made his big mistake. He picked the wrong man.

Policeman: He did what?

Man: He picked the wrong one. He thought he'd got the bloke who'd spilt his beer, but he picked the wrong man. He went up to a big man who was sitting drinking a glass of beer and started shouting at him.

Policeman: In English?

Man: If you can call it that. Most of it was swearwords and – they were all mixed up. I tried to tell him that he'd had too much to drink but he wouldn't listen.

Policeman: So he went up to a complete stranger and started shouting at him. What happened then?

Man: This big man he was shouting at, didn't say a word. He just punched Sid – that's my mate – straight in the eye.

Policeman: Where is this man now?

Man: He's gone. He hit Sid so hard that Sid went down and landed flat on his back. Then this big man finished off his beer as cool as a cucumber and walked straight out of the bar without saying a word.

Policeman: I think that you'd better take your friend home.

Man: I'll do that.

Policeman: And perhaps you will tell him that if he gets drunk again that he is likely to get into serious trouble. I'll also have a word with the barman for serving beer to drunken men.

Man: I'm sober enough. I'll look after Sid – honest I will.

Policeman: All right. Off you go. Don't forget to warn your friend when he sobers up.

Man: Oh I'll tell him. I always tell him, but he never listens to me.

Exercises

1. Answer the following questions:
a) Where were the two Englishmen sitting?
b) What has happened to Sid's face?
c) How did a glass of beer get knocked out of Sid's hand?
d) What did Sid do with the other glass?
e) Why did Sid go to speak to the man who had bumped into him?
f) Sid shouted at the wrong man – what did this man do to Sid?
g) What did the big man do then?

2. Übertragen Sie ins Englische:
a) Es sieht aus, als ob er zuviel getrunken hat.

b) Wie kam es, daß man ihm ins Gesicht schlug?

c) Ich glaube, Sie täten besser daran, Ihren Freund nach Hause zu bringen.

d) Vielleicht sagen Sie ihm, daß er in betrunkenem Zustand möglicherweise in ernsthafte Schwierigkeiten kommt.

e) Ich werde auch den Wirt ansprechen, weil er Bier an Betrunkene verabreicht.

8. THE WRONG ROOM

A policeman is called to a hotel. When he arrives, he is met by the manager and taken to a room on the third floor. A group of people are shouting at one another.

Policeman: Will you all be quiet, please. Who called the police?

Woman: I did. This man tried to rape me.

Policeman: What is your name, madam?

Woman: Sarah Hobbs.

Policeman: Thank you, Mrs. Hobbs.

Woman: Miss . . . I'm not married.

Policeman: I see. Now, Miss Hobbs, will you tell me what happened?

Miss Hobbs: I was in my room asleep when this man burst into my room and attacked me.

Man: I didn't attack her!

Miss Hobbs: Yes, you did!

Policeman: Just a moment. Please, stop shouting. You will wake everyone in the hotel. Now, Miss Hobbs, please calm yourself and tell me what happened after this man came into your room.

Miss Hobbs: He started taking his clothes off.

Policeman: What did you do?

Miss Hobbs: What do you think I did? I screamed.

Policeman: Then what happened?

Miss Hobbs: He tried to run out of the room, but he tripped over that coffee table and hit his head on the wall.

Policeman: What did you do then?

Miss Hobbs: I telephoned the receptionist and asked her to call the police.

Policeman: I see . . . Now sir, did you break into this lady's room?

Man: No, I didn't.

Policeman: What did you do?

Man: I just quietly opened the door and came in.

Policeman: Why did you enter Miss Hobbs room?

Man: I didn't know that it was her room.

Policeman: Whose room did you think it was?

Man: I would rather not answer that question.

Policeman: Unless you wish to find yourself at the police station, you would be well-advised to answer all my questions!

Man: Look, this is very embarrassing.

Miss Hobbs: It certainly is for me.

Man: Look officer, I'm sure that you are a man of the world.

Policeman: Would you answer my question, please.

Man: I thought it was another lady's room.

Policeman: What lady?

Man: A lady I met downstairs.

Policeman: I see. Why did you come to this particular room?

Man: I thought that this was her room.

Policeman: Why did you think that?

Man: She wrote it down for me on this piece of paper.

Policeman: Show me, please.

Man: Here you are. See for yourself.

Policeman: Yes, I see.

Man: She wrote that downstairs in the bar. Now you can see why I came here to room thirty.

Policeman: The number on this piece of paper looks more like thirty-six to me.

Man: What? Let me see!

Policeman: This is room thirty and I think you've got the wrong room.

Man: Oh, my God!

Policeman: Well, at least we can check your story. We can ask the lady in room thirty-six if she gave you this piece of paper.

Man: I don't think she would help me.

Policeman: Why?

Man: She's a married woman and I'm sure she wouldn't admit that she invited me to her room in case her husband found out.

Policeman: Yes, that's a point . . . very well – do you know her name?

Man: Why do you want that?

Policeman: We can look it up in the hotel register.

Man: Well . . . she told me her first name was Ingrid, but I didn't bother to ask her what her surname was.

Policeman: Well, I'm still not sure that I believe your story. I want some form of corroboration that you really mistook the room number.

Man: I don't know how I can possibly prove that I'm telling the truth.

Policeman: Just a moment, there's another lady coming along the corridor, now . . . is that Ingrid?

Man: Where? . . . Oh my God, I didn't think anything more could happen to me. First I get the wrong room, then I fall over and bang my head, then I find my-self accused of rape and being questioned by a policeman and now this – the worst of all.

Policeman: What are you talking about?

Man: That's not Ingrid coming along the corridor – that's my wife!

Exercises

1. Answer the following questions:
   a) Who called the police?
   b) Why was Miss Hobbs alarmed?
   c) Of what offence did Miss Hobbs accuse the man?
   d) Why did the man enter the wrong room?
   e) What was the number of the room occupied by Miss Hobbs?
   f) How did the man bang his head?
   g) How did the policeman discover the man was in the wrong room?

2. Übertragen Sie ins Englische:
   a) Bitte, seien Sie alle ruhig. Wer rief die Polizei?
   b) Nun, Miss Hobbs, erzählen Sie mir bitte, was geschah.
   c) Hören Sie auf zu schreien, Sie wecken alle Leute im Hotel auf.
   d) Warum haben Sie Miss Hobbs Zimmer betreten?
   e) Wenn Sie sich nicht bei der Polizei-wache einfinden möchten, wären Sie gut beraten, alle meine Fragen zu beantworten.
   f) Wollen Sie bitte meine Fragen beant-worten.
   g) Nun, ich bin nicht sicher, daß ich Ihre Geschichte glauben kann. Ich hätte gern eine Bestätigung dafür, daß Sie sich wirklich in der Zimmernummer geirrt haben.

9. THE ATTEMPTED SUICIDE

A police car is being driven slowly along a residential street, when a man runs out of a house and waves the police car to a halt. The man speaks to the policemen in the car.

Man: Come quickly! My wife has killed herself.

Policeman: What has she done?

Man: She's taken an overdose of drugs.

Policeman: I'll come with you. My colleague will call for medical assistance. You lead the way and I will follow.

The man leads the policeman to his bedroom. There, the policeman sees a young woman, wearing a nightdress and a dressing gown, lying on a bed.

Man: I'm sure she's dead.

Policeman: Just a moment. I'll feel her pulse . . . she is still alive, but her pulse is weak. If we can get her to hospital quickly, she should be all right.

Man: What shall we do?

Policeman: We must wait for the ambulance to arrive. Do you know what she has taken?

Man: I think so. That bottle on the bedside cabinet was full of aspirin tablets when I went out a few hours ago. Now it is nearly empty. She must have taken about a hundred tablets.

Policeman: Rather less than a hundred, I think. There are quite a lot of tablets scattered on the floor and on the bed. Why did she try to commit suicide?

Man: She has often threatened to do it before, but I didn't think that she really meant it. She left me a note on the dressing table.

Policeman: Will you give it to me, please?

Man: Here it is.

He hands the policeman a short letter written on a single sheet of paper.

Policeman: Have you read this?

Man: Yes. She says that she cannot face leaving Germany.

Policeman: What does she mean?

Man: Well, as you can hear, I'm English. My wife is German. I met her here when I was in the army. When I left the army, I got a job in Germany and bought this house. Now, I have lost my job and can't get another. So, I am going back to England, taking Lotte, my wife, with me.

Policeman: And your wife doesn't want to go.

Man: No. She dreads leaving her family and friends behind. I didn't realize that she felt so deeply about leaving here.

Policeman: I can hear the ambulance coming. Your wife will soon be in hospital.

Man: If Lotte lives, I must think again about things.

Exercises

1. Answer the following questions:
a) Where were the policemen driving?
b) What drug did the woman take?
c) Why did the woman try to commit suicide?
d) Where was the suicide note left by the woman?
e) Where were the aspirin tablets scattered?
f) How did the policeman discover that the woman was still alive?

2. Übertragen Sie ins Englische:
a) Was hat sie getan?
b) Mein Kollege wird um ärztliche Hilfe bitten.
c) Sie gehen vor und ich komme nach.
d) Wenn wir sie schnell zum Krankenhaus bringen können, wird sie es überstehen.
e) Warum versuchte sie, Selbstmord zu verüben?

10. THE FIRE

Two policemen are patrolling in a wireless car. As they drive along a residential street, a woman runs from a house and waves her arms in front of the police car. The car stops and the woman speaks to one of the policemen.

Woman: You're just in time. I've had an accident and my house is on fire.

Policeman: What happened?

Woman: I was frying some chips in a pan of oil and the oil caught fire.

Policeman: I will come with you. My colleague will call the fire brigade.

Woman: It's in my kitchen at the back of the house.

Policeman: You lead the way and I'll follow.

The policeman and the woman go to her house. When they get into the hall of the house, they see large clouds of black smoke coming from the kitchen. Through the smoke, flames can be seen on the top of a stove.

Policeman: Is that a gas stove or an electric one?

Woman: It's gas.

Policeman: Is the gas still alight under the frying pan?

Woman: I'm afraid so. It was too hot for me to get to the gas tap.

Policeman: Where is the main gas tap for the house?

Woman: Under the stairs, just here.

Policeman: Show me . . . I see. I'll turn the gas off here. That should help to stop some of the smoke. Does anyone else live here with you?

Woman: Only my husband.

Policeman: Is there anyone else in the house at the moment?

Woman: No. Well, not in my part of the house.

Policeman: What do you mean?

Woman: Well, there's the couple in the flat upstairs. They're in.

Policeman: Have you got an old blanket or something like that, which I can use to smother the flames?

Woman: What about a big sack? Will that do?

Policeman: That will be ideal. Where is it?

Woman: It's in the cupboard under the stairs, near the gas meter.

Policeman: Right. I'll get it. Have you got a fire extinguisher?

Woman: Oh no. I've never thought of getting one.

Policeman: All right. I'll use the sack. Now, you go upstairs and evacuate everyone from the house. Everyone. Do you understand?

Woman: You want me to tell the couple upstairs to come down?

Policeman: Yes. I want everyone out of the house and outside on the pavement.

The woman goes upstairs to clear the house of its occupants. When she comes down again, she finds that the fire has been put out by the policeman.

Woman: That's marvellous. It was lucky that you came by when you did. I'm sure the house would have burned down.

Policeman: The smoke has made a terrible mess of your kitchen.

Woman: Yes, but it can soon be cleaned up. I think the cooker is ruined too. The enamel has cracked.

Policeman: Your husband won't be very pleased when he comes home.

Woman: He certainly won't. I'm not too worried though. I've been trying to get him to buy me a new cooker for years. Now he'll have to get one, and the kitchen will have to be repainted, too. It's about time it was done.

Policeman: You aren't very upset about the fire then?

Woman: I wouldn't say that. I now have the problem of trying to give my husband his dinner tonight.

Policeman: It looks as though you'd better go to a restaurant.

Woman: What a good idea. My husband hasn't taken me out to dinner since my birthday. If he's going to be upset by having to redecorate the kitchen, buy a new cooker and get a new frying pan, it won't upset him much more to take me out to dinner!

Exercises

1. Answer the following questions:

a) How did the fire start?
b) Where did it happen?
c) What sort of stove was involved?
d) How did the policeman extinguish the flames?
e) What damage was caused by the fire?
f) Where was the main gas tap for the house?

2. Übertragen Sie ins Englische:

a) Ich werde mit Ihnen kommen, mein Kollege wird die Feuerwehr rufen.
b) Sie zeigen den Weg, und ich werde folgen.
c) Wo ist der Hauptgashahn für das Haus?
d) Ist zur Zeit noch jemand im Hause?
e) Haben Sie ein altes Bettlaken oder sonst etwas, das die Flammen erstikken könnte?
f) Haben Sie einen Feuerlöscher?
g) Sie gehen nach oben und holen (evakuieren) alle aus dem Hause.

PART 2

USEFUL STRUCTURES

1. THE SERIOUS CRIME

"This is an awful nuisance", said Detective Swift as he trudged through the pouring rain, feeling a cold trickle of water running down his neck. "There are better ways of spending an evening", admitted Detective Sergeant Owen. "A burglary like this doesn't seem to be a very important job to send us out on overtime. There was only a small amount of silver and jewellery stolen. The thieves might have been children. Anyway no sensible thief is going to be out on a night like this." The two men walked on in silence, passing large houses, their windows ablaze with light. Detective Swift slipped on some wet leaves and nearly fell. His shoes were letting in water and his feet were cold and wet.

"It's raining cats and dogs," he grumbled.

"I don't care if it's raining white mice," retorted Detective Sergeant Owen. "The superintendent wants us to catch these thieves."

"I can't understand why he is so determined to catch them," said Detective Swift. "They've only broken into one house."

"Yes," said the detective sergeant quickly, "and it was the superintendent's house!"

Exercise 1

Fill in the appropriate form of the indefinite article, either "a" or "an". "A" is used before a word beginning with a consonant, or a vowel that sounds like a consonant. "An" is used before a word beginning with a vowel.

Examples:
an awful nuisance
a night

a) I'll call – ambulance for you.

b) I saw – English car on the road to Cologne.
c) We are looking for – nice hotel in this area.
d) Then he discovered – strange thing.
e) The thief took – artificial diamond pendant and left – genuine diamond ring.
f) The two ladies led the detective to – small room.
g) She had – credit card.
h) Yesterday she bought – dress, – over-all and – raincoat.
i) He showed them – white suitcase and – green bag.
j) The policeman found – open door and – broken window at the scene of the burglary.
k) He was running with – tall young man along the road.
l) He wore – overcoat and carried – large umbrella.
m) They have – dog and – parrot.
n) The robber was armed with – iron bar and – knife.
o) She made – cake and asked her friends for tea.

Exercise 2

Put the following sentences into the plural form. Remember the irregular plural form of

child – children
man – men
woman – women
wife – wives
knife – knives
thief – thieves
foot – feet
tooth – teeth
goose – geese

mouse – mice
louse – lice
tomato – tomatoes
potato – potatoes
fish – fish (or fishes)

a) The man disappeared when we switched on the lights.
b) I like this fish best.
c) Mary said that she saw a louse on her hair.
d) There was a woman standing at the corner.
e) We had a thief here last night; he had a knife.
f) He is really a gentleman.
g) That sound must be caused by a goose.
h) She was frightened by a mouse.
i) My tooth aches when it gets cold.
j) She wanted a tomato with her sandwich.
k) A child ran across the road.
l) She had a potato with her meat.
m) He hurt his foot.
n) He took his wife out for dinner.

2. THE NEW CAR

Mr. King's car was brand new and he was very proud of it. Unfortunately the car no longer looked new. Its front bumper and bonnet were dented and torn. The whole front of the car was wrecked. His heart sank as he surveyed his damaged car. He had spent all his and his wife's savings to buy it only yesterday. It had been their pride and joy. He turned to the woman whose car was directly in front of his. The rear of her car was equally damaged.

"Why did you stop without warning?" he asked.

The woman looked at him reproachfully. "I stopped to put on my safety belt," she said. "I was afraid I might have an accident."

Exercise 1

There are two different forms of genitive in English. Names of persons and animals take the s-genitive. It can also be used with the names of countries and certain institutions. With inanimate objects and abstract nouns the of-genitive ist generally used. (There are exceptions to this rule).

Examples:
Mary's watch (sing.)
Mr. Smith's car (sing.)
Britain's industry (sing.)
our neighbours' house (pl.)
the children's toys (pl.)
the Robinsons' cat (pl.)

the centre of the town
the price of the car
the keys of the house
the causes of war

Fill in the "s"- or "of"-genitive in the following sentences.

Example:
The suitcase (Mr. King) was large and heavy.
Mr. King's suitcase was large and heavy.

a) The owner (dog) lives next door.
b) The speed (car) was more than 30 m. p. h.
c) Clothes (women) are always expensive.
d) I lost the key (safe).
e) The tools (mechanic) are old and out of date.
f) The passport (this man) was forged.
g) The children (the Browns) cause a lot of trouble.
h) The garden (our neighbour) is large and beautiful.
i) That behaviour (the young man) is very suspicious.
j) The bumper (this car) is dented.
k) They broke the lock (gate).
l) She liked to wear high-heeled shoes (her sister).

Exercise 2

Possessive pronouns (my, your, its, his, her, our, their) can be used to replace the persons and/or things mentioned in a sentence.

Example:
The suitcase (Mr. King) was large and heavy.
His suitcase was large and heavy.
Transform the sentences of Exercise 1 in the same way.

Exercise 3

In this exercise "whose" is used in questions concerning a person's ownership whereas "what" is used in respect to things in general, asking about their qualities (= „was für ein?"). Note that it is also possible to say "what people" – was für Leute! Change the sentences of Exercise 1 into questions using either "whose" or "what".

Example:
The suitcase (Mr. King) was large and heavy.
Whose suitcase was large and heavy?

3. A PLEASANT PROSPECT

The young policeman knocked on the door. It was opened by an attractive young woman wearing a revealing négligé. She smiled at him and waved him into the flat. He tried to work out what he should say. He wanted to see Mr. Pitt to question him about a burglary. "I came to see Mr. Pitt," he said.

"I'm his wife," said the young woman. "He is staying at his brother's. They are partners in the clothing business."

"I wanted to see them about one of their shops," said the policeman, "it was broken into."

"You can talk to me," said Mrs. Pitt, "my husband and I are both involved in the business. We share the work."

"I'm afraid that I have to speak to your husband," said the young policeman.

Mrs. Pitt sat down on a settee and in doing so displayed even more of her ample figure. "He will not be home for ten days," she said.

The policeman looked at her dreamily, "I will be very happy to wait," he said.

Exercise 1

The personal pronouns to replace the subject are "I", "you", "he", "she", "it", "we", "you", "they".
Replace the subject by a personal pronoun in the following sentences.

Example:
The door was opened by an attractive young woman.
It was opened by an attractive young woman.

a) Mrs. Gold and Mrs. Jones are sisters.
b) My husband and I are both involved in the business.
c) The shop was broken into.
d) His suitcase was very heavy.
e) The Sergeant said: "Mr. Brown, tell me how the accident happened, please."
f) The policeman searched the flat.
g) The plane runs daily.
h) Suddenly the van stopped.
i) This bracelet is of little value.
j) My car has broken down.
k) The photographs fell out of his wallet.
l) The murderer appeared at the scene of the crime.
m) My sister always goes there by bus.
n) The dog was killed in the accident.
o) His coat was wet and dirty.

Exercise 2

The personal pronouns which can replace the object in a sentence (both direct and indirect object) are "me", "you", "him", "her", "it", "us", "them".
Replace the object by a personal pronoun.

Example:
He wanted to see Mr. Pitt.
He wanted to see him.

a) I gave the key to my brother.
b) She enjoys writing letters.
c) He climbed the fence.
d) They invited Mr. Gregory for dinner.
e) That briefcase belongs to my husband.
f) Did you meet Dick and Mary at the theatre?
g) He sent a present to me and my friend.
h) He told the police all about the accident.
i) I broke that plate.
j) The dog bit his master.
k) She bought some sweets for her mother.
l) Mary will decorate this room.
m) He taught his son to swim.
n) She always makes the cakes herself.
o) I can't understand French.

4. THE OBSERVATION

The following report was submitted by a young detective: "I am still keeping watch on number 54 Königsallee as directed. Every morning at seven o'clock I go to the house on the opposite side of the street. In order to avoid being seen, I enter by the back door. To do this, I walk along an alley and then climb over a tall fence. Sometimes, I get over easily but other times I slip and tear my trousers. I then have to buy new ones.

I am let in by the owner of the house, Frau Wittrisch. I pay her weekly for the use of her front room. As it is very cold, I also pay her for the electricity I need to keep myself warm and pay for the coffee that she makes me.

At exactly eight o'clock each morning, I see the door of number 54 open. The suspect comes out and gets into his car. I watch him drive off and then I go to talk to the suspect's maid. From her I learn what the suspect is doing. For this information, I pay her a few marks each day. I then see the postman and look at the mail for number 54. For his help, I pay him a few marks also. Once a week I see the refuse collector who tells me what is in the dustbin of number 54 when it is emptied. The refuse collector is very expensive.

At twelve o'clock each day, I go to the bar at the end of the street where I listen for gossip about the suspect. The drinks are very costly but I must drink something to avoid suspicion.

I am back at my observation post at four o'clock where I wait until the suspect comes home and watch him go into his house. I then leave via the fence and jump into the alley. This has sharp stones which cut my shoes. I now have four pairs of damaged shoes.

May I please be paid my expenses?"

Exercise 1

Transform the following sentences into third person singular.

Examples:
I climb the fence and jump into the alley.
He climbs the fence and jumps into the alley.
They come out and get into their car.
He comes out and gets into his car.

a) The policemen stop the drivers and ask for their driving licences.
b) They catch criminals and arrest them.
c) Robbers often carry weapons.
d) They see an accident.
e) The men run away, jump into the car and drive off.
f) Burglars watch the houses they want to break into.
g) They want to go to Düsseldorf.
h) They do not believe her stories because they know they are not true.
i) Policemen often direct traffic.
j) Detectives don't wear uniforms.
k) His dogs always attack strangers.
l) Motor-cycles make a lot of noise.

m) Buses go every ten minutes.
n) You drive too quickly.
o) I remember the address.
p) We leave home at 8 o'clock every day.

Exercise 2

The auxiliaries (except "do", "be" and "have") do not take the "-s" of third person singular. Transform the following sentences into third person singular.

Examples:
I must drink something to avoid suspicion.
He must drink something to avoid suspicion.
I am still keeping watch.
He is still keeping watch.

a) Can the detectives find the books the burglars have stolen?
b) Foreigners do not understand when policemen speak quickly.
c) Shall I tell the police what I have seen?
d) Do you live here?
e) Will you identify him if we catch him?
f) Must you leave immediately or do you have time to stay until my colleagues come?
g) They think that they may come later.
h) Can I help you or do you want to manage it yourself?
i) Do you know the way?

Exercise 3

Transform the report into third person singular.

5. THE INJURED BURGLAR (1)

Detective Sergeant Owen was sitting by a hospital bed talking to an injured burglar.
"Does your leg hurt?" he asked.
"It hurts all the time," complained the man.

"You rarely get into trouble like this," said the detective.

"I'm in real trouble now," said the burglar.

"You seldom come just to see me," Detective Sergeant Owen grinned, "you usually want something."

"I've come to talk about a burglary," he said. "I have already talked to your friend. He is usually the one who gets hurt but he is feeling very healthy at the moment."

"I usually feel sorry for him. I hope he is feeling sorry for me today," said the burglar.

"You generally study the house you break into but at the moment you seem to be suffering from the results of carelessness," said the detective. "Will you tell me what happened?"

"You are the detective, you should be finding out what happened," said the burglar.

"Don't worry, I will," said the detective sergeant as he headed for the door.

Exercises

Simple Present – Present Continuous

The simple present is used to express habitual actions: I usually feel sorry for him. Adverbs such as usually, often, always, generally, every day are often followed by the simple present tense.

The present continuous tense is used for an action happening at the moment:
I hope he is feeling sorry for me today.

Exercise 1

Change to present continuous tense using the given adverbs.

Example:
He generally studies the map. /
at the moment.
He is studying the map at the moment.

a) My son never drinks gin. / now
b) He often parks his car in Springstreet. / at present
c) They usually go there by bus. /now
d) We seldom lock the front-door. / just now
e) Occasionally we give her a ring. / at the moment
f) Does your wife argue with you? / continually
g) Does your mother complain? / constantly
h) He generally listens to his records about this time. / now
i) He seldom stays with his parents. / this week
j) My husband never looks at shop windows. / at the moment
k) He always mends the roof himself. / now
l) They watch that building every night. / just now
m) She seldom wears her glasses. / at the moment
n) He never goes for a walk. / now

Exercise 2

Fill in the correct form.

Example:
He normally (feel) very healthy, but he (not feel) healthy at the moment.
He normally feels very healthy, but he is not feeling very healthy at the moment.

a) He generally (speak) quickly, but he (speak) very slowly at the moment.
b) They usually (have) potatoes for dinner, but today they (have) rice.
c) She normally (clean) her husband's shoes, but at the moment he (clean) them himself.
d) His secretary usually (type) his letters, but now he (type) a letter himself.
e) He never (drink) beer, but he (have) a glass of beer now.
f) They (argue) all day, but they (not argue) now.

g) He never plays chess with his son, but he (play) chess with him right now.
h) Normally their children (keep on) shouting but today (keep) quiet.
i) Normally Mr. Brentford (drive) the car himself but now his wife (drive) the car.
j) She usually (drive) carefully but now she (drive) carelessly.
k) He seldom (do) his homework but he (do) his homework now.

6. THE INJURED BURGLAR (2)

Detective Sergeant Owen asked Mr. Vaughan to tell his story in his own words. This is what he said:

When we were having dinner, we suddenly heard footsteps. I went to the back door and looked out through the window. I saw two men standing outside. One of them tried the door handle. As soon as they noticed me, the two men ran off. I opened the back door and went to the shed where Simba was sleeping. I called Simba and he chased the two men. Suddenly they shouted and I went to the tree at the bottom of the garden. The two men had climbed up the tree. They were hanging from one of the lower branches. One of them was bleeding where Simba had clawed his leg. Simba was waiting at the foot of the tree. He tried to reach the men who were screaming with fear.

It seems the burglars did not know that I have a pet lion.

Exercise 1

The simple past is used for an action completed in the past:
"We suddenly heard footsteps."

The use of the past continuous tense often shows a relation between two actions:
"When we were having dinner, we suddenly heard footsteps."

Practise the past continuous tense in the following sentences.

Example:
What were they doing when they suddenly heard footsteps?
They were having dinner.

a) What was Nancy doing when the police arrived? / open the garage
b) What were you doing when Mrs. Miller rang the bell? / take a bath
c) What was Mr. Hunter doing, when you saw him? / clean his shoes
d) What were you doing at nine o'clock? / write a letter
e) What were you doing yersterday evening? / read a book
f) What were the boys doing when their father came home? / watch TV
g) What were you doing when I phoned? / prepare dinner
h) What were you doing when you heard Paul crying? / work in the cellar
i) What was Mr. Turner doing when you entered the room? / talk on the phone
j) What was that man doing when you opened the windows? / try to open the gate
k) What was Peter doing when you met him? / smoke a cigarette
l) What were you doing when father came home? / practise on the piano

Exercise 2

Simple Past or Past Continuous Tense?
Fill in the right form!

Mrs. Castle (take) her driving test. As she (drive) along the main road, she (see) a friend who (walk) on the far side of the road. She (take) her hands from the steering wheel and (wave) to her friend but, unfortunately, at the time she (change) gear with the other hand the car (swerve) across the road. A lorry which (travel) in the opposite direction (stop) suddenly and its load of wine (fall) off. Glass and wine (be) all over the road. A motor cyclist who (follow) the lorry (skid) on the wine, (lose) control of the machine and (crash) into a shop window where it (catch) fire. Mean-

while Mrs. Castle (try) to regain control of her car. She (turn) the steering wheel quickly but the car (go) too fast. It (skid) and (turn) over so that it (land) on its roof. Mrs. Castle (be) unhurt but (hang) upside down in her seat belt. She (scream) loudly. As the lorry driver (walk) across the spilt wine, he accidentally (kick) a dog which (drink) it. The dog (bite) the lorry driver. The lorry driver (aim) another kick at the dog but he (miss). He (fall) on his back, on the broken glass. By now, the fire in the shop (burn) furiously and people (run) out onto the street where a crowd (gather). A fire engine and an ambulance (arrive) at the time from opposite directions. They also (skid) on the slippery road and (collide). The driver of the fire engine (strike) the ambulance driver and a fight soon (break) out. Mrs. Castle (fail) her driving test.

7. THE FAST FRENCHMAN

One day a traffic policeman was sitting in his patrol car which was parked at the side of a busy motorway. He suddenly saw a French Citroën car overtake all the other traffic and pass him at a fast speed. The policeman decided to stop the Citroën and started off after it. It took a long time to catch up with the French car which was being driven at well above the speed limit. Even then, it was some time before the policeman was able to get in front of the car and signal the driver to stop.

The policeman got out of his car and walked back to talk to the driver of the Citroën.

"When did you come to Germany?" asked the policeman. "I came to Germany two days ago," said the driver.

"Then you have had plenty of time to learn the speed limit in this country," he was told.

"I was in a hurry," said the Frenchman.

"I could see that," said the policeman.

"Why were you in such a hurry?"
The Frenchman thought quickly and then he said, "I am short of petrol."

The policeman looked puzzled. "So," he said, "why were you driving so fast?"

"Well," said the Frenchman, "I drove as fast as I could in order to reach a petrol station before running out of petrol."

Exercise 1

"When did you come to Germany?" asked the policeman. "I came to Germany two days ago," said the driver.

In a sentence where the word "ago" occurs the verb is put in past tense. Answer the following questions according to the given example.

Example:
When did you buy your car? (two days)
I bought my car two days ago.

a) When did you buy this case?
   (two weeks)
b) When did he get home? (three hours)
c) When did he ask for help? (a week)
d) When did they return? (four days)
e) When did you meet him? (a few days)
f) When did you go to France? (several years)
g) When did she break her arm?
   (a month)
h) When did we last meet? (two years)
i) When did you hurt yourself?
   (a few minutes)
j) When did the car break down?
   (half an hour)
k) When did the woman say she arrived?
   (four days)
l) When did he take you to his home?
   (a few weeks)

Exercise 2

Use the simple past tense in the following sentences.

Example:
I (ask) him why he (drive) so fast.
I asked him why he drove so fast.

a) I (want) to see him before he (leave).
b) He (tell) me that he (be) innocent.
c) The woman (die) before she (reach) the hospital.
d) The fight (be) much worse than we (think) at first.
e) He (take) the prisoner to the police station immediately after he (catch) him.
f) She (say) that she (call) the police.
g) I (ask) him if he (break) the window.
h) It (be) the butler who (do) the murder.
i) It (seem) an age before the ambulance (arrive).
j) It (feel) like an earthquake when the gas main (explode).
k) When the car (crash) the driver (break) his leg, (cut) his head and (bruise) his arm.

8. THE WORRIED MAN

A senior police officer went to see his doctor. "You look worried," the doctor told him.

"I have every reason for being worried. My wife has gone shopping in Paris," said the police officer.

"Does she usually shop in Paris?" asked the doctor.

"Only when I am stupid enough to give her a credit card," said the police officer dejectedly.

"But your wife doesn't speak French," said the doctor.

"She doesn't need to," was the reply. "She points to what she wants with one hand and holds out her credit card in the other."

"Don't worry about it," said the doctor, "I'll give you some tablets, and you'll soon feel better."

"Don't give me any tablets," said the police officer. "Just lend me five hundred pounds."

Exercise 1

The present tense interrogative is formed with the auxiliary "to do".
Transform the sentences according to the given example.

Example:
She is shopping in Paris.
Does she usually shop in Paris?

a) He is driving his car.
b) The officer is talking about his wife.
c) The doctor is asking the patient questions.
d) The lady is pointing to the things she wants.
e) I am taking some tablets before I start eating.
f) We are stopping the cars for a traffic check.
g) The policemen are asking for the documents.
h) They are all walking to the station.
i) The drivers are doing the breathalyzer test.
j) Her husband is going to his pub for a drink.
k) I am walking to my office.
l) My boss is calling me for an interview.

Exercise 2

The present tense negative is also formed with "to do". Make the following sentences negative.

Example:
She speaks French. (her boyfriend)
But her boyfriend doesn't speak French.

a) They understand. (I)
b) I know the Smith family. (they)
c) Sally spends a lot of money on clothes. (Mary)
d) John has a cooked lunch every day. (his wife)
e) I like going by bus. (my brother)
f) She usually shops in Düsseldorf. (her friend)
g) He pays the bill every evening. (his colleague)
h) That man borrows money from his colleagues. (I)
i) Mrs. Stones buys fresh rolls every morning. (Mrs. Collins)
j) John and his wife smoke a lot. (their daughter)
k) My wife keeps a lot of money in her drawer. (I)
l) The No. 53 bus goes to the airport. (the No. 50 bus. It goes to the station).

9. THE BROKEN LOCK

Two girls went up to a policeman outside a large railway station.

"I lost my suitcase in the station," said one of them.

"Did you really lose it," asked the policeman, "or did someone steal it?"

The girl explained that she put her suitcase down while she went to look for a taxi. When she came back, the suitcase had gone.

"When did this happen?"

"It happened about half an hour ago," replied the girl.

"But didn't your friend see it taken?" queried the policeman.

"No," said the girl. "She came with me to get a taxi."

"Why did you leave your case?" asked the policeman.

"I left it because it had a broken lock," explained the girl.

"I was afraid it would burst open."

The policeman took the girl and her friend to the police office where he showed them a white suitcase.

"That's mine," said the girl, "where did you get it?"

"You were in luck," said the policeman. "A thief picked up your case and walked away with it. No one stopped him."

"But didn't you stop him?" asked the girl.

The policeman smiled. "No," he said. "The broken lock gave way and the suitcase burst open. All your underclothes fell out onto the ground. The thief was so embarrassed that he dropped the case and ran away."

Exercise 1

Past Tense

Both the interrogative and the negative of simple past tense are formed with "did". Form questions:

Example:
I lost my suitcase.
Did you really lose it?

a) She broke the Chinese vase.
b) They took that watch.
c) He wore red trousers.
d) I won £ 1 000.
e) She bought six pairs of shoes.
f) They even stole her personal letters.
g) She understood perfectly what I said.
h) The Smiths sold their new car.
i) I wrote a letter to the chairman.
j) He forgot his wife's birthday.
k) She wore the same dress for three weeks.
l) Her underclothes fell onto the ground.

Exercise 2

Form questions in the negative according to the following example.

Example:
No one stopped him. (you)
But didn't you stop him?

a) No one saw the accident. (Mr. White)
b) No one knew his address.
   (his girl friend)
c) No one helped him. (the police)
d) No one liked sweets. (Claire)
e) No one paid attention. (you)
f) No one wore a blue hat. (Charlie)
g) No one drank that wine. (Mr. Prime)
h) No one came to my house.
   (Mrs. Taylor)
i) No one read this book. (my brother)
j) No one gave me any money.
   (your mother)
k) No one waited for him. (his colleagues)
l) No one visited our house last week.
   (Mr. Miller)

Exercise 3

Ask for the expressions in italics.

Example:
They arrived *about four o'clock.*
When did they arrive?

a) I met him *at the station*
b) She wore *large dark glasses.*
c) She didn't come home *because she was frightened.*
d) *John* went to the pictures.
e) She showed him *their house.*
f) *Last Sunday* we had lunch in a restaurant.
g) We saw *a good film* yesterday.
h) Mr. Taylor phoned *his boss.*
i) He carried *a heavy case.*
j) They travelled *by train* to Austria.

10. FINDING A NEEDLE IN A HAYSTACK

"Right, let's go," said Detective Karl Schreier as he started the engine of the police car. "It won't take us long to get to the railway station."

"I don't think we stand much chance of catching him," said his colleague Detective Peter Kempff. "We haven't much to go on. The description that they gave us would fit about half the young men in Germany."

"I'd very much like to catch him," said Detective Schreier, "I don't like people who smuggle drugs. What exactly was the information?"

"A young Englishman named Eric Sharp arrived at Hook on the boat this morning. He's carrying a load of heroin to sell to the students at the university here," was the reply.

"It's a pity they missed him when he came off the boat," said Detective Schreier.

"The train from Hook is full of German students returning from Holland and Britain. It will be like looking for a needle in a haystack trying to pick out one young Englishman."

They drove on in silence for a few minutes. Then Detective Kempff spoke:

"He might have something on him that shows that he's English."

"Huh," snorted his friend, "he's not likely to wear a Union Jack on his hat, is he?"

"Have you ever seen any heroin?" asked Detective Kempff.

"Yes, I saw some last week," said Detective Schreier. "Have you ever dealt with a drug dealer?"

"No, I haven't," replied his colleague.

At that moment, the police car turned into the road leading to the railway station. Ahead of them, the two detectives could see a crowd of young people emerging from the railway station.

"We're too late," cried Detective Kempff.

"I don't think so," replied Detective Schreier, as he stopped the car and started to get out.

"Unless I'm very much mistaken, that young man over there is British. Let's stop him."

The two detectives ran along the road to where a lone figure had crossed the road and was about to get on a bus.

"Mr. Sharp?" said Detective Schreier to the young man, who looked at them in astonishment.

"Yes, that's me," he said, "but how did you know?"

"It's our job to know these things," said Detective Schreier smugly, glancing at his puzzled colleague. "Come with us please."

Some hours later, after Eric Sharp had been safely placed in a cell, Peter Kempff could contain his curiosity no longer. "All right," he said, "how did you know he was an Englishman?"

Karl Schreier grinned. "Two things told me," he said. "The first was the fact that he crossed the road against the red traffic light. In Britain they do that all the time."

"That's not very conclusive," said Detective Kempff. "Even German people do that sometimes."

"Ah yes," grinned his friend, "but in Britain they drive on the other side of the road and when Mr. Sharp stepped off the kerb he looked only to his right and walked into the road. A German would have looked to his left."

Exercise 1

"Have you ever seen any heroin?" asked Detective Kempff.

"Yes, I saw some last week," was the reply.

If a question is asked in present perfect the answer might be given in simple past tense especially when a certain adverb of time is used.

Answer the following questions in the affirmative:

Example:
Has he ever taken any heroin?
(last week)
Yes, he took some last week.

a) Has he ever done it before? (in 1975)
b) Has she ever run away before?
   (a year ago)
c) Has he ever stolen a car? (last month)
d) Have they ever caused trouble?
   (last time)
e) Have you ever seen him? (yesterday)

f) Have you ever been to France?
   (last year)
g) Have you ever dealt with a drug
   dealer? (last week)
h) Has he ever driven a car?
   (this morning)
i) Have we ever met? (a long time ago)
j) Have you ever met her? (last week)
k) Has she ever telephoned you?
   (last night)
l) Have they chosen you? (yesterday)
m) Has he ever gone to prison?
   (last year)

Exercise 2

"Have you ever dealt with a drug dealer?" asked Detective Schreier.

Answer the questions of Exercise 1 in the negative.

Give short answers.

Example:
Has he ever taken any heroin?
No, he hasn't.

Exercise 3

"Has he ever been to Germany before?" asked Detective Schreier. "No, he never has," replied Detective Kempff.

The word "never" emphasizes the negative. Answer the questions of Exercise 1 using the word "never".

Example:
Has he ever taken any heroin?
No, he never has.

11. THE CRAFTY FOX (1)

Detective Sergeant Owen spoke quietly to his companion in the police car, "Don't forget," he said, "this man, Albert Fox, is crafty. We shall need to keep our wits about us. It's important that we catch him."

"Yes, it is," said Detective Jack Swift. "What do you want me to do?"

"You go to the back of the house," said the sergeant. "When I go to the front door, he'll recognize me and run out of the back door. If you are quick, you can catch him when he comes out."

"Yes, I can," replied Jack confidently.

"Don't let him go," warned the sergeant.

Jack looked hurt. "Of course I won't. You can rely on me," he said. "It will be easy to stop him."

"No, it won't, snapped Sergeant Owen. "It will be quite difficult. Now, here we are. I'll give you a few minutes to get round the back, then I'll knock at the front door. Be sure that you catch him. Albert Fox thinks quicker than you."

"No, he doesn't", snorted Detective Swift as he walked off smiling confidently. He soon reached the back door of the house and stood quietly waiting. After only a few moments, the door opened and a man beckoned to him.

"Come in quickly," the man urged. „Sergeant Owen has got Mr. Fox in the hall and needs your help with him."

Detective Swift rushed into the house and soon reached the front door. He was astonished to find it closed. When he opened it, he saw Detective Sergeant Owen standing outside with his arms folded and a grim expression on his face. "How the hell did you get there?" asked the sergeant fiercely.

"A man let me in through the back door," said Jack. "He said that you needed help with Mr. Fox."

"You idiot," snarled Sergeant Owen. "That was Fox. I told you he was crafty."

Exercise 1

"It's important that we catch him," said Detective Sergeant Owen.

"Yes, it is" said Detective Swift, agreeing with him.

If you agree with a statement, it is often impolite just to answer with "yes" or "no". The auxiliary is repeated in the answer. Give short answers showing agreement with the statement.

Example:
If you are quick, you can catch him when he comes out.
Yes, I can.

a) I think he'll escape if he can.
b) You'll probably catch him quickly.
c) I believe this is the way to the station.
d) You've travelled a long way today.
e) I expect you're tired.
f) They're a very peaceful crowd at present.
g) He says that it is too late.
h) I understand that you are a good shot.
i) It's essential that we get there in time.
j) She really told him off, didn't she!
k) He could have got away if he'd tried.
l) I dare say you would be glad to be on holiday.
m) We're going to have trouble when the football match is over.
n) It's a good idea to keep football fans away from everyone else.

Exercise 2

"It will be easy to stop him," said Detective Swift.
"No, it won't," snapped Detective Sergeant Owen.

Express your disagreement with the following statements by using the same construction as in the example. Remember that "not" is often abbreviated when used in spoken English.

Example:
I am the only one who knows the way.
No, you're not.

a) I've got enough beer.
b) My team will win the championship.
c) This is a good car.
d) He is a good centre forward.

e) I believe he's a very good shot.
f) It's all right, we've plenty of time.
g) You've made a mistake again.
h) It has stopped raining now.
i) There's going to be a party tonight.
j) He's a crafty man.
k) I've arrested the right man.
l) She's a very nice woman.
m) Could he have got out through the back door?
n) Would we give him a permit for his gun?

Exercise 3

"Albert Fox thinks quicker than you," said Detective Sergeant Owen.

"No, he doesn't," snorted Detective Swift.

If there is a verb in the statement it is repeated by a form of "to do" in the short answer. Disagree with the following statements.

Example:
The other team cheated all the time.
No, it didn't.

a) He wants to confess all his crimes.
b) They started earlier than me.
c) The car skidded on the wet road.
d) She asked for police help.
e) I bought the last round of drinks.
f) You drank my beer.
g) We always agree with one another.
h) He likes traffic duty.
i) She drives very carefully.
j) The boat travels very smoothly even on rough seas.
k) He says that the train arrived late last night.
l) This woman claims that her husband beats her.

12. THE CRAFTY FOX (2)

The two detectives went into the house and looked in all the rooms. There was no one in the house. After he had searched the

89

bedrooms, Detective Sergeant Owen called Detective Swift and together they went to the back door of the house. Once outside, the sergeant said to his colleague in a loud voice. "We'll have to search for him. You take the north part of the town and I'll go south. I'll meet you at the car in half an hour."

Detective Swift ran off. He felt very miserable. "We shall never catch Fox now," he thought. He searched everywhere he could think of during the next thirty minutes. Then, breathless and forlorn, he returned to the car. To his surprise, Sergeant Owen was sitting in the car talking to the man who had let him into the house. "You have met Mr. Fox, I believe," said Sergeant Owen sarcastically.

"But how did you catch him?" asked Jack in bewilderment.

"I was just a little more crafty than him," was the reply. "I noticed that his jacket and his wallet were still in the bedroom because he hadn't had time to fetch them. I thought he wouldn't go far without them, so I only pretended to leave to search for him. I waited quietly and he came out from where he was hiding in a garden. Then I caught him."

"And I've just run all over the town looking for him," groaned Jack.

"Ah well, that will teach you not to be quite so gullible in future, won't it," said Detective Sergeant Owen. "One day you'll think before you act instead of afterwards. When that happens, we'll both be happy."

Exercise 1

"We'll have to search for him," said Detective Sergeant Owen.

The future tense is used to express intention. Express the intention in direct speech.

Example:
He wants him to take the north part.
You will take the north part.

a) He wants to meet him at the car.
b) She wants to walk home.
c) She wants to buy a new dress.
d) The police want to chase the car.
e) He wants her to see the doctor.
f) He wants to have dinner at 6 o'clock.
g) Mrs. Smith wants to take a taxi.
h) She wants to go to the cinema.
i) They want to spend their next holiday in Spain.
j) He wants to sell his house.

Exercise 2

"That will teach you not to be so gullible, won't it," said Detective Sergeant Owen.

Add to the following future tense statements a question tag.

Remember: When the statement is positive, the question tag is negative; when the statement is negative, the question tag is positive.

Example:
It will be quite difficult, won't it.

a) One day you'll think before you act.
b) You won't catch him quickly.
c) I think he'll escape if he can.
d) They will give him a permit for his gun.
e) You won't make that mistake again.
f) My team will win the championship.
g) She will start earlier than me.
h) He won't confess all his crimes.
i) My wife will drive carefully.
j) You'll check the other side.
k) We won't come to Germany.
l) She won't buy this case.

Exercise 3

In written English you often find "shall" and "will" to express the future. "Shall" is only used with "I" and "we".

Fill in "shall" or "will" in regard to "I" and "we".

Example:
I . . . see him before he leaves.
I shall see him before he leaves.

a) She says that she . . . call the police.
b) . . . we go to the zoo?
c) She . . . lose her watch.
d) My father . . . pay the bill.
e) . . . they build a new shop?
f) I . . . go out for dinner.
g) . . . you give me your passport, please?
h) . . . it break?
i) . . . we answer all your questions?
j) I . . . go home soon.

13. LOST

A distraught woman was waiting for the police car by the telephone box. She explained to the police officer that her young son had wandered off into the nearby woods and had got lost. Her husband was looking for the boy.

"We are going to get some police dogs," said the policeman. "You'll have to lend us something with your son's scent on it."

"I'm going back to our caravan in a moment. I'll get one of his old shoes," said the woman.

"What does your husband intend to do for the next hour or so?" asked the policeman.

"He will search this part of the wood, then he will go to our caravan," was the reply.

"When do you expect to meet him again?" asked the policeman.

"He will be meeting me at the caravan at four o'clock," said the woman.

The police officer used his radio to call a unit with police dogs on board.

"The police dog van is going directly to your caravan," he told the woman, "so we'll go there, too."

When the policeman arrived at the caravan site with the woman, he was very pleased to see that the boy had found his way back to his caravan.

"I am going to make sure he doesn't frighten us like that again," she promised the policeman as he drove away.

Four hours later the policeman was back at the same telephone box where the same distraught woman awaited him.

"Are you going to tell me your son is lost again?" he demanded.

"Oh, no," was the tearful reply, "he is all right, but will you help me find my husband? He has never returned from looking for my son. You will need your dogs to find him now."

Exercise 1

Modes of expressing the future are:

1. the present continuous tense
2. the "going to"-form
3. the future tense
4. the future continuous tense

The present continuous tense is used when things are very likely to happen, especially when a time adverb of the immediate future is given. Put the following sentences into the present continuous using the given time adverb.

Example:
You should go back to your caravan. / in a moment
We are going back to our caravan in a moment.

a) You have to take your car to the garage. / tomorrow
b) You have to buy a guide. / after lunch
c) You have to stay at your hotel. / tonight
d) He has to see a doctor. / immediately
e) The motorist has to clear the road. / at once
f) You should ask for permission. / soon
g) He has decided to go to America. / next year

h) The Smiths will buy a new car. /
   in October
i) They have to move to Stuttgart. /
   in a fortnight
j) You should phone your wife. /
   immediately
k) You have to order a visa. /
   next week
l) You have to replace the tyres. /
   tomorrow

Exercise 2

The use of "going to" or "will" implies that the future action will be done more deliberately.
Change the following sentences into the "going to"-form.

Example:
We will get some police dogs.
We are going to get some police dogs.

a) My brother will lend me the money.
b) My colleague will ask you some further questions.
c) What will you do on Sunday?
d) He will stay there until 8 o'clock.
e) He will wait for you at the bus stop.
f) She will ring me up every day.
g) I shall go on holiday twice this year.
h) He will sell our car.
i) We will change our wet clothes.
j) We will get something to eat.
k) We shall get a map of the district.
l) They'll find a hotel for tonight.

Exercise 3

Change the following sentences into the simple future tense.

Example:
He intends to search this part of the wood.
He will search this part of the wood.

a) He intends to go to London.
b) They intend to hire the flat.
c) I intend to buy a new car.

d) He wants to leave without paying.
e) You should shut the door.
f) I intend to stay over night.
g) We should leave our luggage at the station.
h) He intends to sell antiques.
i) You should fill in this form.
j) They intend to hire a car.

Exercise 4

The future continuous tense expresses not so much of intention or plan, moreover it tells that a certain action will take place in the future.
Use the future continuous tense.

Example:
What will he be doing at four o'clock? /
to meet me at the caravan.
He will be meeting me at the caravan at four o'clock.

a) What will he be doing in the afternoon? / to work in his office
b) What will they be doing this time next week? / to travel to Holland
c) What will they be doing tonight? /
   to pack their cases
d) What will he be doing on Saturday? /
   to watch a football match
e) What will he be doing this evening? /
   to play golf
f) What will you be doing on Tuesday? /
   to celebrate John's birthday party
g) What will he be doing this afternoon? /
   to paint the house
h) What will the children be doing when we arrive there? / to feed the animals
i) What will Paul be doing when they get home? / to read the newspaper
j) What will she be doing when you come home? / to prepare dinner

14. PEACE AND QUIET

A police patrol car cruised slowly through the dark streets of a large town. The driver, John Hawkins, glanced at his colleague,

Bill Brewer, who had been unusually quiet all evening.

"You haven't told headquarters that we're back on patrol," he said.

"I'll tell them in a minute," growled Bill. "I'm in no hurry to get another assignment."

"Why is that?" asked John, for his colleague was usually anxious to get as many jobs as possible. That way time passes more quickly than just by patrolling for the whole shift.

"I'm on leave from tomorrow," said Bill, "and I don't want to get a big job tonight. Turn down here, we'll have a look around the industrial estate, nothing ever happens there."

John drove between rows of factories and warehouses until he came to a dark, quiet road with high walls on either side. He stopped the car and switched off the engine.

"You haven't switched off the lights", said Bill.

"I'll switch them off immediately," said John, an amused smile on his face, "I didn't realize that you were that determined to keep out of trouble."

"If I can't go on holiday tomorrow, my wife will probably divorce me," said Bill. "We're going to Mallorca for a couple of weeks."

"Will you and your wife go by plane?" asked John.

"Yes, we'll go by plane," replied Bill, "but my wife isn't very keen. She doesn't like flying."

"Will you take the children or will you go alone?" asked John.

"No, we won't take the children, we shall go alone," was the reply. "It's too expensive to take children. Anyway, I need peace and quiet. I never get that when my children are around."

The two men sat quietly for some time, each wrapped up in his own thoughts. Suddenly, the silence was broken by the sound of a gate being opened. The two policemen saw the shadowy figure of a man carefully open a warehouse gate just ahead of them. The man looked furtively around him and then waved to someone inside the warehouse. Immediately a large lorry came out onto the road and stopped while the man closed the gates and ran to a car parked just along the street.

Bill groaned, "Oh no," he said, "of all nights to choose. Tell headquarters that we've got a suspected gang of thieves."

"I'll tell them straight away," said John, "but if they are villains, it may stop you going on leave tomorrow."

"Don't remind me of that," said Bill. "Just start thinking what I'm going to tell my wife."

Exercise 1

"You haven't switched off the lights," said Bill.

"I'll switch them off immediately," was the reply.

Answer the following statements using the future tense:

Example:
You haven't told the truth (now).
I'll tell the truth now.

a) You haven't stopped the engine. (immediately)
b) You haven't produced your passport. (tomorrow)
c) You haven't signed this document. (right away)
d) You haven't been to the office. (this afternoon)
e) You haven't told us what happened. (in a moment)
f) You haven't brought the necessary papers. (next week)
g) You haven't caught the thief. (next time)

h) You haven't paid this bill. (at the end of the month)
i) You haven't sold your car. (as soon as I can)
j) You haven't been able to see her. (Wednesday)
k) You haven't got a ticket. (before seven o'clock)

Exercise 2

"Will you go by plane" asked John.
"Yes, we'll go by plane," replied Bill.
(Note that Bill is replying on behalf of his wife and himself.)

Answer the following questions.

Example:
Will you go by train?" (No)
No, I won't go by train.

a) Will you travel by air? (Yes)
b) Will you use your car? (No)
c) Will you take a statement? (No)
d) Will you arrest him? (Yes)
e) Will he be on the train? (Yes)
f) Will he be at the meeting? (No)
g) Will she identify the thief? (Yes)
h) Will they come to the meeting? (Yes)
i) Will you be there to meet them? (No)
j) Will they hold a rally in the square? (No)
k) Will they march to the town hall? (Yes)

Exercise 3

John asked, "Will you take the children or will you go alone?"
Bill replied, "No, we won't take the children, we shall go alone."

This form combines a positive and a negative structure in one sentence. Reply to the following questions.

Example:
Will you take the children or will you go alone?
I will take the children, I won't go alone.

a) Will you stay here or will you go home?
b) Will you drive the car or will you walk?
c) Will you arrest him or will you let him go?
d) Will you tell her or will you let her find out for herself?
e) Will you deal with it or will you let John do it?
f) Will you write a letter or will you telephone?
g) Will she come here or will she go straight to the office?
h) Will he tell her the truth or will he tell her lies?
i) Will they plead guilty or will they fight the case?
j) Will we catch him or will he escape again?

15. THE BARE TRUTH

An identification parade was being held at a police station. A police inspector had asked a number of men to line up with the suspect who was thought to have attacked a young woman. When everything was ready, he went to explain to the victim of the attack what she had to do.

"You told us you were attacked by a naked man. I want you to walk along that line of men. If you see the man who attacked you, point him out to me."

"He isn't here, is he?" gasped the woman. The inspector resisted the temptation to say that he hoped so, otherwise the wrong man had been arrested. Instead, he said reassuringly, "You have nothing to fear."

"I suppose I haven't really," said the young woman. "You will be there, won't you?"

"Of course," said the inspector. "Now, you said that a tall, well-built, naked man chased you and started to tear your clothes off. Then a passing motorist rescued you and the man ran away. That's right, isn't it?"

94

"That's right," said the woman.

"So, when you get into the room where these men are lined up, you must look at all their faces and then point to this man if he is there. You understand, don't you?"

"Yes," replied the woman. "Are they all wearing clothes?"

"Of course they are," replied the inspector impatiently.

"Then I don't think I can pick him out," she said, "I didn't really look at his face."

Exercises

This text shows more question tags.
"You will be there, won't you? You understand, don't you?"
Question tags follow the same rule as short answers.
Add question tags to the following sentences.

Example:
He is on duty.
He is on duty, isn't he?

a) She shouldn't be there.
b) She speaks good English.
c) He lives here.
d) You mustn't do that.
e) He ran well.
f) He is a crook.
g) I shouldn't be here.
h) I need to arrive early.
i) He drove the car too fast.
j) He was convicted.
k) You are in uniform.
l) They never used to carry guns.
m) The car seldom broke down.
n) You are not in plain clothes.
o) They hope to catch him.
p) They will be stopped.
q) They make a good pair.
r) She spoke to you.
s) I was right.
t) He didn't arrive.
u) She hates him.
v) They could come later.

w) He broke in through the window.
x) He wouldn't dare.
y) You answered the telephone.
z) It hardly ever needs new tyres.

16. MORE ABOUT A PIANO

The ambulance was already leaving when the policeman arrived at the house. There was little that he could do other than to find out what had happened. The hall of the house was a scene of utter confusion. A large piano was partly embedded in the floor and splintered wood and pieces of plaster were strewn all around. A woman and two young men were sitting on the stairs looking sadly at the wreckage.

"Hello," said the woman. "Be careful where you walk. Do you think these stairs are safe?"

"Yes, but the hall is safer," said the policeman.

"I will stay here. What happened?"

"It was the strangest thing I have ever seen," she replied. "My husband and my two sons were trying to get this piano upstairs. My youngest son Rudolph got his fingers pinched between the piano and the stairs' banisters so he let go of the piano."

"Is his hand painful?" asked the policeman.

"Yes, but his foot is more painful," said the woman, "the piano fell on it."

"He must have been annoyed," said the policeman sympathetically.

"Yes, but his brother was much more annoyed," was the surprising reply. "It was his piano."

"I see," said the policeman.

"It was a nasty accident. I am sure that all three of you are very upset."

"We certainly are," said the woman. "Of course, my husband is the most upset."

"Why is that?" asked the policeman.

The woman waved her hand to indicate the devastated hall. "He was underneath the piano when it happened," she said, "and it fell on top of him. He will be very angry when he wakes up in hospital."

"I'm sure he will," said the policeman. "Yes," said the woman, "he is the most unmusical man I know."

Exercise 1

Use the correct comparative of an adjective following the example.
Remember that one- and two-syllable adjectives form their comparative and superlative by adding "-er" and "-est"; two-syllable adjectives ending in "-ful" or "-e" and three-syllable adjectives form their comparative and superlative by putting "more" and "most" before the positive.

Example:
Is your hand painful?
Yes, but my foot is more painful.
Is the Audi fast?
Yes, but the Mercedes is faster.

a) Is the boy truthful? (girl)
b) Are the sandwiches fresh? (rolls)
c) Is the road straight? (motorway)
d) Is the coffee hot? (tea)
e) Is the written examination difficult? (oral test)
f) Are the drawings helpful? (photographs)
g) Is the restaurant cheap? (canteen)
h) Are the pistols accurate? (rifles)
i) Is the blonde pretty? (brunette)
j) Is the French girl attractive? (her friend)
k) Is the car economical? (motor cycle)
l) Are burglaries common? (thefts)

Exercise 2

The word "much" before the comparative emphasizes the comparative.

Example:
Mrs. Smith was angry when she had a car crash. (Mr. Smith)
Yes, but Mr. Smith was much more angry.

a) The lorry was damaged in the collision. (car)
b) John was happy when the marriage took place. (Mary)
c) The boy was relieved when he left school. (school)
d) He was grateful for being given a new job. (wife)
e) The boy's mother was pleased when he passed his exam. (boy)
f) The drive up the mountain was dangerous. (drive down)
g) Taking action was risky. (doing nothing)
h) He was annoyed. (his brother)

Exercise 3

Use the correct superlative.

Example:
Is your brother a careful driver?
He's the most careful driver I know.

a) Is your father a courteous man?
b) Is your mother a hard-working woman?
c) Is your boss a difficult man to work for?
d) Is your son an athletic boy?
e) Is your sister a pleasant girl?
f) Is your friend a likeable man?
g) Are your neighbours helpful people?
h) Is Annette an attractive girl?
i) Are the members of the crowd peaceful people?
j) Is he a patient man?
k) Is the car reliable?
l) Is the mountain road dangerous?
m) Is the route direct?

17. THE HARDER THEY FALL

Detective Sergeant Owen had a new young detective named Swift working with him for the day.

"My feet are sore," complained Detective Swift. "This place is not so close as I thought."

"It's farther than I thought, too," said Detective Sergeant Owen. "I hope you can handle Joe Bloggs, you're not so fit as he is. You're not as big as he is either." "The bigger he is, the harder he will fall," said Detective Swift confidently. "He may have some of his mates with him, too," said the detective sergeant.

"The more the merrier," said the constable. "I'm not so sure," said the sergeant. "Joe Bloggs is as tough as nails." "I'm as tough as Joe Bloggs," boasted the young detective constable. The two men arrived at their destination. Joe Bloggs was standing with a very fat woman outside his house.

"He is bigger than I thought he was," muttered Detective Swift.

"You're not as stupid as I thought you were," grinned Detective Sergeant Owen. "Leave Joe Bloggs to me, you deal with his wife."

When the two detectives got close to Mr. and Mrs. Bloggs, Detective Sergeant Owen quickly slipped a handcuff on one of Joe Bloggs' wrists and fastened the other handcuff to an iron railing.

However, Detective Constable Swift was immediately seized by Mrs. Bloggs who threw him to the ground and sat heavily on top of him. Detective Sergeant Owen looked down at him with a grin on his face. "She is as heavy as a ton weight," cried Detective Constable Swift. "Get her off me." The sergeant laughed. "There's no hurry," he said. "You are learning a useful lesson and the younger you are, the more you have to learn!"

Exercise 1

Comparison of unequal things is expressed by the following structures:
This place is not so close as I thought.
This place is further than I thought.

Transform the given examples.

Example:
His behaviour was not so bad as his brother's. (good)
His behaviour was better than his brother's.

a) This house is not so large as I thought. (small).
b) He was not so bright as his son. (dull)
c) They were not so sure as the shop-keeper. (uncertain)
d) The cupbord was not so high as the wardrobe. (low)
e) This car is not so slow as I thought. (fast)
f) Her skirt is not so dark as this one. (light)
g) Mrs. Webster's clothes are not so old-fashioned as her daughter's. (modern)
h) The black bag is not so cheap as the green one. (expensive)
i) My TV-set is not so new as their TV-set. (old)
j) My watch is not so good as Peter's watch. (bad)
k) His suitcase was not so light as his bag. (heavy)
l) This scarf is not so long as the one he wore yesterday. (short)

Exercise 2

Comparison of equal things is expressed by "as ... as".

Transform the following sentences using this structure.

Example:
I am tough (Joe Bloggs).
I am as tough as Joe Bloggs.

a) Charles Brentley is well known. (John Haddocks)

b) His wife was obstinate. (Mr. Dean)

c) The young man looked crafty.
   (the old one)

d) The Jaguar was badly damaged.
   (the Rover)

e) Mr. Smith seemed to be busy.
   (Mr. Pitt)

f) Playing cards is interesting and enter-
   taining. (playing chess)

g) Their son Tim is an impudent rascal.
   (their son Eddie)

h) The kitchen was untidy. (the living
   room)

i) His coat was dirty. (his trousers)

j) The hostess was generous. (the host)

k) Mr. Jandy is very co-operative.
   (Mr. Hawkins)

l) The morning was rainy.
   (the afternoon)

m) His father looked miserable.
   (his mother)

18. THE NAKED MAN

The two elderly ladies were waiting at
the door when Detective Sergeant Owen
arrived. They introduced themselves as
Alice and Eva Smith.

"I understand that you reported seeing a
naked man," he said.

"That's right," said Alice. "First Eva saw
him then I saw him as well."

"Yes," said Eva, "I called Alice and she
came and saw him, too."

"It could do us a lot of harm," said Alice.
Detective Sergeant Owen tried hard to
hide his smile.

"Our doctor told us we should avoid excitement, it's bad for our hearts. Neither Eva
nor I have strong hearts."

"That's right," echoed Eva, "both Alice
and I have to avoid excitement.

"Well," said the detective, "will either you
or your sister show me where I can see this
naked man?"

The two ladies led the detective to a small
room at the top of the house. Alice pointed
to a house on the other side of the street.
"You can see him at the bathroom window
of that house," she said. "But you can't see
into that window," protested Detective
Sergeant Owen.

"Oh no," said Alice, "but you can if you
stand on this chair."

Exercise 1

There are different ways to express the
German word "auch", which are all very
common in English.
"As well", "also", and "too" all mean the
same.

Translate the following sentences using "as
well".

Example:
Eva saw him and I saw him as well.

a) Eva sah ihn, und ich sah ihn auch.

b) Herr Müller erkannte den Mann, und
   Herr Schmidt erkannte ihn auch.

c) Peter hatte zu viel getrunken (too
   much to drink) und Richard auch.

d) Sie sollten zuhören, und Ihr Bruder
   sollte auch zuhören.

e) Ich kaufte (mir) einen Anzug und auch
   einen Mantel.

f) Er entriß (to rob s.o. of sth.) mir die
   Handtasche und auch die Armband-
   uhr.

g) Fräulein Steiner wohnt hier und Herr
   Lingemann auch.

h) Mein Mann raucht Zigarren und mein
   Sohn auch.

i) Sie durchsuchten den Schrank und
   auch die Schubladen.

j) Ich werde Ihre Firma benachrichtigen
   und auch Ihre Frau.

Exercise 2

Translate the sentences of Exercise 1
using "too".

Example:
She came and saw him, too.

Exercise 3

Translate the sentences of Exercise 1 using "also".

Example:
Eva saw him and I also saw him.

19. THE KIND LADY

One cold and rainy evening a young man was standing at the bus stop waiting for a number seven bus. After some time a number fifteen bus arrived and an elderly lady got off. She joined the young man and spoke to him, "Nasty night, isn't it? But perhaps I won't have to wait for long."

A little curious, the young man asked her which bus she wanted. The lady seemed to be pleased with herself when she said, "I'm waiting for a number fifteen." "But you just got off a number fifteen," said the man, "why did you get off before you had reached your destination?"

"Well," she stammered shyly, "there was a badly crippled young man on that bus. He could hardly stand, but no one offered him a seat. I thought he'd be upset if an old lady like me got up for him, so I just pretended it was time for me to get off and I rang the bell. He took my seat and wasn't embarrassed and I – well, there's always another bus."

Exercise 1

„Sie schloß sich dem jungen Mann an" means translated into English:
"She joined the young man."
Note that the word „sich" which is part of the German reflexive verb is dropped. This is the case with most German reflexive verbs when translated into English.

Give a correct translation of the following sentences:

a) Wir werden uns am Bahnhof treffen. (to meet)
b) Wir können es uns nicht leisten, in den Ferien wegzufahren. (to afford)
c) Er weigerte sich, das Geschenk anzunehmen. (to refuse)

d) Bilde dir nicht ein, daß ich dir zu jeder Zeit Geld leihen kann. (to imagine)
e) Wir freuen uns darauf, dich wieder-zusehen. (to look forward to)
f) Sie beklagt sich über sein schlechtes Benehmen. (to complain about)
g) Ich frage mich, ob er es schaffen wird. (to wonder)
h) Kann ich mich auf diese Karte verlassen? (to depend)
i) Seine Kenntnisse haben sich verbessert. (to improve)
j) Sie streiten sich oft ohne Grund. (to quarrel)
k) Er schloß sich dem Jugendclub an. (to join)
l) Er erhob sich, um mich willkommen zu heißen. (to rise)

Exercise 2

Reflexive pronouns like "myself", "your-self" etc. mainly emphasize nouns or pronouns.

Example:
She seemed to be pleased.
She seemed to be pleased with herself.

Use a reflexive pronoun in the following sentences for emphasis.

a) He repairs his car. . . .
b) Did you paint your house . . . ?
c) Although she has a housekeeper she cleans the windows . . . .
d) I don't want to make a fool of . . . .
e) My parents sent us some money, although they haven't got much . . . .
f) Dick and Mary make their carpets . . . .
g) We enjoyed . . . .
h) Was his secretary on the phone or did you speak to Mr. Warren . . . ?
i) I am not going to give you these books, girl. Buy them . . . .
j) He always cooks his meals . . . .

20. THE CALLER

Jane Owen glanced at the clock. Her two children had left for school and her husband was at work. So she had three hours to get her housework done unless someone interrupted her. She liked her friendly neighbours although she was sometimes glad when they left her alone to get on with her work. No sooner had she started making the beds than she heard the doorbell. She decided to answer the door despite her wish to get on with her work. She opened the door to find a tall young man standing outside.

"I'm a police officer," he said. "I'm making enquiries about an incident in the next road. May I come in for a moment?" Jane showed him into the sitting-room. She wished now that she had started work downstairs rather than in the bedrooms because the sitting-room was still as untidy as her husband usually left it.

"How can I help?" she asked. "The house opposite yours in the next road was broken into yesterday," she was told. "A woman was killed by the man who broke in."

"Yes," said Jane. "I heard about it." "Did you see anyone come out of that house yesterday?" she was asked. "Your bedroom window faces that way." Jane noticed that her questioner was looking at her intently. His hands were clasped tightly together and he was sweating profusely. She tried to keep her voice steady in spite of her nervousness. She was now certain that this man was not a police officer. "No," she said, "I couldn't see anything. We do have a bedroom facing that direction; however it is only used when we have visitors. You can see for yourself if you like."

This offer was received with a grateful nod and Jane led the way upstairs. When they reached the small back bedroom, the tall man rushed to the window and stared out at the house opposite.

Quickly but quietly Jane took the key from the inside of the door, left the room and locked the door from the outside. Then she ran to the telephone and called her husband. Upstairs the sounds of shouting and banging told her, that the man had discovered he was locked in. Jane was grateful that she lived in an old house because the doors were of solid wood with strong locks.

It seemed an age before she heard her husband's car arrive although, in fact, it was only three minutes since she had phoned him. She rushed to open the front-door.

Detective Sergeant Owen was already running up the path. He looked anxiously at his wife.

"Are you all right?" he asked. Jane smiled in reply. "He's still locked in upstairs," she said.

"Well done," said her husband, "but in future remember it's my job to catch murderers, not yours."

Exercises

The following exercise practises conjunctions which are already shown in the text above.

The conjunctions are "unless" (wenn nicht), "however" (jedoch), "in spite of" (trotz), "because" (weil).

Combine the following sentences by the appropriate conjunction.

Example:
We have a bedroom facing that direction.
It is only used when we have visitors.
We have a bedroom facing that direction; however, it is only used when we have visitors.

a) I prefer travelling by plane. It is quicker than the boat.
b) Mr. Scott doesn't like flying. His secretary booked a flight to New York last week.
c) You should go to the hospital. You have got a bad cut on your head.
d) Joe Bloggs is a plausible liar. His friends believe what he says.

100

e) The police examined the car. No fingerprints were found.

f) The children could not find their parents. They eventually met at the hotel.

g) You will get wet. You have to carry an umbrella.

h) The door was firmly locked. The thief managed to break in.

i) Charles Smith walked over fifty miles. He had an injured leg.

j) They went to the beach. The forecast was rain.

k) Your brake lights won't come on. You have to turn on the ignition key.

l) Please move your car to that lay-by. You are blocking the road.

m) I arrived at the office in time. There was a traffic jam.

n) Don't drive so fast. There is a speed limit.

o) I can't read. I have to wear glasses.

p) I'll take you to the police station. Further inquiries have to be made.

q) The vandals will break more windows. Something has to be done.

r) Crowds gathered to see the popstar. The tickets were expensive.

s) The ship still sailed to Norway. The sea was rough.

t) This man will die. He must get medical treatment.

21. THE LITTLE MAN

It was just beginning to get dark. It was raining hard and a cold wind was blowing. Police Constable Peter Williams felt rather sorry for himself. He was on foot patrol, a duty he was never enthusiastic about at the best of times and which he really was not interested in. He much preferred car patrols, work which he was good at and felt satisfied with. It was also dry and warm in a police car.

He had just decided that it would be rather nice to go and get a cup of coffee when he noticed a little man standing in the middle of the pavement looking anxiously about him. Peter felt himself becoming curious about this forlorn figure who clutched a small piece of paper in one hand. Suddenly, the man noticed him and walked quickly towards him.

"Good evening," said the man. "I'm sorry to bother you, but are you busy at the moment?" "No," replied Peter. "It seems I was right about you, you do need help." "I certainly do," replied the man, "I'm lost."

"I'm not surprised at that," said Peter comfortingly. "Where are you trying to get to?"

The man replied, "I feel rather ashamed of myself. I left my wife in this store and now I can't find her."

He held up the piece of paper for Peter to see. It was an empty sugar packet from the restaurant of a big department store. "Don't worry about it," said Peter. "That store is in the next road."

"That's why I'm so angry with myself," said the man. "I've just come from there. I went into the restaurant where I was to rejoin my wife but she's not there. At first it seemed similar to the restaurant I had tea in, but then I realized it was quite different."

"If you are certain of that," said Peter, "I think you have confused two branches of the same store."

"You mean there are two of them?" gasped the little man. "No wonder this restaurant seemed different to the one I was in earlier. I shall have to hurry to the other as my wife will be very angry about being kept waiting. I'm desperately short of time."

"Are you familiar with this city at all?" asked Peter. "No, but I am quick at learning directions," replied the man. After he had been told how to find the other branch of the department store, the little man set off at a brisk rate through the rain. Peter stepped back into a doorway out of the wind and rain and safe from the umbrellas of people walking by. He now felt rather

101

sorry about his earlier feeling and reflected that he should be happy about his present situation. At least he didn't have an angry wife waiting for him.

Exercise 1

This text contains various adjectives followed by certain prepositions. List all the adjectives plus prepositions!

Exercise 2

Answer the following questions using the appropriate preposition:

Example:
Was he curious? / this forlorn figure
He was curious about this forlorn figure.

a) Did he feel sorry? / the little man
b) Was she curious? / their new house
c) Is she satisfied? / food and conditions
d) Am I right? / the departure of the train
e) Were they angry? / their children
f) Were you happy? / the birthday present
g) Is she sorry? / hurting my feelings
h) Are you ashamed? / the old suitcase
i) Were they surprised? / his early arrival
j) Was he enthusiastic? / playing football
k) Is she anxious? / getting married
l) Is the party different? / the party last year

Exercise 3

In a question you often find the preposition at the end of a phrase.
Form questions from the following statements.

Example:
I am surprised at that.
What are you surprised at?

a) I am anxious about flying.
b) He was happy about getting home early.
c) We were surprised at his good report.
d) Joe Bloggs is angry with the informer.

e) He is curious about her age.
f) They were satisfied with their accommodation.
g) He is familiar with the bank procedures.
h) They are good at playing golf.
i) Mary is quick at learning to read.
j) The family are enthusiastic about going on holiday.
k) She is ashamed of her exam results.
l) They were right about the way to Paris.
m) We all felt sorry for John.
n) This camera is different to Paul's.

22. THE CAR CHASE

The police car was parked in a lay-by in a busy street. The driver John Bush and the wireless operator Bill Clark were watching the traffic and discussing their holidays.

"I'm going to get my foreign currency next week," said Bill. "The rate of exchange may be better."

"My wife is getting our pesetas today", said John. "We are going to Mallorca next week." "I went to Mallorca two years ago," said his friend. "I want to go there again next year."

At that moment Bill touched John's arm. "Look!" he said.

He pointed to a large new car which was being driven by a young man. "He looks too scruffy to own a car like that," he said. "We'll have a word with him in a moment." John started the police car und followed the suspect car while Bill radioed to headquarters to check whether it had been reported stolen. In a matter of moments the message came back, the car had been stolen an hour previously. By now the driver of the stolen car had realized he was being followed and had accelerated to a dangerous speed.

"He's moving now," said Bill as he flicked the switches. That set off the police siren and flashing lights. "He'll crash in a minute if he doesn't slow down," shouted John. "Get on the radio and tell them what's happening."

Bill pressed the button on his microphone. He gave their position and then said, "He's heading south. I think he will turn left in a moment. Yes, he has turned left. He jumped a red traffic light a moment ago, he has just done it again. Now he is trying to lose us in the back streets. We shall lose him in a minute if he keeps this up."

The police car lurched and turned on. John gritted his teeth and pursued the stolen car which was by now being driven more and more recklessly. Suddenly Bill gave a shout. "We've got him. The bloody fool has turned into the back entrance to the Police Station."

Exercise 1

The following exercises are substitution exercises. The given words replace a part of the sentence. Both exercises practise the use of tenses.

Example:
My wife is getting our pesetas today. / my parents
My parents are getting our pesetas today. / their
My parents are getting their pesetas today. / etc.

a) My wife is getting our pesetas today.
b) my parents
c) their
d) to collect
e) new car
f) an hour ago
g) to crash
h) Mary
i) her
j) to clean
k) tomorrow
l) last week
m) the boys
n) the windows
o) now
p) to open
q) the safe
r) Joe Bloggs
s) to find
t) the detectives
u) him
v) to arrest

Exercise 2

a) We'll have a word with him in a moment.
b) drinks
c) yesterday
d) to buy
e) for the party
f) new furniture
g) in the department store
h) next week
i) our neighbours
j) look for
k) since then
l) our daughter
m) for us
n) to wait
o) in London
p) at the station
q) now
r) with her friend
s) at the hotel
t) for another week

23. THE OUT-OF-DATE BURGLAR

The two detectives arrived at the shop. "I apologize for calling you out at this time of the night," said the shopkeeper.

"There is no need to apologize to us," said Detective Sergeant Owen. "We prefer to be called at the time something happens. We were on duty anyway."

The shopkeeper took the detectives to a room at the back of the shop. As he went in, Detective Sergeant Owen saw a man tied to a water pipe with a rope. A large woman was standing by him. She was holding a knife in her hand and was pointing it at the man's throat. The detective recognized the man at once. "I'm surprised at you," he said, "you must have been very short of cash to have broken in here."

"I'm not interested in what you think," snarled the burglar. "I'm just angry at myself for getting caught by this woman. How was I to know that she was good at judo?" The detective smiled. "At the moment you should be careful what you say about her, there's nothing to prevent her from sticking that knife in your throat."

"I insist on my rights," said the burglar, "you belong to the police and you should protect me from her and warn her about stabbing people."

The detective burst out laughing at the sight of the frightened burglar.

"Don't you laugh at me," howled the man. "I shall complain about you when I get to the police station."

"I'm ashamed of you," said Detective Sergeant Owen. "You were only released from prison yesterday. I'm rather interested in the reason why you broke into this butcher's shop. It's different from your usual pattern, you usually prefer to steal from jewellers."

"I thought this shop belonged to a jeweller," said the burglar. "It did before I went to prison two years ago."

"In this age of rapid change," grinned the detective, "you should make sure you keep up-to-date. There is nothing worse than an out-of-date burglar!"

Exercises

English prepositions differ very much from German prepositions.

a) There is no need to apologize *to* us.
   (sich *bei* jemandem entschuldigen)

b) ... and was pointing *at*... (zeigen *auf*)
c) I'm not interested *in*... (interessiert sein *an*)

Exercise 1

Scrutinize the text for verbs followed by a preposition.

Exercise 2

Answer the following questions using the correct preposition.

Example:
Did he insist? (rights)
He insisted on his rights.

a) Did he prefer walking? (going by car)
b) Did you apologize? (your neighbour)
c) Was he ashamed? (being met in her flat)
d) Are you interested? (history books)
e) Did the children laugh? (old man)
f) Was he released? (prison)
g) Were they surprised? (loud noise)
h) Was he very angry? (his wife)
i) Did they complain? (his bad behaviour)
j) Is this watch different? (my husband's)
k) Did they warn you? (driving in Germany)
l) Were his hands tied? (gas pipe)
m) Will she apologize? (coming late)
n) Does he feel safe? (police)
o) Did he insist? (going home)

24. THE PINK HANDBAG

Miss Alison Field, the fashion editor of a women's magazine, was explaining to a detective how some money had been stolen. The money belonged to one of their young women employed as fashion writers and had been hidden in her handbag which was left in the main office where the writers worked.

"We were in the main office having our coffee when she told everyone about her holidays," said Miss Field. "She mentioned how much money she had drawn out of the building society and how she had hidden it in her pink handbag." Detective Sergeant Owen interposed, "Who was there when she said this?"

"The four girls, myself and John Wright," was the reply. "John is the boy friend of one of the other girls, he often joins us for coffee."

"When was it stolen?" asked the detective.

"We all came to my office after we had had our coffee," said Miss Field. "We had a conference for about an hour but each of the girls left the room at least once during that time. After we had finished the conference we went back to the general office. It was then that we found that all four of the handbags had been taken."

"Where did you find them?" asked Detective Sergeant Owen.

"In a store room along the corridor. The two grey handbags and the green one had been opened but nothing taken. The pink handbag had been ripped to pieces and the money was gone."

Detective Sergeant Owen leaned forward. "Are any of the people involved colour blind?" he asked.

Miss Field looked at him in surprise.

"Why, yes, I think John Wright is," she said, "It stopped him getting a job as a photographer."

Detective Sergeant Owen nodded. "I thought so," he said. "Only someone who was colour blind would have to take all four handbags to find out which one was pink. He and I must have a little talk."

Exercise 1

The past perfect tense is used to show that, out of several actions in the past, one action took place before another.

Example:
They (come) here after they (eat) their dinner.

They came here after they had eaten their dinner.

a) We (come) to the station after we (arrest) the prisoner.

b) He (hear) that a shot (be fired) in the house.

c) I (ask) him why he (come) to Germany.

d) I (ask) him what other countries he (visit).

e) He (tell) me that he (catch) a plane from Holland.

f) He (say) that he already (be questioned) by the police.

g) I (ask) him what (happen) to his passport.

h) He (say) that he (not mislay) his passport on purpose.

Exercise 2

The word "after" is often used to show that two actions took place in the past. "After" is always followed by the past perfect tense.

Example:
He stole the coat and sold it.
After he had stolen the coat he sold it.

a) Detective Sergeant Owen sat down and started to ask questions.

b) John Wright found the money and dumped the handbag.

c) The detectives questioned John Wright and he confessed.

d) The girls had coffee and then went to the conference.

e) The policeman stopped the car and spoke to the driver.

f) The police car crew arrived at the scene and asked for an ambulance.

g) The store closed and the burglar then broke in through the skylight.

h) I chased him for several miles; then he gave up running.

25. THE LATE DETECTIVE

Jack Swift had been a detective for only a few weeks. As he walked quickly through the pouring rain, he wished that he had never become a detective. He was cold and wet but, more important, he was late. He should have met Detective Sergeant Owen over ten minutes ago and the sergeant would not be pleased to be kept waiting.

As he rounded the corner of the street where he was to meet the sergeant, he broke into a run. Running with his head down to shield his face from the rain, he almost collided with Detective Sergeant Owen who was walking to meet him.

"Where the hell have you been?" snarled the detective sergeant as Jack stood in front of him trying to regain his breath. "I'm sorry I'm late," said Jack. "How long have you been waiting?"

"I've been waiting since midnight," growled the sergeant. "That's when you should have been here."

"I've been to see my girl friend," said Jack, "I had a job to get away."

"I can imagine that," said Detective Sergeant Owen sarcastically. "How often do you see her?"

"I see her about three times a week," replied Jack, "Why do you ask?"

"I just want to know how often you would be late," was the disconcerting reply. "Anyway, now that you are here perhaps we can get on with the job."

"What are we going to do?" asked Jack.

"We're going to keep watch on that factory," said the sergeant. "A reliable informant has told me that it's going to be broken into tonight." He then led the way to a narrow alley where they could watch the factory. "We'll sit here," he said, "it's not very comfortable but at least we're out of the rain."

They sat in silence for what seemed like an age. Jack became colder and colder; his legs stiffened and he began to shiver in his wet clothes. "How long have we been here?" he whispered.

"We've been here for about two hours," was the quiet reply. "If they don't come within the next hour then we'll give up." They sat in silence for a few more minutes and then Detective Sergeant Owen touched Jack on the shoulder. "Listen," he said, "I think I can hear something." Jack listened but all he could hear was the rain falling. "I can hear something," said the sergeant. "You check this side of the factory and I'll meet you back here in a few minutes."

With that he was gone and Jack set off uncertainly towards the factory.

Shielding his torch with his hand, Jack walked quietly round the factory, pausing every few moments to listen intently.

Suddenly he caught his breath. He could hear the faint sounds of movement a few yards away. He stopped, switched off his torch and waited quietly with his back to the wall. Dimly, he could make out the dark figure of a man creeping furtively towards him. He waited until the man was level with him and then grabbed him quickly from behind. After a short struggle, he had the man on his back and was sitting triumphantly on his chest. He reached for his torch and shone it onto the face of his captive. There, glaring up at him malevolently, was the unsmiling face of Detective Sergeant Owen.

Exercise 1

"How long have you been waiting?" Jack asked the sergeant. "I've been waiting since midnight," was the reply.

Apply the same structure which shows the use of the present perfect continuous to the following sentences.

(However, note the use of the present tense in the German translation: „Wie lange warten Sie schon?")

Example:
How long have you been waiting?
(ten o'clock)
I've been waiting since ten o'clock.

a) How long have we been waiting?
(two o'clock)

b) How long have we been drinking?
(noon)

c) How long has it been bleeding?
(half an hour)

d) How long has he been phoning?
(nine o'clock)

e) How long has he been watching TV?
(four o'clock)

f) How long has it been raining?
(eleven o'clock)

g) How long have you been painting?
(six in the morning)

h) How long have you been training?
(work was finished)

i) How long has he been driving?
(daybreak)

j) How long have they been watching?
(midnight)

k) How long have they been travelling?
(yesterday morning)

l) How long has he been following her?
(this morning)

Exercise 2

Answer the following questions.

Example:
How long have you been waiting?
(about two hours)
I've been waiting for about two hours.

a) How long have you been waiting?
(about an hour)

b) How long has it been bleeding?
(about two hours)

c) How long has he been phoning?
(more than an hour)

d) How long has he been watching TV?
(six months)

e) How long has it been raining?
(nearly three hours)

f) How long have you been painting?
(just over an hour)

g) How long have you been training?
(all afternoon)

h) How long has he been driving?
(about six hours)

i) How long have they been watching?
(half the night)

j) How long have you been travelling?
(a day and a half)

k) How long has he been following her?
(almost four hours)

26. IF

Police Constable John Friend walked across the park looking about him in desperation. It was his first day on his new duty and things had gone badly from the start. Inspector Brown had let John know very forcibly that life was not going to be easy working for him.

As he passed a children's play area he heard someone call and, looking round, he saw a woman and a small boy running towards him.

"Oh dear," he thought, "Here comes more trouble."

"I've just been bitten by a dog," said the woman.

"And it's run off with our ball."

"Show me where it bit you", said John.

The woman held out her hand. Small red marks showed clearly where she had been bitten.

"You must go to hospital," said the policeman. "The dog may have rabies and that could be very dangerous."

"I'll go to hospital, if you think I should," said the woman.

"There's no doubt about it," was the reply. "We also must try to trace the dog. Would you recognize the animal if we found it?" "I would recognize it if it still had our ball in its mouth," said the woman. "But I didn't really get a chance to study the dog. I'd know the ball again. It's a bright red plastic one."

"I'm not sure that's much help," said John. "If I had a description, I could see if anyone around here knew the dog."

"He's very big and looks like a wolf," said the little boy.

"Oh well," said John resignedly, "that's something to go on, I suppose. You must go to hospital now."

Some time later, after the woman had been sent off to the local hospital, John walked back to the police station. He was worried. He tried to think what he was going to say to Inspector Brown. As he climbed the steps, he saw the inspector standing just inside the police station entrance, obviously waiting for him.

"Where the hell have you been?" said Inspector Brown crossly.

Before John could reply, the inspector went on, "And just what sort of police dog handler are you supposed to be? Your dog came back alone two hours ago."

The police constable started to explain but was quickly interrupted by the irate inspector.

"Furthermore," said Inspector Brown, "if you have a police dog, you should not play games with it."

Stung by the unfairness of this last remark, John was about to protest when he saw his dog. It was lying in the entrance hall looking rather like a well-groomed wolf. Between its front paws rested a bright red plastic ball.

Exercise 1

In this exercise the if-clause in present tense has to be linked with the main clause in future tense. Complete the following sentences.

Example:
If you read this, you (see) what I mean.
If you read this, you'll see what I mean.

a) If he drives like that, he (crash).
b) They (steal) your wallet, if you leave your jacket undone.
c) He (escape), if I don't watch him.
d) I (write) the report, if you want me to.
e) If you come early, you (get) a good seat.
f) It (bite) you, if you try to take the ball away.
g) If you stand there, you (get) knocked down.
h) If she does that, he (sue) for a divorce.
i) If the car overheats, we (have) to stop.
j) He (be) late, if his car breaks down.

Exercise 2

In this exercise the main clause is in conditional while the if-clause has to be in past tense.
Complete the following sentences.

Example:
Would you recognize the animal if we (find) it?
Would you recognize the animal if we found it?

a) Would you identify the man if we (catch) him?
b) He would give you the right answers if you (ask) the right questions.
c) I would be pleased if you (come) to the police station.
d) Would it matter if we (make) a mistake?
e) Would you go home if I (let) you go?
f) He would crash if he (is) allowed to drive as drunk as that.
g) I would be pleased if they (be) caught.
h) Would you go if she (come) too?
i) Would it help if I (explain) it to you?
j) I would help if I (can).

Exercise 3

Fill in the right tense.

a) If it still had our ball in its mouth,
   I (recognize) it.
b) He will join the police, if you (suggest)
   it.
c) I would be late, if I (miss) the bus.
d) If you want, I (call) a breakdown
   truck.
e) If you tell me where it is, I (show) you
   the way.
f) Would she come, if I (ask) her?
g) I will help you, if you (tell) the truth.
h) Would she come, if I (ask) her?
i) Would they miss me, if I (be) not there?
j) If you tell me when you are ready,
   I (come) and help you.
k) It would be better, if you (stand) over
   there.
l) If you missed the train, you (be) late.

27. THE THREAT

The policeman on duty in the police station
groaned when he recognized the woman
who walked through the door. It was Mrs.
Parkinson, a widow who lived near the
police station and who often called the
police when she was troubled by one of her
many men friends.

She strode up to the counter and banged on
it with her fist. "I want police protection,"
she said.

"You must be joking!" said the policeman.
"Why should we protect you?"

"Don't take that attitude," snapped Mrs.
Parkinson. "I've heard the rumours about
my men friends. People tell stories about
me."

"Stories are told about you," admitted the
policeman, "but what has this to do with
protection?"

"Someone sent a threatening letter to me,"
said the woman. "Did you hear me?
A threatening letter was sent to me!"

"Who sent it?" asked the policeman.

"I don't know," was the reply, "she didn't
sign her name. The letter said that if I don't
leave her husband alone, she will kill me!
That is a threat to my life."

The policeman laughed. "That's easy," he
said, "all you have to do is to stop seeing
her husband."

"Don't be so stupid," said Mrs. Parkinson,
"how do I know which one is her husband
when I don't know her name?"

Exercise 1

"People tell stories about me."
"Stories are told about you."

The passive voice is used when the action
itself is emphasized rather than the person
who did it.
Change the following sentences to passive
voice present tense.

Example:
They hold up the traffic.
The traffic is held up.

a) They hide the money.
b) People buy expensive presents for
   Christmas.
c) He sells cars.
d) We speak English.
e) They take the car to the garage.
f) They hide the stolen money.
g) The shopkeeper closes his shop
   at 6 o'clock.
h) She breaks a cup every day.
i) People speak English all over the
   world.
j) They build a new shop every
   6 months.
k) I don't allow you to touch these things.
l) They follow the instructions.

Exercise 2

Change the following sentences to passive
voice past tense.

Example:
They found the stolen car.
The stolen car was found.

a) He hurt his leg in an accident.
b) You chose the right man.
c) She lost her watch.
d) He stopped the lorry.
e) They took the car to the garage.
f) Did they pay the bill?
g) They gave the thief a fair trial and sent him to prison.
h) He finished his work by 5 o'clock.
i) Did they answer all the questions?
j) They told me to be quick.
k) They punished me for something I didn't do.
l) They built the bridge last year.

28. THE ANTIQUE RING

Mrs. Webster was very upset. "I don't know how you can take it so calmly," she shrieked at her husband who sat quietly in a corner of the hotel room, "you hadn't even insured it!"

Detective Sergeant Owen gave a cough to remind Mrs. Webster of his presence.

"I'm sorry," said Mrs. Webster turning to him, "I'm very angry with my husband. Do you know he didn't want me to call the police when I found that someone had stolen my beautiful antique ring this morning."

"Can you describe the ring?" asked the detective.

"It's made of gold and has three very large diamonds, it is a very unusual design," replied Mrs. Webster. "Do you think I shall get it back?"

"I doubt it," said Detective Sergeant Owen, "as it is so unusual, the thief will probably sell the diamonds separately. He will break up the ring."

"Did you hear that?" shouted Mrs. Webster at her husband, "the ring will be broken up!"

The following day, Detective Sergeant Owen went to the hotel and spoke to Mr. Webster alone.

"We have found the ring," he said.

Mr. Webster went pale. "The ring has been found!" he gasped. "Where did you find it?" "The thief returned it to the hotel," said the detective, "he didn't want a fake ring."

"Fake?" cried Mr. Webster. "It can't be. The man who sold it to me told me that it was a valuable antique."

"What else did he tell you?" asked the detective grimly.

"He told me to keep quiet about it because it was stolen property. That's why I didn't want to call the police. Will you arrest me?"

Detective Sergeant Owen smiled, "No, you won't be arrested. I think you will be punished enough when you tell your wife the truth!"

Exercise 1

Practise passive voice future tense.

Example:
They will sell the car.
The car will be sold.

a) We will discuss the matter tomorrow.
b) They will need help.
c) I'll answer your questions.
d) They will take her to hospital soon.
e) We'll have to examine you again.
f) The police will arrest the thief.
g) Somebody will meet the boys at the station.
h) They will laugh at you if you tell them all this.
i) They will call a breakdown truck.
j) I'll let you off with a warning.
k) I'll tell your wife about this accident.
l) They'll help you at the garage.

Exercise 2

Practise passive voice present perfect.

Example:
They have found the ring.
The ring has been found.

a) Somebody must have taken it while I was out.
b) He has taken the car to the garage.
c) They have hidden the watch.
d) She has posted the letters.
e) Has he taken the car to the garage?
f) Nobody has answered my question properly.
g) They have taken all the money.
h) Somebody has left the gate open.
i) Somebody has found the man the police wanted.
j) Someone has stolen my jewellery.
k) We have asked that car driver to give us some petrol.
l) The clerk has shut the safe properly.

29. THE BURGLARY

Detective Sergeant Owen was sitting in a flat which had been burgled, talking to the elderly lady who lived there, Mrs. Howard.

"Have you any idea what is missing?" he asked.

"I haven't really looked," said Mrs. Howard. "When I telephoned the police, they told me not to touch anything."

"That's quite right," said the detective. "The burglar may have left some fingerprints. But we can have a look around, you may notice that something is missing."

Mrs. Howard looked about her. "There were some valuable coins in that drawer," she said. "And I had some jewellery in a music-box that has gone."

She walked to the door of the bedroom and looked at the clothes and personal belongings scattered around the room.

"I can't see if anything is missing from here," she sighed.

"It's all such a mess. I shall have to give you a list of everything that is missing when I have tidied up."

"That's a good idea," said Detective Sergeant Owen," but if you discover that any unusual articles have been taken I would like you to give me a ring so I can circulate their descriptions." As he started to leave, the detective turned to Mrs. Howard.

"There is one thing that puzzles me," he said. "I can't see how the burglar got in. Has anyone a key to your flat?"

"Only me and my husband," was the reply.

"Well, somebody got in here without leaving any signs of entry," said the detective. "Someone must have got a key from somewhere."

"Oh dear," said Mrs. Howard, "I do leave a key under the mat outside the door. I didn't think anybody would look under there."

Detective Sergeant Owen lifted up the mat. There was no key.

"Ah well," he said, "at least that's one problem solved. We know how he got in, now all I have to do is to find out who did it."

Exercise 1

"Some" and its compounds are used in affirmative sentences.

"Any" and its compounds are used in negative sentences and questions.

Fill in "some" or "any" or one of their compounds:

a) Are there . . . foreign visitors among the passengers?
b) I have only got . . . presents.
c) She doesn't have . . . documents with her.
d) Does . . . body know where she is?
e) You must tell us . . . thing more about your hobby.
f) There isn't . . . thing you can do now.
g) Yes, there is . . . body in that room.
h) There is not . . . one you can ask for information.
i) Is there . . . thing wrong with your car?
j) I saw . . . body in the car.
k) We bought . . . drinks at the bar.

l) ... body must have stolen my tickets.

m) Have you got ... idea where your keys are?

n) I have seen you ... where before.

Exercise 2

Make the following sentences negative.

Example:
He had some drinks.
He didn't have any drinks.

a) He had some drinks.

b) I know something.

c) You can get some oil there.

d) There is somebody who saw him.

e) I shall find it somewhere.

f) He gave me something to drink.

g) They gave me some information.

h) You will see him somewhere along that road.

i) There are some maps in the glove compartment.

j) There is somebody you can ask.

k) He knows someone who lives there.

l) You can have some of these books.

30. THE ELECTRIC DRILL

The lady ringing the police station was very upset. "I like watching television," she said, "but I'm being stopped from doing it." "Why is that?" asked the policeman. "It's the man upstairs," she said. "Having been given an electric drill for his birthday, he keeps mending things with it and it makes an awful noise. Can you come and prevent him from doing it?" The policeman thought for a moment, then he said, "Can't you ask him yourself?" "I don't like to," replied the lady, "you see, it's my dining room furniture that he's mending."

Exercise 1

Find out all words ending by "-ing".
Which of these words are gerunds?

Exercise 2

Answer the following questions using a gerund.

Examples:
What does Mr. Smith like? (drink)
Mr. Smith likes drinking.
What did the witness deny? (tell lies)
The witness denied telling lies.

a) What does Mr. Forbes hate? (work)

b) What does the policeman dislike? (direct traffic)

c) What is a detective's job? (arrest thieves)

d) What did the prisoner admit? (take the wallet)

e) What must he try to avoid? (leave his car unlocked)

f) What was the burglar caught doing? (break into a house)

g) What was the tourist proud of? (speak French)

h) What won't the judge allow? (shout in court)

Exercise 3

The phrase "would you mind ..." is used for a polite request. Any verb following it takes the form of gerund.
Transform orders into polite requests.

Example:
Order:
Wait.
Request:
Would you mind waiting, please?

a) Stop here.

b) Turn round.

c) Sit down.

d) Sign here.

e) Stand up.

f) Give me your passport.

g) Show me your driving licence.

h) Come with me.

Exercise 4

Complete the following sentences using a gerund.

Example:
I can't help (feel) cold.
I can't help feeling cold.

a) Don't carry on (drive) like that.
b) It is no use (try) to escape.
c) Do you mind (I, come) in your house?
d) There's no (deny) that he's trying to be honest.
e) I think the shopkeeper will remember (she, buy) the coat.
f) I can't understand (he, attempt) to steal that.
g) Please forgive (we, come) without any warning.
h) If you persist in (refuse) to co-operate, I will insist on (you, be) detained.

31. THE SECONDHAND CAR

Two traffic policeman were in a patrol car driving along a country lane. Ahead of them they saw the most dilapidated car they had ever seen. Smoke was pouring from its exhaust and it was obviously struggling to get up a small hill.

"It's never going to make it, Joe," said Bill to his colleague who was driving the police car.

Suddenly Bill let out a shout.

"Watch out! It's stopping... now it's rolling backwards, what the hell does the driver think he's doing?"

The old car gently rolled backwards until it hit the bank at the side of the road. Joe stopped the police car a short distance away and the two policemen got out. By the time they reached the old car the driver had lifted the bonnet and was peering into the engine compartment. The policemen heard him mutter, "this sparking plug needs changing."

Looking at the rest of the car, with its rust patches and holes clumsily filled with fibreglass, Bill could not help smiling. Joe spoke sternly to the driver.

"You are taking a chance driving a car like this," he said. Glancing up from under the bonnet, the driver winced as he realized that the two policemen where eying his car with interest. Joe, having taken his notebook out, was already making notes. "I've only just bought it," the driver informed Bill who was still looking at the car and quietly whistling to himself.

"I'm not sure," said Joe, "but I think you could be committing a record number of offences for using a car in a defective condition." "What's wrong with it?" protested the driver. He soon realized that he had asked the wrong question as Joe began listing the defects.

"The tyres need changing," he started.

"The bodywork needs welding, the brakes need re-lining, the steering needs adjusting, the electrical system needs re-wiring and by the look of the exhaust the engine needs complete overhauling."

"Oh dear," said the man in despair, "it looks as though I've wasted my money." Bill spoke at last. "Whatever you paid for this car, it certainly wasn't a bargain."

Exercise 1

Find out all words ending by "-ing".
Which of these words are gerunds?

Exercise 2

The gerund is often used as a direct object. Practise the use of the gerund.

Example:
What does the sparking plug need?
(replace)
The sparking plug needs replacing.

a) What did his spare time go into?
(drive to the garage)

b) What does Bill enjoy? (listen to pop music)
c) What did the thief deny? (have taken the bag)
d) What does McTarish dislike? (pay a lot of money)
e) What did John Brown admit? (have taken the car keys)
f) What can't he resist? (drive at high speed)
g) What could you give up easily? (smoke in bed)
h) What will he avoid? (drink too much)
i) What is he fond of? (collect stamps)
j) What did they insist on? (come again next week)
k) What was he afraid of? (have a breakdown on the autobahn)

32. THE CROOK

Detective Sergeant Owen sighed as he walked along the narrow street. Somehow or other he had to find a place from which he could watch one of the houses without being seen. Even a plain van would be conspicuous in such a quiet, respectable neighbourhood. He paused and glanced across the street. Two elderly ladies were peering at him from a ground floor window. It suddenly occurred to him – here was the perfect place. Moments later, he was standing on the doorstep as the door was opened by the two ladies. "Good morning", said Detective Sergeant Owen, "I'm a police officer, may I have a word with you, please?"

"I'm Mrs. Chester," said one of the ladies. "This is my sister, Mrs. Trimble. You'd better come in."

Once inside, the detective tried to think of a way of getting what he wanted without having to reveal too much confidential information.

"I'm afraid I can't tell you the full reason but I need your help," he began, "would you mind if I used your front room to watch the street?"

"We quite understand," said Mrs. Chester. "We'll do anything we can to help you catch him."

Detective Sergeant Owen looked at her in astonishment.

"Catch who?" he asked

"Why, Mr. Smith of course," replied both ladies simultaneously.

"I think we'd better have a talk about this," said Owen. He felt in his pocket for his pipe.

"Do you mind me smoking?" he asked. "We don't mind, but I'm afraid it might upset Henry," said Mrs. Trimble.

"Who's Henry?" asked the detective.

"There he is," said Mrs. Trimble, pointing to a large dog that was eying Detective Sergeant Owen suspiciously.

The detective hastily put his pipe back into his pocket. "Now," he said, "what do you know about Mr. Smith?"

"He lives in the house opposite," said Mrs. Chester. "We think he's a crook and we're very pleased that you will arrest him."

"I shan't be able to arrest him yet," said Owen. "I shall keep observation on him for a few days. I hope you will allow me to use this window."

"Of course we will, if it will help you to catch him," said Mrs. Trimble. "Shall I tell you how we knew he was a crook?"

"Yes, please," said the detective.

"We knew as soon as he came here about six weeks ago," explained Mrs. Trimble. "We were out walking with Henry when we met Mr. Smith. Henry wanted to make friends, but Mr. Smith shouted at him and threatened to kick him."

"Really?" said Detective Sergeant Owen nervously as Henry walked menacingly towards him.

"Yes," said Mrs. Trimble, "and anyone who can't be friends with Henry must be a crook."

Exercise 1

Practise the polite question following the given example.

Example:
I use the telephone.
Would you mind if I used the telephone?

a) I drive the car.
b) We come in your house.
c) I leave my overcoat here.
d) I speak to your son.
e) They come with us.
f) He stops with me.
g) I travel with you.
h) We search your car.
i) You have to walk home.
j) I start without you.
k) She goes first.

Exercise 2

"Do you mind my smoking?" is another structure to form a polite question.
Use this structure to make up questions from the sentences above.

Example:
I use the telephone.
Do you mind my using the telephone?

33. THE LADDER

A policeman was walking home late one evening when he saw a young man carrying a ladder on his shoulder. His curiosity aroused, he stopped the youth. "Where are you going with that ladder?" he asked.

"What business is it of yours? Who are you?" retorted the young man.

The policeman addressed him sternly. "I am a police officer," he said, "What are you doing with that ladder?"

"I'm a window cleaner," said the young man, "I'm going to visit my girl friend." The policeman eyed him with disbelief. "I'll come with you," he said, "then I can see if you're telling the truth."

The two walked along in silence for a little while, then the policeman asked the young man why he needed a ladder to see his girl friend.

"She lives with her father who is a narrow-minded old man. He works at night and locks her in the house, so I have to climb in her bedroom window. I've been doing it for weeks."

"I see," said the policeman. "Where does your girl friend live?"

"Just along this street," said the young man.

"Which house does she live in?" asked the policeman.

"Here we are now," said the young man as he lowered his ladder quietly to the ground. The policeman put his hand gently but firmly on the youth's shoulder. "What," he asked, "is the name of this young lady?"

"Eva Baker," said the young man impatiently. "If you don't mind, I would like to put up my ladder now."

"You needn't bother," said Police Constable Baker. "You can come in through the front door and we'll see what my daughter Eva has to say then!"

Exercise 1

Most of the questions in this text begin with "who", "what", "which" or "where".
Add one of these question-words to the following questions:

Example: "... does she live?"
Where does she live?

a) ... is your name?
b) ... is the nearest way to the station?
c) ... did you lose him?
d) ... bus goes to the theatre?
e) ... is the driver of this car?
f) ... hotel is the nearest to the sea?
g) ... did the accident occur?
h) ... gave you this ticket?
i) ... town do you want to go to?
j) ... went with you to Germany?

k) . . . sort of car was it?
l) . . . is Tom?
m). . . is your nationality?
n) . . . did you last see him?
o) . . . things were stolen?

Exercise 2

Turn the following statements into questions. Replace the words in italics:

Example:
Eva Baker is my girl friend's name.
What is your girl friend's name?

a) Mr. Brown went to a *telephone box.*
b) I received *a telephone call.*
c) *One of our detectives* wishes to see you.
d) *My father* gave it to me.
e) *All my jewellery* was stolen.
f) I picked up my *shopping basket.*
g) *This* shop sells the best wine.
h) The policeman told her *to go to hospital.*
i) *A burglar* came in.
j) *That* one is better.
k) I went in through the *main door.*
l) They were wearing *nylon stockings* over their faces.
m) *The other two men* wore gloves.
n) He stayed *at the counter.*
o) *He* lost his wallet.

Exercise 3

You are told to question a suspect. Ask him questions by changing the following phrases.

Example:
(We want to know) what he is doing.
"What are you doing?"

a) . . . what is the number of his car.
b) . . . who let him into the shop.
c) . . . where his home is.
d) . . . who is with him.
e) . . . what books he stole.
f) . . . which window he broke, back or front.
g) . . . where he hid the money.

h) . . . who he sold the books to.
i) . . . what he did with his gun.
j) . . . which prison he escaped from.
k) . . . what he did with his prison clothes.
l) . . . where he dumped the stolen car.

34. THE COAT

Detective Sergeant Owen was bored. His wife who had decided she needed a new coat had insisted that he must help her choose one. He sat on a chair which had been conveniently placed so that he could see his wife try on coat after coat. He now regretted the impulse that had caused him to offer his wife the money.

Suddenly he was alert. His police instincts were aroused by something he had seen. A girl shop assistant who had just served a customer slid a ten pound note under a pile of paper bags on the cash desk. By now he was on the move and he could see the amount the girl had rung up on the cash register. He knew the price of the coat the customer had bought, for his wife had shown him one half an hour earlier. For a man who had been bored only a few minutes before, he was now very active. He soon took charge of the crime that he had just seen committed.

Mrs. Owen, who was unaware of what had happened, emerged from behind a rack of coats. The chair on which her husband had been sitting was empty. There was no sign of her husband. She snorted angrily. Trust her husband to disappear just when she had found the very coat that she had been looking for!

Exercise 1

"Who", "which" and "that" are relative pronouns. "Who" is related to persons, "which" is related to objects like coat, roof etc. or to abstract nouns like crime etc. "That" may be used in relation with persons, objects and abstract nouns.
Note: "That" can also mean „daß" or „jene(r)".

Examples:

A girl shop assistant *who* had just served a customer slid a ten pound note under a pile of paper bags.

He sat on a chair *which* had been conveniently placed.

He soon took charge of the crime *that* he had just seen committed.

Combine the following sentences by either "who" or "which":

Example:

A girl shop assistant slid a ten pound note under a pile of paper bags.
She just served a customer.

A girl shop assistant who had just served a customer slid a ten pound note under a pile of paper bags.

a) The driver went into that store. He parked his car at the bus stop.
b) The man spoke in German. He robbed me.
c) Please hand me the map. It is in the glove compartment.
d) I talked to the motorist. He said he was going to Italy.
e) The boy stole from a shop. He was taken to the police station.
f) The car disappeared quickly. It had an English number plate.
g) The train should arrive at 8.30 p.m. It is late.
h) That woman is a policeman's wife. She crossed the road when the traffic-lights were red.
i) The man came here in a Mercedes car. He is now watching the house.
j) A man escaped from prison. He was a dangerous criminal.
k) A vase was stolen from the museum. It was 2000 years old.
l) The pistol was found to be the murder weapon. It was owned by Joe Bloggs.
m) Valuable jewels were stolen from an exhibition. They belonged to Diana Kerr.
n) They arrested a gang of thieves. They had broken into a bank.

Exercise 2

Use the relative pronoun "that" to combine the sentences of Exercise 1.

35. THE MARRIED MAN (1)

Detective Sergeant Owen was investigating a case of bigamy. The two women in the case were sitting tearfully in his office. Both of them, Emma and Lotte, had married a Mr. Webb who had disappeared a few weeks previously.

The detective asked Lotte where Mr. Webb was. She said she did not know where he had gone.

Emma said, "I don't know where he has gone. He left without even saying good-bye." Detective Sergeant Owen turned to her and said, "What did he take with him?" She said, "He took all his belongings." Lotte said that he had taken all his belongings from her house, too.

"Has he taken any money from either of you?" asked the detective. Both women looked indignant.

Lotte said. "I've lost nothing. Henry is a gentleman."

Emma added that she had lost nothing. She also confirmed that Henry was a gentleman.

"Well," said Detective Sergeant Owen, "we will look for Mr. Webb and arrest him."

Both women leapt to their feet in alarm. "We don't want Henry arrested," said Emma. Lotte nodded her head to show that she too did not want him arrested. "We just want you to tell him that we will be happy to share him," the two women said as they both burst into tears.

Exercise 1

Simple present in a quoted statement of direct speech changes to simple past in indirect speech, if the introductory verb of the sentence ("she said") is in past tense.

117

Transform the following sentences from direct into indirect speech.

Example:
She said, "We don't want Henry arrested."
She said that they didn't want Henry arrested.

a) He said, "I am British."
b) They told me, "We are going to Berlin."
c) She answered, "I don't know his name."
d) He said, "I am not living in that house."
e) They asked, "How can we get to Frankfurt?"
f) She confirmed, "I know that man from the night club."
g) She mentioned, "John visits his friend every evening."
h) She said, "I like that blue dress best."
i) The doctor said, "Smoking is bad for you."
j) Mrs. Briand said, "My husband is not at home."

Exercise 2

Simple past in direct speech (quoted statement) changes to past perfect in indirect speech.
Change the following sentences from direct to indirect speech:

Example:
She said, "He took all his belongings."
She said that he had taken all his belongings.

a) John said, "I handed the envelope to Mr. Green."
b) The policeman said, "The car was stolen."
c) She said, "That man took my handbag."
d) Mr. Smith said, "I saw him three days ago."
e) I said, "I registered the number of our car."

f) He said, "I tried to open that door, but it was locked."
g) She said, "I waited for you all day long."
h) Mr. Miller said, "I got that watch as a birthday present."
i) Peter said, "I hurt myself."
j) The man said, "I bought that gun from a shop."

36. THE MARRIED MAN (2)

Detective Sergeant Owen told the two women that Mr. Webb was living in the next town.

"What's more," he said, "he is living with his wife."

"That can't be," said Lotte, "we are his wives."

Sergeant Owen told the women that a detective had been watching Mr. Webb for several days. He said, "The detective was keeping watch on him when he discovered a strange thing."

"What was that?" asked Emma.

"He found that Mr. Webb was planning to get married yet again," replied the detective sergeant. "I said that I would speak to you two ladies about it. If we arrest him, will you give evidence against him?"

Lotte replied angrily, "If what you say is true, it will be a pleasure."

Detective Sergeant Owen nodded smugly, "I said I thought you would be willing to help. Four wives is at least one too many."

Exercise 1

Practise the continuous form when changing from direct to indirect speech. Present continuous changes to past continuous.

Example:
He said, "He is living with his wife."
He said that he was living with his wife.

a) He said, "My wife is sitting in the waiting-room."

b) The motorist said, "I am looking for a car park."
c) I asked him, "What are you doing?"
d) Mr. Smith said, "The Browns are having a party."
e) He mentioned, "I am leaving Dortmund tomorrow."
f) She said, "I am waiting for Mr. Webb."
g) She said, "He is telling lies."
h) Mr. Miller said, "Bob and Richard are playing tennis."
i) Mrs. Morton said, "You can't speak to my husband; he is still sleeping."
j) They answered, "We are just going for a walk."

Exercise 2

Change from direct to indirect speech. Past continuous changes to past perfect continuous.

Example:
He said, "The detective was keeping watch on him and had discovered a strange thing."
He said that a detective had been keeping watch on him and had discovered a strange thing.

a) He said, "When I saw him, the man was running across the field."
b) He reported, "I was bathing in the river when the boy cried for help."
c) They said, "We were having breakfast when we heard a strange noise."
d) The witness said, "I was cleaning the window, when the accident took place."
e) He said, "While we were having a party, thieves broke into the house and stole two valuable pictures."
f) She said, "When I arrived, Mr. Haley was just leaving."
g) She said, "The car was travelling more than 30 m. p. h. when it passed her house."
h) The man said, "They were still listening to the evidence when I left court."

i) The boy said, "While I was swimming someone stole my clothes."
j) "When I last saw her she was wearing a red leather coat," said Mrs. Gold.

37. THE SWINDLER

Mr. Field sat on a chair in the police station. He was angry but self-assured. He complained to Detective Sergeant Owen about the way he had been arrested the previous day.

"I was treated like a common criminal yesterday," he said. "I told the detectives I would be returning the following week. 'I'll be back next week', I said, but they took no notice."

Detective Sergeant Owen frowned at him. "Where were you going yesterday?" he asked.

"I was going to Brazil for a short holiday," said Mr. Field.

"Did you offer to sell Buckingham Palace to an American?" asked the detective. Mr. Field shrugged his shoulders.

"Did you take ten thousand dollars from him as a deposit?" Again the detective received no reply. He paused before asking his next question and moved closer to the man in front of him.

"Did you tell the American you would give him a receipt the following day?" he asked in a biting tone.

Mr. Field smiled. "What I actually said was, 'I'll give you a receipt tomorrow if I see you.' I just didn't see him the next day."

Detective Sergeant Owen looked at the airline ticket in his hand. "That day you bought a one-way ticket to Brazil," he said. "You swindled the American but you won't fool me."

"You can't prove anything," said Mr. Field. "I was arrested last year but I was acquitted of fraud."

119

The detective recalled that Mr. Field had been arrested the previous year for trying to sell the Eiffel Tower to a Japanese scrap metal dealer.

"Well," he said, "a British jury may not care what you do with a French monument, but they will not like it when they hear that you tried to sell the Palace to an American."

Exercises

Note the change of certain adverbs when transforming a sentence from direct into indirect speech. Adverbs and adverbial phrases such as "today", "yesterday", "tomorrow", "next week", "last week" and "here", cannot be made in indirect speech, if the speech is not made and reported on the same day or at the same place:

today (direct speech) – that day (indirect speech)
yesterday – the day before
tomorrow – the following day
next week (month, year, etc.) –
the following week (month, year, etc.)
last week (month, year, etc.) –
the previous week (month, year, etc.)
"here" and "there" are the same in indirect speech as in direct speech.

Change the following sentences into indirect speech using the proper tense and adverb.

Example:
I will marry you tomorrow.
He said he would marry her the following day.

a) She said, "They left the house yesterday."
b) He said, "I am going to Paris tomorrow."
c) On Sunday he said, "I'll mend the roof today."
d) She said, "He was here last week."
e) On Wednesday he said, "I'll take the day off today."
f) John said, "I met that man yesterday."

g) Mr. Bolt said, "You will have your money back next month."
h) He said, "Last year I was employed in a large store."
i) On Christmas Day my husband said, "I will go on a diet tomorrow."
j) They said, "We went to Spain last year, but we won't go there again."
k) She promised, "Tomorrow I'll come and see you."
l) Bill said, "I can't do it today, I'll do it next week."
m) The Browns said, "We were not able to go shopping last week because we were ill."
n) Jim said, "We don't have much rain here."
o) In the evening he said, "I am going to a party tonight."
p) She told us, "It's very calm and quiet here."
q) He declared, "I'll buy the books this morning."

38. DECISIONS, DECISIONS!

A high-ranking police officer had a nervous breakdown. He was sent by his doctor to work on a farm for a few weeks. When he arrived at the farm, he was quickly put to work by the kind-hearted farmer.

"I'll just give you an easy job to start with," said the farmer, "Can you drive a tractor?"

"I'm a very careful driver," said the superintendent.

"Then drive carefully through that green gate, pass the red barn and park the tractor underneath the big tree you can see in the distance over there."

The police officer drove the tractor slowly and steadily through the thick mud and neatly parked it where he had been told.

"Very good," said the farmer. "Are you any good with animals?"

"I'm fairly good with most sorts of farm animals," said the police officer confidently.

"Good," said the farmer. "This grey colt is very dirty and his mane is badly matted. Brush him thoroughly, but handle him gently around the head or he may bite you. Be very gentle and avoid sudden movements and he will behave perfectly." The superintendent did exactly as he was told and soon had the horse beautifully groomed. The farmer was very pleased. He showed him a huge pile of potatoes. "One last job for today," he said. "Sort these potatoes out into three piles. The large ones go here, the medium size potatoes go there and the small ones can be thrown into that corner."

Three hours later, he returned to find the superintendent sitting down looking at the pile of potatoes. He had not even started to sort them out.

"What's the matter with you?" shouted the farmer.

"I'm still trying to make a decision," said the police officer, "I can't make up my mind which size potato is large, which size is medium and which size is small."

Exercise 1

Adverbs are usually formed by adding "-ly" to the corresponding adjective:

bad – badly
rough – roughly

Only a few adverbs have the same form as their adjectives: hard, little, much, early, late, high, low, fast.

Practise the use of adverbs as it is shown in the example.

Example:
She is a beautiful singer.
She sings beautifully.

a) He was a bad golf player.
b) She is an efficient typist.
c) John is a fast driver.

d) My friend is a quick dancer.
e) David is a careful painter.
f) Joe Bloggs is a rough fighter.
g) I am a slow thinker.
h) He is a regular drinker.
i) Little Paul is a courteous cyclist.
j) He is a good climber.
k) My friend is a careless writer.
l) He is a hard worker.

Exercise 2

Fill in the appropriate adjective or adverb!

Examples:
He will behave –. perfect / perfectly
He will behave perfectly.

The farmer showed him a – pile of potatoes. huge / hugely
The farmer showed him a huge pile of potatoes.

a) His car is – damaged. bad/ badly
b) Joe Bloggs is a – driver. careless / carelessly
c) Drive –! careful / carefully
d) Mr. Philip is a – known solicitor. good / well
e) He drove at a – high speed. fair / fairly
f) He behaved –. perfect / perfectly
g) She talked to us in such a – manner. polite / politely
h) He hit that lamppost –. accidental / accidentally
i) Even his voice was –. aggressive / aggressively
j) He must be very –. intelligent / intelligently
k) He went to work –. regular / regularly
l) He spoke to me in a – manner. suggestive / suggestively
m) She shut the door –. violent / violently
n) They searched the house –. thorough / thoroughly
o) He is known as an – person. honest / honestly

PART 3

READING TEXTS

1. OPERATIONAL POLICE STRUCTURES

By basing their recommendations on a job evaluation exercise, the working party was able to make objective statements as to the level of responsibility that should be attached to each of the six ranks considered necessary. Some of the recommendations of the working party were as follows:

Rank	Post
Chief Superintendent:	Officer in charge of a division normally with between 150 and 450 personnel.
Superintendent:	Deputy to officer in charge of a division. Officer in charge of a subdivision with more than 100 personnel.
Chief Inspector:	Deputy to officer in charge of a subdivision with more than 100 personnel.
	Officer in charge of a subdivision with between 25 and 99 personnel.
Inspector:	Deputy to officer in charge of a subdivision with 25–99 personnel.
	Officer in charge of a subdivision with between one and 24 personnel.
	Officer in charge of a relief.
Sergeant:	Foot-patrol sergeant. Section sergeant (detached section).
Constable:	Beat constable.
	Motor patrol officer. Resident constable.

At the top of the pyramid, the chief constable (or commissioner in the two London forces) has the responsibilities that are discussed in the following Chapter. The main line of command for operational purposes then goes from the chief constable through an assistant chief constable who is usually designated as Assistant Chief Constable (Operations). From him, it goes to the divisional commander, who normally holds the rank of chief superintendent and from there to the subdivisional commander, usually a superintendent, but it may be a chief inspector. Up to this point, the distribution has been by operational responsibility and geographical area, but now the question of time also comes into the scheme. A subdivision must operate continuously day and night and therefore it needs shifts and the organizational structure split into shifts (responsibility by time) and sections (responsibility by area). At the bottom of the pyramid are the constables who actually perform the primary functions of the organization and work in

Quellennachweis:

Nr. 1–7 und 9–11: By permission from R. S. Bunyard "Police: Organisation and Command", 1978, Macdonald and Evans.

Nr. 8: By permission from Marna Price "Woman and Home", Febr. 1979.

Nr. 12: By permission from P. Evans "The Police Revolution", George Allan & Unwin, London.

terms of shifts and beats, the same mixture of time and area as their immediate supervisors, the sergeants and (usually) inspectors.

2. THE ROLE OF THE CHIEF CONSTABLE

The position of a chief constable (or commissioner in the case of the two London forces) is well established in British law. In addition to section 5, Police Act 1964, the courts have emphasized that a chief constable is independent of the executive:

"No minister of the Crown can tell him he must or must not keep observation on this place or that, he must or must not prosecute this man or that – nor can any police authority tell him so. The responsibility is on him. He is answerable to the law and the law alone." *(R. v. Commissioner of Police of the Metropolis, ex p. Blackburn [1968] 2 Q.B. 118.)*

But, whilst he may not be subject to operational control, every chief constable is, of course, accountable for what he does. There is a line of accountability running right through the police service. Every police officer, by virtue of his holding the office of constable, is "an officer whose authority is original, not delegated, and is exercised at his own discretion by virtue of his office: he is neither a crown servant nor a servant of the police authority" *(Royal Commission on the Police, Final Report, 1962).* For the exercise of that authority, a constable is answerable to the courts, civil and criminal. Additionally, the chief constable is accountable for the actions of himself and members of his force, not only to the law but also to this police authority, central government and the public. By section 12 of the Police Act 1964, he may be required to submit to the police authority "a report in writing on such matters as may be specified in that requirement, being matters connected with the policing of the area". There is a right to refuse to submit such a report if it contained information

which "in the public interest ought not to be disclosed, or is not needed for the discharge of the functions of the police authority". Where there is disagreement between the police authority and the chief constable, the request for information can be referred to the Home Secretary, who must decide whether or not it should be given. Section 11 of the Police Act provides for arrangements to make the police authority accountable to the county council through a member of the council who is also a member of the police authority and is nominated by that authority for the purpose.

As has been indicated earlier, the Secretary of State also has the right to require a chief constable to submit to him a report on any matter connected with the policing of this area. Here then is another continuation of the line of accountability for, as the chief constable is accountable to the Secretary of State, so is the latter accountable to Parliament for police matters. Many of the Secretary of State's requests for reports from chief constables are to enable answers to be given to questions from Members of Parliament.

3. BASIC POLICE OBJECTIVES

The principal objectives of the police in Britain today can be stated as follows:

1. The protection of life and property.

This covers a wide range of responsibilities and may indeed be a summary of many of the remaining objectives. It is worth stating, however, that one of the prime functions of police is to help to save life, to minimize injury to people and to assist them to protect their property against attack by other persons or the effects of natural disaster.

2. The prevention and detection of crime.

This objective, more than most, needs to be differentiated from the means that the police used to achieve it. The basic responsibility has not changed greatly over the centuries but there have been considerable changes in the police approach to it.

Whilst the basis of crime prevention may still be the presence of uniformed police officers patrolling the streets, police activity is no longer restricted to acting as watchdogs and detectives. Emphasis has moved towards the police preventing crime by teaching people how to safeguard their property, and by helping to educate people in the rule of law and so to discourage them from committing crime.

3. The maintenance of public order.

The traditional method of keeping the peace by patrolling has been supplemented by the use of social methods to achieve the same ends. The involvement of the police in community relations is now an important way of preventing conflict within the community by helping to reduce the tensions that cause conflict.

4. To respond to and deal with emergency calls.

The service provided by the police in answering '999' and other emergency calls goes beyond the basic police role. The definition of the police function with respect to emergency calls can best be related to the two other emergency services: the police deal with all calls which are not within the province of the fire or ambulance service; and the police also work with the other two services in dealing with many other emergencies, for example, accidents involving injury, and certain fires.

5. To provide a 24-hour, first-line social service.

This function of the police must again be seen in relation to other agencies, as it reflects a diverse role assumed by the police, in the absence of any other organization, to provide advice, guidance and assistance to people who cannot obtain it elsewhere. This may be because of the time of day or because there is no other social agency which deals with the particular problem, e. g. tracing missing persons, informing relatives of accidents and illnesses, and dealing with domestic disputes.

6. To prevent road-traffic accidents, to improve driver behaviour and to enforce traffic law.

This is an area of police responsibility which has grown steadily as the volume of traffic and the number of accidents has increased. Police involvement is not confined to enforcement alone but extends to road-safety activities, traffic-management advice and investigations into causes of accidents.

4. FOOT-PATROLS

Careful consideration is needed as to the possible uses to which foot-patrols can be put if they are to form part of a flexible policing system. There is value to be obtained from the ability of people on foot to hear suspicious sounds without the distractions of engine noise and see suspicious sights without having to focus most of their attention on the road ahead. They are quiet and so do not excessively advertise their presence at night, yet they are prominently visible as a deterrent during the day. They are available to anyone who wants to stop them to talk, or seek advice or help. At the social level, they are most obviously at one with the people they police. They can form relationships with the public as they walk amongst them. They become known as individual men and women, their personalities become known; the people are able to select the one police officer that they feel able to speak to about a given problem. In return, the police officers are given information that they can feed into the system or use to solve crimes or problems in their own areas.

Provided that they are equipped with effective radio-sets, they can call for aid to enable them to tackle problems that are too much for one person on foot and can carry out inquiries in their areas when directed by radio.

Given sufficient scope and support, plus an element of stability, a foot-patrol officer can know the area he polices at a depth impossible in any other system. His patrolling is not dictated by one-way streets or width of roads. For certain types of area, the police officer on foot-patrol is the most effective means of policing. Above all, he can stimulate social activities to prevent crime by working within the community. He can identify tensions before they erupt; he can remonstrate with children, advise families and diagnose welfare problems; work of this kind cannot be done from a motor vehicle.

Yet, foot-patrols are expensive in the sense that the area that a man or woman can cover on foot is limited. Such patrols are open to the elements and quickly become fatigued in very hot or very cold or wet weather.

Furthermore, the foot-patrol officer makes a very small contribution to the response of the police to emergency calls. Walking is the least efficient of the means of moving from one place to another and so much of an individual's physical energy is used just for this. It is often said that foot-patrols are unpopular amongst police officers. This is an overstatement. Some police officers prefer to walk around a beat than to do duty in a motor vehicle, but there are provisos. The foot-patrol officer needs to be given the responsibility for policing an area at his own discretion and not according to a set route. The area must also be suitable for foot-policing in that it has people in it to whom the police can talk. Dormitory areas and factory estates do not provide interesting beats because there is no one to whom the police officer can relate. Densely populated city areas containing small shops, houses and flats are ideal, yet even here there may be problems if the population contains violent elements.

For this reason, it may be necessary to use policemen in pairs rather than put individuals at risk. The foot-patrol police officer is always vulnerable even in relatively passive areas and may need very urgent assistance to save him from injury if he is involved in a skirmish. A foot-patrol system needs a mobile support system that can give a quick response to calls for help.

The police officer needs to be given the time in which to build up his relationship with the people of the area and this precludes too many changes. In order that people can know him or her, the police officer has to be in the area often enough and long enough to become recognizable as an individual. Many foot-beat schemes fail because this essential feature of the method is not recognized. To change a foot-patrol officer frequently from one area to another on a rotation system is to destroy one of the main advantages of the system.

5. MOTOR CYCLES AND SCOOTERS

When the foot-patrol system came in for criticism on grounds of manpower costs, the motor cycle was introduced as a labour-saving device. The theory was that the motor cycle would enable a patrolman to cover a much larger area in eight hours than if he was on foot. He would ride the motor cycle to a place of special police interest then get off his machine and patrol on foot. After checking one area, he would travel to the next and patrol that on foot and so on. In practice, the system was not a success due to the limitations of the motor cycle and the fact that policemen, once on or in a vehicle, are reluctant to quit it and parked motor cycles were vulnerable to vandalism. Furthermore, the increased areas allotted to each police officer meant an increased number of routine inquiry calls that tended to take up much of his time.

The motor cycle has a number of disadvantages:

1. They are dangerous for the rider, particularly in inclement weather and are virtually unusable in snow or heavy frost.

2. The rider is open to the elements and cannot operate at his very best in cold or wet weather.

3. Motor cycles are noisy, consequently they can be heard coming, but the rider cannot hear what is happening around him.

4. Great concentration is needed on the road ahead and so there is relatively little possibility of looking around to see matters worth investigating.

5. It takes valuable time to get off a motor cycle and put it on its stand, when about to question a suspect or give chase on foot.

6. A motor cycle cannot convey prisoners or bulky property.

7. Reception of messages requires the motorcyclist to stop his machine to be able to make a written note.

Against all these disadvantages, the solo motor cycle has two real advantages. First, it can be comparatively cheap, particularly if a low-powered motor scooter or a small motor cycle is used. Second, a motor cycle can get to the scene of incidents in crowded city streets by travelling on the outside of streams of vehicles in traffic jams.

Thus the only legitimate function of a motor cycle is for traffic work, or to provide a cheap means of transport for short journeys.

6. PEDAL CYCLES

The use of a pedal cycle at once increases slightly the range of a patrolling officer but decreases his contact with the public. Whilst the pedal cycle does not suffer from all of the disadvantages of the motor cycle, it has enough of them to be of limited value.

The best use of a pedal cycle is probably as an optional aid for the foot-patrol officer to use at his discretion at times of the day or night when a slow, silent patrol is of value. Alternatively, it may be used for a beat of moderate size which contains areas needing the use of police foot-patrols separated by areas of little concern.

7. MOTOR CARS AND POLICE VANS

Given a motor car, a police officer can patrol large areas, carrying useful equipment, with very little physical effort. For areas where police patrolling is necessary but close contact with the public is not needed, the police car provides an effective way of spreading available manpower thinly over the ground.

Probably the most serious disadvantages of the motor car for police patrolling are, first, that the driver needs to concentrate on where he is going and, secondly, that the crew are isolated from the public by the metal and glass of their car. At one time, there was a tendency to underestimate the effects of using police cars on the relations between police and public. As was said in relation to motor cycles, any system that relies for its contacts on the police officers getting out of their cars to walk around is adversely affected by the reluctance of police officers to do that. Checks on such systems have shown that as little as five per cent of the time will be spent on foot by the police officers who are supposed to be out meeting the public. This reluctance to patrol on foot has led to systems of policing in which a number of constables are conveyed in a vehicle under the supervision of a sergeant who directs them where and when to perform periods of foot-patrol.

Closed motor vans are of value to transport property, prisoners and the like but have little value for patrolling purposes. Vision is usually restricted and noise is high, as is fuel consumption. Their use tends to produce a militaristic image and in some sensitive areas they can be regarded as provocative.

8. JOAN'S THE VILLAGE BOBBY

She is a pleasant, dark-haired girl who stands just five feet four inches high but – following the Sex Discrimination Act which enables women police to do the same work as their male colleagues – Joan Spence has made police history by becoming one of the very few women village bobbies in her country. Furthermore, she reckons she loves every minute of her unusual job.

Woman Police Constable Spence, who comes from Yorkshire, joined North Wales Police four years ago, and took up her job at the village substation of Bwlchgwyn near Wrexham in August 1976. There she copes with all the normal duties involved in covering a seven-miles-square rural area which takes in two villages and part of a mountain and serves the two and a half to three thousand people who live within its boundaries.

Joan explained to me her decision to apply for such a post: "I have always liked the country better than the town so when the post at Bwlchgwyn became vacant, I thought I had nothing to lose by applying for it. A village post like this differs from town work mainly because you spend much more of your time actually meeting the people who live there. In a place like Bwlchgwyn the population is static, so in time you get to know people really well."

Cartwheel of joy

When news came through that Joan had got her village job she was at a training session at Wrexham (where she was based), and it is on record that she was so thrilled to hear of her success that she turned a cartwheel in the gymnasium. "It was fantastic news – I was over the moon with joy," she says now.

Soon after hearing the glad tidings, Joan moved into the small Police Station she now calls home. She lives there alone, apart from her crossbred Alsatian dog, Simba. "That's Swahili for lion and I called him that because he looked like a lion when he was small," she explained.

Joan says she has found it very easy to integrate into village life – in fact, she was made most welcome from the start. A few days after her arrival, Joan answered a ring on her front door bell and there stood five village boys (aged from eight to nineteen) who said: "Are you the new policewoman who has come to live here?" Joan answered yes, and they promptly offered to dig and tidy her rather large garden for her.

"They did, too," laughed Joan, "they came at nights and weekends until it was really shipshape. The substation had been empty for a while before I moved in so it had become rather untidy outside."

Meanwhile she continued to get to know her villagers generally. "I think a lot of people were just fascinated at the idea of my being a woman village constable at the beginning, but this is a very close-knit community and once you get to know people here you are accepted really well.

"I think one of the advantages of being a woman in a job like this is that young people seem to approach you much more easily. Both boys and girls seem to be able to talk to me – I think that might be because I represent a kind of mother figure to them.

Of course, if there was a problem that a man could deal with better, one of my colleagues would step in, and I would give similar help in another area if a woman were more fitted to cope. It is very much a give-and-take arrangement among us."

Not that Joan didn't have a few difficulties on her new beat – especially at the start. "I had a bit of trouble finding my way around in the first week," she confessed, "and some of those Welsh names are pretty difficult to spell for a learner. I can't speak Welsh except for a few words but everyone around – even those who speak Welsh at home – can speak English as well. Another problem for me can be lack of sheer physical strength. Say there is a heavy farm gate to be moved – well, I can't lift it easily like a man could. I might need to get help."

Every day is different

Joan Spence has always been interested in working with people and when she left school in Ilkley, Yorkshire, she went into social service, working in old people's homes in the north of England. One such home she worked in had a holiday-type annexe at Colwyn Bay on the North Wales coast and it was working there that first took Joan to Wales. While acting as a matron, she became interested in police work and decided to join the North Wales Police who have their headquarters in the town.

After initial training she was posted to the town of Wrexham where she did general duties for two years, and then she moved to Bwlchgwyn. Now she works an eight-hour day divided into four shifts (the last one ends at two in the morning) for five days a week, and maintains that she enjoys every minute of her new life as a village bobby.

Because her work is so varied it is almost impossible to describe a typical day in Joan's life, but "you can say that it is very quiet one day and then the next I might be running about all over the place."

Missing Mother

One day, for example, Joan was called to a certain house because a small boy had phoned 999 to say that he was at home but he had lost his Mummy. Slightly bemused, Joan went to the house – to find an even more bemused mother answering the door to the police. It emerged that the seven-year-old had been trained by his mother to dial 999 in an emergency and, when he woke one morning to find her missing, he had done just that! Actually, his mother

had gone out shopping in the early morning, leaving the little boy and his grown-up brother asleep in bed upstairs. But the little boy had woken up early, found Mummy missing... and resourcefully summoned Joan.

Well, that started her day and she went next to the local electricity shop where a theft from a meter had been reported. After that, it was off to another village to collect some road signs and then, at 12.30 p.m., Joan was due to control traffic at a large funeral taking place in her area. "After all that," she added, "I had some lunch and then I went out on mobile patrol with the police van."

After her patrol, Joan delivered a warrant, and then did another patrol (this included the checking of security on industrial buildings) before handing over to the next police officer when she had completed her eight-hour shift.

Duties also vary with day and time, of course. On a recent Saturday night duty, Joan went along to a village dance to make certain there was no trouble and then did mobile patrol. At 11.30 p.m. she was at the scene of an accident involving two cars, and then she patrolled again until 1 a.m.

Sheep-worrying, too

Because she has a country beat, Joan has to deal with cases of sheep-worrying (including going with the farmer to the scene of the incident), and she also copes with sudden deaths in her villages. A neighbour might report that a pensioner's milk bottles are piling up on the doorstep... so off goes Joan to investigate. "Sometimes we knock up someone having a lie-in. At other times we're really needed," she told me.

But when the worst has happened and there is a death, the village bobby gives all the practical help she can. "Apart from the formalities of getting the body identified and taking statements, I often get in touch with a funeral director and I also contact relatives for people," she said. "Families are more scattered now, and an old person might have sons and daughters living away who need to be informed. I do all that sort of thing."

Joan shares a police van with colleagues but does some of her village work in the traditional way, on foot. "Sometimes I just call casually on people," she said. "I might see somebody out in their garden, so I have a few words. I find that once I have made the initial contact it is easier to get friendly with people. I spend quite a bit of time hearing about the old folks' grandchildren!"

But Joan meets the young ones, too. She visits the schools in her area to give talks on road safety and she says that the children instantly want to see her handcuffs and her radio.

The dangerous side

But there is sometimes a more violent side to her work, too. Once Joan, with colleagues, had to chase a fleeing youth over fields, hedges and ditches until she caught him. "I'm not a very fast runner but I can run for a very long time and I did get my man," she laughed. "I was just annoyed that my stockings got ripped on some barbed wire!" Joan also takes the prospect of arresting drunks very much in her stride. "I think arresting your first drunk is a little difficult, but you soon gain experience. We find that no matter how drunk a man is, he will often go better with a policewoman than he would with a man. They all seem to think twice before hitting a woman and most will listen to reason and 'go quietly'. But drunken women can be very violent. If a woman is violent, she tends to go on being violent . . . and, of course, she does not have the same reservations about hitting another woman."

The village bobby who worked 24 hours a day is now very much a thing of the past. When Joan is not on duty, another officer covers her area, and she fills in for him in a similar manner. She also helps out in other areas if the need arises.

Work apart, Joan likes dancing and her other interests include badminton, tennis and a little swimming. "I also love taking long walks," she told me, "and I generally whisk around with a vacuum cleaner doing my housework on my day off."

What is Joan's ambition for the future? "Well, it would be nice to be the first woman Chief Constable," she smiled, "but at present I'm very, very happy where I am."

9. SOCIAL VIOLENCE

It is clear from the history of Britain that social violence is nothing new. Aspects of modern life now accepted as important parts of democracy, like universal suffrage and trade unions, were the causes of social violence in the past by Chartists, suffragettes and trade unionists. In every society there will always be militant minorities who seek to impose their views on the majority. The aim of the police in a free society must be to allow people to express their views, of whatever nature, within the bounds of free speech, yet to prevent minorities from imposing their wishes upon other people by force or by the use of threat or violence.

The use of terrorist tactics has a long history but the modern terrorist is aided by two things:

"The first is the greater sophistication and striking power of the violence inspired by political motives. The second is the certainty that it will attract public attention on a scale undreamed of by earlier generations. Newspapers, radio and, above all, television have made violence a cause for concern by millions irrespective of the country in which it occurs." *(Policing a Perplexed Society, Sir Robert Mark, George Allen and Unwin, 1977)*

International terrorism has become big business and every country can expect its share of hijackings, armed groups seizing hostages, bomb incidents and political murders. The probability of incidents will, in part, depend on the success of previous terrorist activities. It is therefore essential that the police should prepare themselves to deal with a wide range of terrorist situations firmly, but without overreacting.

The emergence of rival political groups using violence to attract attention to themselves is a familiar feature of British life. Conflicts between the National Front and left-wing extremists are reminiscent of the fascist/communist clashes of the 1930s. The aims of the British fascists of 1930 were directed against Jews. The National Front uses coloured immigrants in much the same way and in doing so places the police in the familiar position of having to intervene to prevent riots. Once again there is the danger that the police may be associated with extremist views since they must protect those who hold them from attack by those who oppose them. The reputation of the police for complete impartiality is its greatest asset at such times.

Finally, a most disturbing trend towards violence has been in relation to industrial disputes where the police have been confronted by large numbers of 'pickets' using mass violence as a means of putting pressure on the government. The limitations of legal action in dealing with industrial confrontations were mentioned before and there are extremists who are willing to exploit these limitations for political advantage. The role of the police is to ensure that intimidation and violence cannot be used by extremists to subvert democracy. Occasionally this will mean thousands of police officers upholding the law against even more thousands of militant pickets but within our society there is no alternative. If militant minorities are allowed to break the law in order to intimidate the government then democracy itself is in danger.

10. POLICE DEVELOPMENTS

The police service has made considerable advances during recent years both in terms of organization and technology. The need for the police to provide a response to terrorism and mass intimidation has led to unprecedented co-operation between police forces, not only in supplying aid in terms of men and equipment, but also in exchanging information and training facilities. Faced with a need for massive assistance, any police force can request its neighbours to supply a number of 'police-support units' of thirty constables with their own supervisory officers, an inspector and three sergeants. Such aid can be summoned quickly and a steady build-up of men can be arranged for lengthy problems.

Local government has also developed its response to emergencies; contingency plans in which the police have participated are now generally available for serious floods, fires or other disasters.

The police use of advanced technology has been greatest in the field of communications, one of the key requirements of good policing. The development of the Police National Computer has greatly aided the operational police officer, and command and control systems being installed one by one throughout the police forces of the country are improving their response to emergency calls and providing a valuable source of management information.

Changes are also taking place in policing systems as police forces try to use their limited resources to deal with the demands imposed upon them by rising crime rates and increased violence and social tensions, particularly in large cities. Trends that may be noted here are increasing specialisation as policing problems become more complex, the increasing involvement of police within communities in order to prevent violence and the increasing recognition that the police must come to terms with the public media.

11. POLICE AND DEMOCRACY

All countries have to arrive at a balance between allowing total freedom for the individual and restricting that freedom in order to preserve law and order. They then have to fit the police into the framework of their legal and social systems and provide safeguards to ensure that the police act within that balance. In a much simplified form, this process has provided a plot for countless western films: a small town is terrorized by a gang of outlaws; the senior citizens of the town hire a gunfighter to kill the outlaws and restore law and order; the town may then find itself being ruled by the gunfighter and so one oppressive regime has been replaced by another.

In totalitarian countries where the police are an instrument of the state dedicated to the preservation of the dictatorship, their role is clear-cut and they can operate with few inhibitions. In a democratic society, the police need to be constrained so that their powers are balanced against the freedom of the individual. The means that different countries use in order to achieve this balance vary considerably, as does the amount of power given to the police.

The Royal Commission on the Police gave serious consideration to the question as to whether a national police force should replace the existing local organization. Despite a formidable array of arguments favouring a unified police service, the Commission concluded that "the police forces of this country should not be brought under the direct central control of the Government. In our view the improvements which the advocates of such a change wish to see can be achieved without seriously disturbing the local basis on which the present police system rests, and thus sacrificing much that is valuable" *(Final Report, 1962, p. 49)*.

"It was put to us that, so long as the police in Great Britain are not controlled by the Government, tyranny will be impossible in this country; but that, if the present system of local forces were to be abolished in favour of a unified police service, any future Government would have ready to hand the means of establishing a police state. We find this argument unconvincing, for it rests, in our view, on fallacious assumptions. British liberty does not depend, and never has depended, upon a dispersal of police power. It has never depended upon any particular form of police organization. It depends on the supremacy of Parliament and on the rule of law" (ibid., p. 45).

In his Memorandum of Dissent to this Report, Dr. A. L. Goodhart was more positive about the role of police in preserving freedom in a democracy: "The danger in a democracy does not lie in central police that is too strong, but in local police forces that are too weak. It was the private gangs of the Fascists and of the Nazis that enabled Mussolini and Hitler to establish their dictatorships when the legitimate police proved impotent."

The Nazi Germany example is one that is often cited to illustrate what can happen when ruthless politicians set out to take control of a country.

12. TRAFFIC POLICING AND SELF-CONTROL

One of the main principles behind traffic policing – the same principle underlying much else of police work in Britain – is of such importance that without it law and order would collapse; the principle of self-control. Self-control is never far away from traditional law enforcement in this country. It is epitomized by the queue. There is, of course, no law covering queues in general, but observers looking at the British might conclude that there could be. The principle behind it is, put at its simplest, first come, first served. So strong is public belief in this principle that the Conservative Government in the early 1970s was able to use it to political effect. Asians with U. K. passports and deprived of their livelihood in Tanzania – indeed, sometimes of their right to be there – set off for Britain without proper entry papers, only to be sent back again on arrival or thrown into gaol until their cases had been examined. The government's reason, calculated to win public support, was that they were 'queue-jumpers'.

In some provincial cities motorists respect the idea of a queue so much that, even where there is room for two lines of vehicles waiting a traffic lights, vehicles instead form one queue. The motorist who tries to sneak up the side of a single line of traffic is regarded as breaking the informal rules, and is liable to be hooted at or to find a vehicle asserting its right over him by trying to prevent him from overtaking. In London, where the principle of give and take is more flexibly practised, people become indignant less easily. Although such informal enforcement of the law can in certain circumstances be dangerous – for instance, if a line of traffic closes up and the overtaking motorist finds himself marooned in the face of oncoming traffic – police do rely upon it.

That is why small traffic islands have in some places replaced traffic lights at junctions, so that they are 'self-policing'. In other words, motorists arriving at a junction decide for themselves when it is safe to emerge into the circling traffic stream. People finding themselves involved in minor collisions on roads may discover that the police are not very interested unless some offence has been committed, or injury has occurred, or traffic is held up; it remains the responsibility of the people involved to exchange names and addresses for insurance purposes. An accident in Britain is greeted with a calm that seems almost deliberate in contrast with the arm-waving and general vehemence in, say, Italy.

Whenever streets are closed as pedestrian precincts, or bus lanes are created, the police hope that the effects will be self-policing, although the responsibility for making them work is theirs. In London computer systems linked to traffic lights are concerned with the flow and density of traffic so that vehicles do not get snarled up. Frustration can be dangerous.

The British, however, have never been so orderly when a diminution of their personal freedom has been involved. The weakness of demands for 'law-and-order' is that its advocates lump together two concepts that are not exactly similar. Only the lawless would object to the general principle of the rule of law, provided that it is applied fairly (a fair cop is an old cliché). But the rule of order would get a very different response.

The pedestrian in this country, even more than the motorist, believes in freedom of movement, and does not like it if demands for apparently unnecessary order restrict it.

The point at which law hardens into order can be a sore one. Tracts of a thin red line can still be seen beside the pavement in Fleet Street as evidence of a futile attempt to control pedestrians. These were part of an experiment in which pedestrians were to be allowed to cross the street only at the points which authority indicated. The public was treated to the spectacle of elderly businessmen waiting until a policeman's back was turned and then, risking life and reputation, delightedly hopping over the line and back again in a vigorous response to a challenge. But in Sweden, on the day that traffic switched from left-hand to right-hand drive, the populace allowed itself to be very strictly controlled, crossing streets when they were told and only at selected points. In Denmark, too, pedestrians wait for traffic lights to tell them when to cross roads, even when there is no traffic about.

PART 4
VOCABULARY

DIALOGUES
I. Asking Directions

1. ASKING THE WAY (1)

corner ['kɔ:nə]	– Ecke, Straßenecke
busy ['bizi]	– geschäftig, *hier:* belebt
railway station ['reilwei 'steiʃən]	– Bahnhof
I beg your pardon [beg jɔ: 'pa:dn]	– wie bitte?
slower ['sləuə]	– langsamer
of course [kɔ:s]	– natürlich
bridge [bridʒ]	– Brücke
beyond [bi'jɔnd]	– jenseits, hinter
to go straight ahead [streit ə'hed]	– geradeaus gehen
till [til]	– bis
traffic lights ['træfik laits]	– Verkehrs- ampel
to turn right [tə:n rait]	– nach rechts abbiegen
to turn left [tə:n left]	– nach links abbiegen
post-office ['pəust 'ɔfis]	– Postamt
you're welcome ['welkəm]	– bitte *(als Antwort auf danke)*

2. ASKING THE WAY (2)

pavement ['peivmənt]	– Bürgersteig
main road [mein rəud]	– Hauptstraße
to stay [stei]	– bleiben
square [skwɛə]	– Platz
turning ['tə:niɲ]	– Abbiegung
to follow ['fɔləu]	– folgen
tram-lines [træm lainz]	– Straßenbahn- schienen

road sign [rəud sain]	– Straßenschild, Verkehrs- schild
to be so kind as to write [kaind]	– so freundlich sein zu schrei- ben
sketch [sketʃ]	– Zeichnung
don't mention it ['menʃən]	– gern gesche- hen!

3. ASKING THE WAY (3)

to face [feis]	– ansehen, ent- gegensehen
carriageway ['kæridʒwei]	– Fahrdamm
to mistake [mis'teik]	– verfehlen
river ['rivə]	– Fluß
alongside [ə'lɔɲsaid]	– entlang
junction ['dʒʌɲkʃən]	– Kreuzung
space [speis]	– *hier:* Parklücke
parking meter ['pa:kiɲ 'mi:tə]	– Parkuhr
multi-storey car park ['mʌlti 'stɔ:ri ka: pa:k]	– Hochgarage
to drop s.o.[drɔp]	– jm. absetzen

4. ASKING THE WAY (4)

bank [bæɲk]	– Flußufer
outside ['aut'said]	– außerhalb
to catch a bus [kætʃ]	– den Autobus nehmen
to change buses [tʃeindʒ]	– umsteigen
to get off	– aussteigen
conductor [kən'dʌktə]	– Schaffner

5. ASKING THE WAY (5)

square ['skwɛə]	– Platz
to walk [wɔ:k]	– gehen
towards him [tə'wɔ:dz]	– auf ihn zu

map [mæp] – Landkarte
to represent [repri·zent] – darstellen
to afford [ə·fɔ:d] – (sich) leisten
service [·sə:vis] – Dienst, hier: (Verkehrs-) Verbindung
opera house [·ɔpərə ·haus] – Opernhaus
statue [·stætju:] – Statue
to enjoy [in·dʒɔi] – Gefallen finden an, genießen
you will enjoy it – es wird Ihnen gefallen

6. THE DETOUR

detour [·di:tuə] – Umleitung
to waste [weist] – verschwenden, vergeuden
lane [lein] – Weg, Pfad, Sträßchen
via [·vaiə] – über
wedding [·wediŋ] – Hochzeit
bridegroom [·braidgrum] – Bräutigam

7. THE LOST MOTORIST

kerb [kə:b] – Straßenkante, Straßenseite
you are not allowed to – es ist Ihnen nicht erlaubt
office [·ɔfis] – Büro
to illuminate [i·lju:mineit] – beleuchten
to get cracking [·krækiŋ] – eilends losfahren, sich beeilen
to break the law – gegen das Gesetz verstoßen
to fine [fain] – mit einer Geldstrafe belegen
provided [prə·vaidid] – vorausgesetzt
safe journey! – gute Fahrt!

8. THE LONG TAXI RIDE

argument [·a:gjumənt] – Auseinandersetzung
stationary [·steiʃnəri] – hier: stehend
to resolve [ri·zɔlv] – lösen, auflösen
to overcharge [əuvə·tʃa:dʒ] – zuviel rechnen
to hire [·haiə] – mieten
Town Hall [·taun hɔ:l] – Rathaus
via [·vaiə] – über
liar [·laiə] – Lügner
reasonable [·ri:znəbl] – hier: annehmbar
tip [tip] – Trinkgeld

II. Traffic Incidents

1. THE WITNESS

to collide [kə·laid] – zusammenstoßen
dead [ded] – tot
to shake s.o. up [ʃeik] – aufrütteln, erschüttern
towards [tə·wɔ:dz] – gegen, auf etwas zu
to involve [in·vɔlv] – verwickeln
to swerve [swə:v] – abweichen, abschweifen
to collapse [kə·læps] – zusammenbrechen
to slump forward [slʌmp ·fɔ:wəd] – plötzlich nach vorne fallen
unconscious [ʌn·kɔnʃəs] – bewußtlos
to avoid [ə·vɔid] – vermeiden, verhüten
necessary [·nesisəri] – notwendig

2. A BREAKDOWN (1)

to overheat [ouvə·hi:t] – überhitzen, heißlaufen
fan belt [fæn belt] – Keilriemen
radiator [·reidieitə] – Kühler
to boil [bɔil] – kochen
breakdown truck [breikdaun trʌk] – Abschleppwagen
attendant [ə·tendənt] – Bediensteter

136

garage ['gæraːʒ] – Autorepara-
turwerkstatt
mechanic [mi'kænik] – Techniker,
Monteur
to tow [təu] – ziehen
to fix [fiks] – herrichten

3. A BREAKDOWN (2)

bonnet ['bɔnit] – Motorhaube
owner ['əunə] – Eigentümer
to cut out – ausfallen,
aufhören
forecourt ['fɔːkɔːt] – Vorhof, *hier:*
freier Platz,
freie Stelle
handbrake ['hændbreik] – Handbremse
out of gear [giə] – auf Leerlauf
geschaltet
space [speis] – *hier:*
freier Platz,
freie Stelle
fuel system – Kraftstoff-
[fjuəl 'sistəm] anlage

4. THE LADY DRIVER

to collide [kə'laid] – zusammenstoßen
obvious ['ɔbviəs] – offenbar
improbable [im'prɔbəbl] – unwahrscheinlich
substantiate – nachweisen
[səb'stænʃieit]
to hoot [huːt] – hupen

5. THE LOW BRIDGE

wedged – eingekeilt,
eingezwängt
identification marking – Kennzeichen
[ai'dentifi'keiʃən
'maːkiŋ]
joking matter – Sache zum
['dʒəukiŋ 'mætə] scherzen
to mislay [mis'lei] – verlegen
to reverse [ri'vəːs] – *hier:*
zurücksetzen
arch [aːtʃ] – *hier:*
Brückenbogen

to release [ri'liːs] – freilassen,
hier: Luft
herauslassen

6. AN ACCIDENT (1)

to swerve [swəːv] – abweichen,
ausweichen
lamppost [læmp pəust] – Laternenpfahl
to hit [hit] – stoßen,
treffen
to be injured ['indʒəd] – verletzt sein
alone [ə'ləun] – allein
drivable ['draivəbl] – fahrbar
damaged ['dæmidʒd] – beschädigt
headlamp ['hedlæmp] – Scheinwerfer
wing [wiŋ] – Kotflügel
dented ['dentid] – verbeult
bumper ['bʌmpə] – Stoßstange
twisted [twistid] – verbogen
particulars [pə'tikjuləz] – nähere
Einzelheiten,
hier:
Personalien
to reverse [ri'vəːs] – rückwärtsfah-
ren, zurück-
setzen
lay-by ['lei 'bai] – Seitenstreifen
(auf Haupt-
straßen)
driving licence – Führerschein
['draiviŋ 'laisəns]
certificate of insurance – Versiche-
[sə'tifikit əv rungsschein
in'ʃuərəns]
documents – Papiere
['dɔkjumənts]

7. AN ACCIDENT (2)

main road [mein rəud] – Hauptstraße
crowd [kraud] – Menge, *hier:*
Gruppe
to pile up [pail] – anhäufen
the traffic is beginning – es bilden sich
to pile up Verkehrs-
schlangen
to argue ['aːgjuː] – streiten
fool [fuːl] – Narr, Tor

VOCABULARY

amber ['æmbə] – gelb (an der Verkehrs-ampel)
to brake [breik] – bremsen
anyway ['eniwei] – jedenfalls
to block [blɔk] – versperren
to move [muːv] – *hier:* wegfah-ren
to check [tʃek] – kontrollieren
insurance [inˈʃuərəns] – Versiche-rungsschein

8. AN ACCIDENT (3)

essential [iˈsenʃəl] – wichtig
right of way [rait əv wei] – Vorfahrt
major road ['meidʒə rəud] – Hauptstraße
minor road ['mainə rəud] – Nebenstraße
to occur [əˈkəː] – geschehen, sich ereignen
to fail [feil] – verfehlen
to approach [əˈprəutʃ] – sich nähern
priority [praiˈɔriti] – Vorrang
verge [vəːdʒ] – Seitenstreifen
to faint [feint] – in Ohnmacht fallen
pain [pein] – Schmerzen
narrow ['nærəu] – eng
junction ['dʒʌŋkʃən] – Straßen-einmündung
fault [fɔːlt] – Fehler, Schuld
to concern [kənˈsəːn] – betreffen
to fill in [fil] – ausfüllen
to apologize [əˈpɔlədʒaiz] – sich entschuldigen

9. A FATAL ACCIDENT

fatal accident ['feitl] – tödlicher Unfall
rear part [riə] – Rückseite, der hintere Teil
to trap [træp] – einfangen, einschließen

wreckage ['rekidʒ] – Autotrümmer
to stop dead [ded] – plötzlich anhalten
safety strap ['seifti stræp] – Sicherheits-gurt
seat belt [siːt belt]
windscreen ['windskriːn] – Windschutz-scheibe
to release [riˈliːs] – befreien, erlösen
anaesthetic [ænisˈθetik] – Betäubungs-mittel
to ease [iːz] – erleichtern, beruhigen
wrecked ['rekd] – zertrümmert
instantly ['instəntli] – augenblicklich
sedative ['sedətiv] – Beruhigungs-mittel

10. NO PARKING

close [kləus] – nah, dicht
pedestrian crossing [piˈdestriən ˈkrɔsiŋ] – Fußgänger-überweg
distance ['distəns] – Entfernung
less [les] – weniger
to leave [liːv] – verlassen
offence [əˈfens] – Vergehen
stud [stʌd] – Beschlagnagel
to be allowed [əˈlaud] – dürfen
road regulations [rəud regjuˈleiʃənz] – Verkehrs-regeln
to let s.o. off [let] – jm. gehen lassen, es bewenden lassen
warning ['wɔːniŋ] – Warnung, Mahnung
to find, found, found [faind, faund] – finden
to move on [muːv] – weitergehen, weiterfahren

11. TRAFFIC CHECK

check [tʃek] – Kontrolle
to carry out ['kæri aut] – ausführen
to switch on [switʃ] – anzünden, anschalten
main beam [mein biːm] – Fernlicht

138

0

0

to dip [dip]	– hier: abblenden
to apply the brakes [ə'plai]	– die Bremsen betätigen
breath [breθ]	– Atem
to smell [smel]	– riechen
breathalizer test ['breðəlaizə test]	– Alco-Test
tube [tju:b]	– Röhre
to blow [bləu]	– blasen
to continue [kən'tinju:]	– fortfahren

12. THE LORRY THAT STOPPED

grit [grit]	– Staub (auch:Splitt)
log sheet ['lɔg ʃi:t]	– Fahrtenbuch
record ['rekɔ:d]	– Aufzeichnung
carnet de passage	– Zollpassierscheinheft
transit document ['trænsit 'dɔkjumənt]	– Transitpapiere
load [ləud]	– Ladung
movement certificate ['mu:vmənt sə'tifikit]	– Transportbescheinigung
record player ['rekɔ:d 'pleiə]	– Plattenspieler
hi-fi equipment [hai fai i'kwipmənt]	– Hi-Fi-Anlage(n), -Gerät(e)
destination [desti'neiʃən]	– Bestimmungsort
to be aware of [ə'wɛə]	– sich bewußt sein
emergency [i'mə:dʒənsi]	– plötzliche Notlage
to take action ['ækʃən]	– Schritte unternehmen
genuine ['dʒenjuin]	– wirklich, echt

13. THE NOISY MOTORIST

residential street [rezi'denʃel stri:t]	– Straße in einem Wohnviertel
continuous [kən'tinjuəs]	– andauernd
sound [saund]	– Ton
car horn [ka: hɔ:n]	– Hupe
noise [nɔiz]	– Lärm, Geräusch

flat [flæt]	– Wohnung
horn button [hɔ:n 'bʌtn]	– Hupenknopf, Signalring
hooter [hu:tə]	– Hupe
to explain [iks'plein]	– erklären
to live [liv]	– wohnen
top floor [tɔp flɔ:]	– obere Etage
to climb up [klaim ʌp]	– hinaufsteigen
stairs [stɛəz]	– Treppe, Treppen
to waste [weist]	– verschwenden, vergeuden
to annoy [ə'nɔi]	– belästigen

14. THE EMPTY CARAVAN

caravan ['kærəvæn]	– Wohnwagen
entirely [in'taiəli]	– gänzlich, uneingeschränkt
inadvertently [inəd'vətəntli]	– unabsichtlich
to sweep away [swi:p]	– fortreißen
avalanche ['ævəla:nʃ]	– Lawine
lay-by [lei bai]	– Seitenstreifen hier: Rastplatz
apparently [ə'pærəntli]	– augenscheinlich
overcooked ['əuvəkukd]	– zu weich gekocht

III. Crime
1. THE ROBBED WOMAN

to rob [rɔb]	– berauben, stehlen
what's the matter?	– was ist los?
handbag ['hændbæg]	– Handtasche
hurt [hə:t]	– verletzt
cosh [kɔʃ]	– kleiner Totschläger
to cosh	– auf den Schädel schlagen
bump [bʌmp]	– Beule
to bleed [bli:d]	– bluten
ambulance ['æmbjuləns]	– Krankenwagen

139

X-ray ['eksrei] – Röntgen-aufnahme
hospital ['hɔspitl] – Krankenhaus
to grab [græb] – packen, an sich reißen
dazed [deizd] – betäubt
beetle ['biːtl] – Käfer
to identify [ai'dentifai] – identifizieren
spotlight ['spɔtlait] – Sucher, Scheinwerfer
roof [ruːf] – Dach
to describe [dis'kraib] – beschreiben
wavy ['weivi] – gewellt
fawn [fɔːn] – gelbbraun
by radio ['reidiəu] – über Funk

2. ARRESTING A THIEF

thief [θiːf] – Dieb
unshaven [ʌn'ʃeivn] – unrasiert
booking hall ['bukiŋ hɔːl] – Schalterhalle
to carry ['kæri] – tragen (Lasten)
suitcase [sjuːtkeis] – Koffer
leather ['leðə] – Leder
left-luggage locker [left 'lʌgidʒ 'lɔkə] – Gepäck-schließfach
enquiry [in'kwaiəri] – Erkundigung, Untersuchung
belongings [bi'lɔŋgiŋz] – Eigentum, Habselig-keiten
underclothes ['ʌndəkləuðz] – Unterwäsche
contents ['kɔntents] – Inhalt
jewels ['dʒuːəlz] – Schmuck, Juwelen
necklace ['neklis] – Halsband
means [miːnz] – Mittel
to be satisfied ['sætisfaid] – zufrieden sein

3. THE BURGLARY (1)

burglary ['bəːgləri] – Einbruch
floor [flɔː] – Etage
flat [flæt] – Wohnung
to discover [dis'kʌvə] – entdecken

to hide, hid, hidden [haid] – verstecken, verbergen
to ensure [in'ʃuə] – absichern, sicherstellen
to rejoin [ri'dʒɔin] – wiederkom-men
mess [mes] – Verwirrung, Durcheinan-der
clue [kluː] – Spur, Anhaltspunkt
to force open [fɔːs] – aufbrechen
undoubtedly [ʌn'dautidli] – unzweifelhaft
mat [mæt] – Matte
spare [spɛə] – Ersatz

4. THE BURGLARY (2)

awful ['ɔːful] – schrecklich
to disturb [dis'təːb] – zerstören, in Unordnung bringen
drawer ['drɔə] – Schublade
coin [kɔin] – Münze
wardrobe ['wɔːdrəub] – Kleider-schrank
to scatter ['skætə] – zerstreuen, hier: werfen
receipt [ri'siːt] – Quittung
to eliminate [i'limineit] – ausschalten, hier: ausschei-den
to deter [di'təː] – abschrecken, hindern

5. THE BURGLARY (3)

detective [di'tektiv] – Kriminal-beamter
to accompany [ə'kʌmpəni] – begleiten
to suspect [səs'pekt] – verdächtigen
trinket ['triŋkit] – Schmuckstück
to produce [prə'djuːs] – vorlegen
contents ['kɔntents] – Inhalt
to recognize ['rekəgnaiz] – wieder-erkennen
handle ['hændl] – Griff

label ['leibl] – Etikett, Schildchen
brooch [brəutʃ] – Brosche
bracelet ['breislit] – Armband
to rescue ['reskju:] – retten

6. THE STOLEN CAR

car park [ka: pa:k] – Parkplatz
to accelerate – beschleunigen
[æk'seləreit]
to brake [breik] – bremsen
suspect ['sʌspekt] – verdächtig
to reply [ri'plai] – antworten
nationality [næʃə'næliti] – Nationalität
hurry ['hʌri] – Eile
to cause [kɔ:z] – verursachen
to risk [risk] – aufs Spiel setzen
registration book – Kraftfahr-
[redʒis'treiʃən buk] zeugschein
he is not supposed to – er darf nicht,
[sə'pəuzd] hier: er soll nicht
colleague ['kɔli:g] – Kollege
glove compartment – Handschuh-
[glʌv kəm'pa:tmənt] fach
boot [bu:t] – beim Auto: Kofferraum
statement ['steitmənt] – Darlegung, Aussage
to take care [teik kɛə] – achtgeben, aufpassen

7. THE SHOPLIFTER

innocent ['inəsnt] – unschuldig
to investigate – untersuchen,
[in'vestigeit] ermitteln
counter ['kauntə] – Ladentisch
item [aitəm] – Gegenstand
a pack of lies – ein Bündel Lügen
receipt [ri'si:t] – Quittung
stuff [stʌf] – Zeug, Sachen
to prevent [pri'vent] – hindern, verhindern
smug [smʌg] – selbstgefällig, spießig
brand [brænd] – Sorte, Art
theft [θeft] – Diebstahl

8. THE LETTER BOMB

letter bomb ['letə bɔm] – Briefbombe
to waste [weist] – verschwenden
package ['pækidʒ] – Päckchen
store room ['stɔ:rum] – Lagerraum
to suspect ['sʌspekt] – befürchten, argwöhnen, verdächtigen
suspect (adj.) ['sʌspekt] – verdächtig
a suspect (noun) – Verdachts-
['sʌspekt] person
to deliver [di'livə] – liefern, schicken
Jewish ['dʒuiʃ] – jüdisch
suspicious [səs'piʃəs] – verdächtig
size [saiz] – Größe
customer ['kʌstəmə] – Kunde
distinctive [dis'tiŋktiv] – besonders
to wrap [ræp] – einwickeln
to seal [si:l] – versiegeln, verschließen
adhesive [əd'hi:siv] – klebend
explosive [iks'pləusiv] – Sprengstoff
to tamper with ['tæmpə] – sich zu schaffen machen an
disturbance [dis'tə:bəns] – Störung
detonator ['ditəuneitə] – Zündkapsel, Sprengkapsel
capital ['kæpitl] – Hauptstadt

9. THE KIDNAPPED BOY (1)

nanny ['næni] – Kinder-mädchen
to grab [græb] – ergreifen
to panick ['pænik] – in panischen Schrecken geraten
ransom demand – Lösegeld-
['rænsəm di'ma:nd] forderung
to hire s.o. – jm. anstellen
to extort [iks'tɔ:t] – erpressen, abnötigen

10. THE KIDNAPPED BOY (2)

to abduct [æb'dʌkt] – entführen
upholstery – Polsterung
[ʌp'həulstəri]

141

sapphire ['sæfaiə] – Saphir
diamond ['daiəmənd] – Diamant
to separate ['sepəreit] – (sich) trennen
to divorce s.o. [di·vɔ:s] – sich scheiden
lassen von
court order [kɔ:t ɔ:də] – gerichtliche
Anordnung
custody ['kʌstədi] – Sorgerecht,
Aufsicht
to emerge [i·mə:dʒ] – sich heraus-
stellen

11. THE WATER INSPECTOR

inspector [in·spektə] – Kontrolleur
to occur [ə·kə:] – sich ereignen
daughter-in-law – Schwieger-
['dɔ:tə in lɔ:] tochter
message ['mesidʒ] – Nachricht
water pressure ['preʃə] – Wasserdruck
water tap [tæp] – Wasserhahn
purse [pə:s] – Geldbörse
to doubt [daut] – zweifeln
genuine ['dʒenjuin] – echt, wahr
to pose [pəuz] – sich ausgeben
als
meter reader – Zählerableser
['mi:tə ·ri:də]
fake [feik] – Schwindler

12. THE AU PAIR GIRL

burglary ['bə:gləri] – Einbruch
to squeeze [skwi:z] – drücken,
ausdrücken
sound [saund] – gesund,
kräftig, fest
to blush [blʌʃ] – erröten
truthful ['tru:θfəl] – ehrlich, wahr-
heitsgetreu
to promise ['prɔmis] – versprechen
to depend on [di·pend] – abhängen von
to whistle ['wisl] – pfeifen
to suggest [sə·dʒest] – vorschlagen

13. THE FOOTBALL FAN

kick-off [kik ɔ:f] – Anstoß
(b. Fußball)
to approach [ə·prəutʃ] – sich nähern
copper (slang) [kɔpə] – Polizist

to doubt [daut] – zweifeln
mate [meit] – Freund,
Kamerad
supporter [sə·pɔ:tə] – Anhänger
(einer Fuß-
ballmann-
schaft)
pub [pʌb] – Wirtschaft,
Kneipe
hang on (slang) [hæŋ] – Warten Sie
mal!
to nick (slang) [nik] – klauen
announcer [ə·naunsə] – hier: Stadionsprecher
to be well-behaved – sich gut
[bi·heivd] betragen
to fancy ['fænsi] – sich vorstellen
telly (slang) ['teli] – Fernsehen

14. THE ROBBERY (1)

emergency call – Notruf
[i·mə:dʒənsi kɔ:l]
gash [gæʃ] – tiefe Schnittwunde
forehead ['fɔrid] – Stirn
nasty [nas:ti] – böse, schlimm
plaster ['pla:stə] – Pflaster
distinctive [di·stiŋktiv] – besonders,
charakteri-
stisch
windcheater – Windjacke
['windtʃi:tə]
to obtain [əb·tein] – erhalten
employer [im·plɔiə] – Arbeitgeber
cash [kæʃ] – Bargeld
to deposit [di·pɔzit] – einzahlen
stickler ['stiklə] – hier: Pedant
foolproof ['fu:lpru:f] – idiotensicher
to ram [ræm] – rammen
dizzy ['dizi] – schwindlig,
benommen

15. THE ROBBERY (2)

ability [ə·biliti] – Fähigkeit
cart track [ka:t træk] – Feldweg
hedge [hedʒ] – Hecke
level ['levl] – Höhe
to attack [ə·tæk] – angreifen
iron ['aiən] – Eisen

bar [ba:]	– Stange, Stab
to glance at	– anblicken
glancing ['gla·nsiŋ]	– *hier:* streifend
blow [bləu]	– Schlag
briefcase ['bri:fkeis]	– Aktentasche
to trace [treis]	– aufspüren, auffinden, Spur verfolgen
getaway car ['getəwei]	– Fluchtauto
to abandon [ə·bændən]	– verlassen
to be due to [dju:]	– müssen, sollen

16. THE ROBBERY (3)

to exaggerate [ig·zædʒəreit]	– übertreiben
reactionary [ri·ækʃənəri]	– Reaktionär
villain ['vilən]	– Schurke
to stage [steidʒ]	– inszenieren
to caution ['kɔ:ʃən]	– warnen
to grass *(slang)* [gra:s]	– denunzieren
share [ʃɛə]	– Anteil

17. THE DRUG ADDICT

drug [drʌg]	– Droge
addict ['ædikt]	– Süchtiger
dirty ['də:ti]	– schmutzig
pale [peil]	– blaß
to hitch-hike ['hitʃhaik]	– per Anhalter fahren
to throw, threw, thrown [θrou, θru:, θrəun]	– werfen
gutter ['gʌtə]	– Rinnstein
to contain [kən·tein]	– enthalten
to crumple ['krʌmpl]	– zerknüllen
cannabis ['kænəbis]	– Marihuana
to possess [pə·zes]	– besitzen
hemp (Indian hemp) [hemp]	– Marihuana
sleeve [sli:v]	– Ärmel
to cover ['kʌvə]	– bedecken
needle ['ni:dl]	– Nadel
syringe ['sirindʒ]	– Spritze *(medizinisch)*

18. THE BANK RAID

raid [reid]	– Überfall
counter ['kauntə]	– Schalter, Zahltisch
to be rooted to the spot ['ru:tid]	– wie angewurzelt dastehen
to be aware [ə·wɛə]	– sich bewußt sein
gun [gʌn]	– Gewehr
double-barrelled ['dʌbl ·bærəld]	– doppelläufig
butt [bʌt]	– Gewehrkolben
cashier [kæ·ʃiə]	– Kassierer(in)
immediately [i·mi:djətli]	– unverzüglich
cartridge case ['ka:tridʒ keis]	– Patronenhülse
to eject [i·dʒekt]	– hinauswerfen, wegwerfen
to be lodged in [lɔdʒd]	– *hier:* festsitzen
tattooed [tə·tu:d]	– tätowiert

IV. Asking for Help

1. THE LOST CHILD

to lose, lost, lost [lu:z, lɔst]	– verlieren
to cry [krai]	– weinen, schreien
last [la:st]	– der letzte, *hier:* zuletzt
market place ['ma:kit pleis]	– Marktplatz
to wear [wɛə]	– tragen (Kleidung)
canteen [kæn·ti:n]	– Kantine
cab-driver ['kæb ·draivə]	– Taxifahrer
to be frightened ['fraitnd]	– sich fürchten
to calm [ka:m]	– beruhigen

2. THE SICK MAN

sick [sik]	– krank
beat [bi:t]	– *hier:* Streife

suddenly ['sʌdnli] – plötzlich
kerb [kə:b] – Bordstein
heart attack – Herzanfall
['ha:t ə'tæk]
to undo [ʌn'du:] – lösen
to stagger ['stægə] – taumeln
telephone-box – Telefon-
['telifəun bɔks] häuschen
postal address – Postanschrift
['pəustl ə'dres]
to inform [in'fɔ:m] – informieren
assistance [ə'sistəns] – Hilfe
attendant [ə'tendənt] – Bediensteter
illness ['ilnis] – Krankheit
message ['mesidʒ] – Mitteilung,
Botschaft

3. THE LOST HOTEL

worried [wʌrid] – beunruhigt
on duty ['dju:ti] – Dienst haben
to realize ['riəlaiz] – erfassen,
erkennen
to remember – sich erinnern
[ri'membə]
curtain ['kə:tn] – Vorhang
receptionist – Empfangs-
[ri'sepʃənist] dame
fair-haired ['fɛə 'hɛəd] – blondhaarig
light brown – hellbraun
['lait 'braun]
I'm afraid [ə'freid] – ich fürchte,
leider
to identify [ai'dentifai] – identifizieren,
bestimmen
main entrance – Haupteingang
['mein 'entrəns]
most probably – höchstwahr-
['məust 'prɔbəbli] scheinlich
key [ki:] – Schlüssel
key tag ['ki: 'tæg] – Schlüssel-
schild

4. THE WORLD TOUR

cramp [kræmp] – Krampf
recently ['ri:sntli] – unlängst,
vor kurzem
to hitch-hike ['hitʃhaik] – per Anhalter
fahren

in particular [pə'tikjulə] – besonders
truck [trʌk] – Lastwagen
rough [rʌf] – grob, flüchtig
hostel ['hɔstel] – Herberge
to provide [prə'vaid] – bereitstellen
to accommodate – unterbringen
[ə'kɔmədeit]
to commit a crime – ein Verbre-
[kə'mit] chen begehen

5. THE CHEAP THEATRE TICKETS

goddam (slang) – verflucht
['gɔdæm]
available [ə'veiləbl] – erreichbar
sale [seil] – Verkauf
sucker (slang) ['sʌkə] – Depp
to introduce oneself – sich vorstellen
[intrə'dju:s]
to describe [dis'kraib] – beschreiben
average ['ævəridʒ] – Durchschnitt
guy (slang) [gai] – Kerl
honest ['ɔnist] – aufrichtig,
ehrlich
genuine ['dʒenjuin] – echt
to alter ['ɔ:ltə] – ändern
forgery ['fɔ:dʒəri] – Fälschung

6. THE PROWLER

prowler ['praulə] – Herumtreiber
residential area [rezi- – Wohnviertel,
'denʃəl] Villenviertel
suburb ['sʌbə:b] – Vorort
trace [treis] – Spur
chilly [tʃili] – kühl, frostig
to catch cold – sich erkälten
[kætʃ kəuld]
shrub [ʃrʌb] – Strauch
scraping [skreipiɲ] – kratzend,
scharrend
shutter [ʃʌtə] – Fensterladen
gap [gæp] – Lücke, Spalt
claustrophobia – Furcht vor
[klɔ:strə'fəubjə] geschlossenen
Räumen
to insult [in'sʌlt] – beleidigen
conspicuous – auffallend,
[kən'spikjuəs] deutlich
sichtbar

to crash [kræʃ]	– stürzen
desire [di·zaiə]	– Wunsch

7. THE SPILT BEER

to spill, spilt, spilt [spil]	– verschütten
proprietor [prə·praiətə]	– Eigentümer, Besitzer
bloke [bləuk]	– Kerl, Bursche
to punch [pʌntʃ]	– schlagen, boxen
to have a skinful *(slang)* [·skinful]	– betrunken sein
weak [wi:k]	– schwach
counter [·kauntə]	– Theke
apology [ə·pɔlədʒi]	– Entschuldigung
let alone	– *hier:* geschweige denn
cucumber [·kju:kʌmbə]	– Gurke
sober [·səubə]	– nüchtern, ernsthaft, vernünftig
to sober up	– nüchtern machen (werden)

8. THE WRONG ROOM

to shout [ʃaut]	– schreien
to rape [reip]	– vergewaltigen
to burst into [bə:st]	– hineinstürzen
to attack [ə·tæk]	– angreifen
to calm [ka:m]	– beruhigen
to scream [skri:m]	– schreien
to trip over [trip]	– fallen über
receptionist [ri·sepʃənist]	– Empfangsdame
to embarrass s.o. [im·bærəs]	– jm. in eine peinliche Lage bringen
particular [pə·tikjulə]	– besonders, speziell
to admit [əd·mit]	– zugeben
to bother [·bɔðə]	– sich kümmern
corroboration [kə,rɔbə·reiʃən]	– Bekräftigung, Bestätigung
to prove [pru:v]	– beweisen

9. THE ATTEMPTED SUICIDE

to attempt [ə·tempt]	– versuchen
suicide [·sjuisaid]	– Selbstmord
overdose [·əuvədəus]	– Überdosis
nightdress [·naitdres]	– Nachthemd
dressing gown [·dresiŋ gaun]	– Morgenrock
weak [wi:k]	– schwach
bedside cabinet [·bedsaid ·kæbinit]	– Nachttisch
to scatter [·skætə]	– verstreuen
to commit [kə·mit]	– begehen (ein Verbrechen etc.)
to threaten [·θretn]	– drohen
to dread [dred]	– sich fürchten

10. THE FIRE

wireless car [·waiəlis ka:]	– Funkwagen
to be on fire [faiə]	– brennen
to fry [frai]	– braten, backen
to be alight [ə·lait]	– brennen
fire brigade [·faiə bri·geid]	– Feuerwehr
main [mein]	– Haupt-
gas tap [·gæs ·tæp]	– Gashahn
blanket [·blæŋkit]	– Bettlaken
to smother [·smʌðə]	– ersticken, dämpfen
fire extinguisher [·faiə iks·tiŋgwiʃə]	– Feuerlöscher
to evacuate [i·vækjueit]	– fortschaffen, evakuieren
occupant [·ɔkjupent]	– Bewohner
cooker [·kukə]	– Herd
enamel [i·næməl]	– Email

USEFUL STRUCTURES

1. THE SERIOUS CRIME

nuisance [·nju:sns]	– Ärgernis, unangenehme Sache

to trudge [trʌdʒ] – stapfen
trickle ['trikl] – tröpfeln, sikkern
to admit [əd·mit] – zugeben
overtime ['əuvətaim] – Überstunden
sensible ['sensibl] – vernünftig
to be ablaze [ə·bleiz] – in Flammen stehen
to be ablaze with light – hell strahlen, beleuchtet sein
to grumble [grʌmbl] – murren, schimpfen
to retort [ri·tɔ:t] – (scharf) entgegnen
artificial [a:ti·fiʃəl] – künstlich
pendant [pendənt] – Anhänger

2. THE NEW CAR

bumper ['bʌmpə] – Stoßstange
bonnet ['bɔnit] – Motorhaube
to dent [dent] – einbeulen, eindrücken
tear, tore, torn [tɛə, tɔ:, tɔ:n] – reißen, zerreißen, herausreißen
wrecked [rekt] – zertrümmert, zerstört
to survey ['sə:vei] – überblicken, genau betrachten
savings [seiviŋs] – Ersparnisse
pride [praid] – Stolz
rear [riə] – Heck
reproachful [ri·prəutʃful] – vorwurfsvoll
safety belt ['seifti ·belt] – Sicherheitsgurt
speed [spi:d] – Geschwindigkeit
tools [tu:lz] – Werkzeug(e)
behaviour [bi·heivjə] – Benehmen
high-heeled ['hai hi:ld] – hochhackig

3. A PLEASANT PROSPECT

prospect ['prɔspekt] – Aussicht
revealing [ri·vi:liŋ] – enthüllend, hier: durchsichtig

burglary ['bə:gləri] – Einbruch
to be involved in [in·vɔlvd] – beteiligt sein an
to share [ʃɛə] – teilen
I'm afraid [ə·freid] – hier: leider
settee [se·ti:] – kleineres Sofa
to display [dis·plei] – zeigen, offenbaren
ample [æmpl] – reichlich, voll

4. THE OBSERVATION

report [ri·pɔ:t] – Bericht
to keep watch [ki:p wɔtʃ] – wachen über
to avoid [ə·vɔid] – vermeiden
fence [fens] – Zaun
suspect ['sʌspekt] – Verdächtiger
refuse collector [ri·fju:z kə·lektə] – Müllabholer
dustbin ['dʌstbin] – Mülleimer
suspicion [sə·spiʃən] – Verdacht
expenses [iks·pensiz] – Auslagen
weapon ['wepən] – Waffe
burglar ['bə:glə] – Einbrecher

5. THE INJURED BURGLAR (1)

to complain [kəm·plein] – sich beklagen
to grin [grin] – grinsen
healthy ['helθi] – gesund
to head for [hed] – sich auf etwas zubewegen

6. THE INJURED BURGLAR (2)

to stare [stɛə] – anstarren
to chase [tʃeis] – jagen, verfolgen
to claw [klɔ:] – kratzen, zerren
pet lion ['pet ·laiən] – zahmer Löwe

7. THE FAST FRENCHMAN

speed limit ['spi:d ·limit] – Geschwindigkeitsgrenze
puzzled ['pʌzld] – verwirrt
innocent ['inəsnt] – unschuldig
immediately [i·mi:djətli] – sogleich
murder ['mə:də] – Mord
to bruise [bru:z] – quetschen

146

8. THE WORRIED MAN

to be worried ['wʌrid]	– besorgt sein, sich Sorgen machen
senior officer [si:njə]	– höherer Offizier, Vorgesetzter
dejected [di·dʒektid]	– niedergeschlagen
roll [rəul]	– Brötchen

9. THE BROKEN LOCK

to query ['kwiəri]	– fragen, in Zweifel ziehen
to burst open [bə:st]	– aufbrechen
to be in luck [lʌk]	– Glück haben
to pick up [pik]	– aufheben, aufnehmen
to be embarrassed [im·bærəsd]	– verlegen sein, peinlich überrascht sein

10. FINDING A NEEDLE IN A HAYSTACK

haystack ['heistæk]	– Heuschober
load [ləud]	– Ladung
to snort [snɔ:t]	– schnauben
peddler [pedlə]	– Hausierer hier: Händler
to emerge [i·mə:dʒ]	– herauskommen
lone [ləun]	– einsam, einzeln
cell [sel]	– Zelle
curiosity [kjuəri·ɔsiti]	– Neugier
to grin [grin]	– grinsen, lächeln
conclusive [kən·klu:siv]	– schlüssig

11. THE CRAFTY FOX (1)

crafty ['kra:fti]	– schlau, listig
to keep one's wits about	– einen klaren Kopf behalten
to rely [ri·lai]	– sich verlassen
to snap [snæp]	– hier: anschnauzen
to snort [snɔ:t]	– schnauben

to beckon ['bekən]	– zuwinken, zunicken
fierce [fiəs]	– grimmig, wütend
to snarl [sna:l]	– knurren

12. THE CRAFTY FOX (2)

breathless ['breθlis]	– atemlos
forlorn [fə·lɔ:n]	– verlassen, einsam
bewilderment [bi·wildəmənt]	– Verwirrung, Bestürzung
wallet [wɔlit]	– Brieftasche
to fetch [fetʃ]	– holen
to pretend [pri·tend]	– vorgeben, vortäuschen
to hide [haid]	– verbergen
gullible ['gʌlibl]	– leichtgläubig

13. LOST

distraught [dis·trɔ:t]	– verwirrt, bestürzt
scent [sent]	– Geruch
to intend [in·tend]	– beabsichtigen
caravan ['kærəvæn]	– Wohnwagen
site [sait]	– Gelände

14. PEACE AND QUIET

to cruise [kru:z]	– herumfahren
to glance at [gla:ns]	– einen Blick werfen
assignment [ə·sainment]	– Anweisung, Aufgabe, Auftrag
shift [ʃift]	– Schicht
on leave [li:v]	– in Urlaub
estate [is·teit]	– hier: Gelände
warehouse ['wɛəhaus]	– Lagerhaus
determined [di·tə:mind]	– entschlossen
to divorce s.o. [di·vɔ:s]	– sich scheiden lassen von
to be keen [ki:n]	– hier: begeistert
to be wrapped up in one's own thoughts	– in Gedanken versunken sein

147

15. THE BARE TRUTH

to line up [lain]	– sich in einer Reihe aufstellen
suspect ['sʌspekt]	– Verdächtiger
to suspect [sə'spekt]	– verdächtigen
victim ['viktim]	– Opfer
to resist [ri'zist]	– widerstehen
temptation [temp'teiʃən]	– Versuchung
reassuring [ri:ə'ʃuəriŋ]	– beruhigend
to tear off [tɛə]	– wegreißen
to rescue ['reskju:]	– befreien, retten

16. MORE ABOUT A PIANO

ambulance ['æmbjuləns]	– Krankenwagen
utterly ['ʌtəli]	– äußerst, völlig
to embed [im'bed]	– einschließen, -graben
splintered ['splintəd]	– zersplittert
to strew, strewed, strewn [stru:]	– ausstreuen
wreckage ['rekidʒ]	– Trümmer
to pinch [pintʃ]	– kneifen, auch: stehlen
to pinch one's fingers between	– die Finger einklemmen zwischen
banister ['bænistə]	– Treppengeländer
to annoy s.o. [ə'nɔi]	– jm. ärgern, belästigen
to be annoyed	– sich ärgern
sympathetically [simpə'θetikəli]	– mitfühlend
to indicate ['indikeit]	– anzeigen
to devastate ['devəsteit]	– verwüsten

17. THE HARDER THEY FALL

sore [sɔ:]	– wund
mate [meit]	– Kumpel
tough [tʌf]	– zäh
to boast [bəust]	– sich rühmen
destination [desti'neiʃən]	– Bestimmung, Ziel
to mutter ['mʌtə]	– murmeln

handcuff [hændkʌf]	– Handschelle
wrist [rist]	– Handgelenk
railing [reiliŋ]	– Gitter, Geländer
immediately [i'mi:djətli]	– sofort, direkt
to seize [si:z]	– ergreifen

18. THE NAKED MAN

to introduce oneself [intrə'dju:s]	– sich vorstellen
to avoid [ə'vɔid]	– vermeiden
excitement [ik'saitmənt]	– Aufregung
to lead, led, led [li:d]	– führen
to search [sə:tʃ]	– durchsuchen
to inform [in'fɔ:m]	– benachrichtigen

19. THE KIND LADY

curious ['kjuəriəs]	– neugierig
to be pleased [pli:zd]	– zufrieden sein
destination [desti'neiʃən]	– Ziel
to stammer ['stæmə]	– stammeln, stottern
crippled ['kripld]	– verkrüppelt, behindert
to be embarrassed [im'bærəsd]	– verlegen sein
to pretend [pri'tend]	– vorgeben, vortäuschen

20. THE CALLER

to interrupt [intə'rʌpt]	– unterbrechen
enquiry [in'kwaiəri]	– Erkundigung
incident ['insidənt]	– Vorfall, Ereignis
to face [feis]	– hier: gegenüberliegen
intent [in'tent]	– hier: aufmerksam, gespannt
to clasp [kla:sp]	– umklammern
profuse [prə'fju:s]	– (über-)reich
nod [nɔd]	– Kopfnicken
solid ['sɔlid]	– massiv, fest

21. THE LITTLE MAN

to be employed [im'plɔid]	– beschäftigt sein

enthusiastic [in,θju:ziˈæstik] – begeistert

curious [ˈkjuəriəs] – neugierig

to clutch [klʌtʃ] – fassen, packen, halten

to bother [ˈbɔðə] – jemanden belästigen

to comfort [ˈkʌmfət] – trösten

to feel ashamed [əˈʃeimd] – sich schämen

department store [diˈpaːtmənt stɔː] – Warenhaus

to rejoin [riˈdʒɔin] – wieder treffen

similar [ˈsimilə] – gleich, ähnlich

branch [braːntʃ] – *hier:* Filiale

to gasp [gaːsp] – keuchen

desperate [ˈdespərit] – verzweifelt

familiar [fəˈmiljə] – vertraut, bekannt

brisk [brisk] – rasch, lebhaft

procedure [prəˈsiːdʒə] – Verfahren

22. THE CAR CHASE

chase [tʃeis] – Verfolgung

lay-by [ˈleibai] – Seitenstreifen

wireless operator [ˈwaiələs ˈɔpəreitə] – Funker

foreign currency [ˈkʌrənsi] – Devisen

scruffy [ˈskrʌfi] – vergammelt, schmutzig

previous [ˈpriːvjəs] – vorher

to accelerate [ækˈseləreit] – beschleunigen

to flick [flik] – anknipsen

siren [ˈsaiərin] – Sirene

to lurch [ləːtʃ] – sich ruckartig bewegen

to grit one's teeth [grit] – mit den Zähnen knirschen

to pursue [pəˈsjuː] – verfolgen

reckless [ˈreklis] – rücksichtslos

23. THE OUT-OF-DATE BURGLAR

to apologize [əˈpɔlədʒaiz] – sich entschuldigen

rope [rəup] – Seil

throat [θrəut] – Kehle

cash [kæʃ] – Bargeld

to snarl [snaːl] – knurren

to stab [stæb] – erstechen, erdolchen

to howl [haul] – heulen, schreien

to complain about [kəmˈplein] – sich beklagen über

to release [riˈliːs] – entlassen

behaviour [biˈheivjə] – Benehmen

24. THE PINK HANDBAG

pink [pink] – rosa

fashion [ˈfæʃən] – Mode

editor [ˈeditə] – Schriftleiter

employed [imˈplɔid] – angestellt

to join [dʒɔin] – *hier:* sich anschließen an

storeroom [ˈstɔːrum] – Lagerraum

to rip [rip] – zerreißen

to involve [inˈvɔlv] – *hier:* beteiligen

prisoner [ˈpriznə] – Gefangener

on purpose [ˈpəːpəs] – mit Absicht

to dump [dʌmp] – wegwerfen

to chase [tʃeis] – jagen, verfolgen

25. THE LATE DETECTIVE

to shield [ʃiːld] – schützen, beschirmen

to regain [riˈgein] – wiedergewinnen

to growl [graul] – brummen, grollen

disconcerting [diskənˈsəːtiŋ] – verwirrend, beunruhigend

reliable [riˈlaiəbl] – zuverlässig

alley [ˈæli] – Gasse

to stiffen [stifn] – starr, steif werden

to relapse [riˈlæps] – zurückfallen

faint [feint] – schwach, matt

dim [dim] – undeutlich, blaß

furtive [ˈfəːtiv] – heimlich, hinterhältig

to be level with [ˈlevl] – auf gleicher Höhe sein

149

captive ['kæptiv]	– Gefangener
malevolent	– feindselig,
[mə'levələnt]	böswillig

26. IF

desperation	– Verzweiflung
[despə'reiʃən]	
forcible ['fɔːsəbl]	– eindringlich
rabies ['reibiːz]	– Tollwut
to trace [treis]	– aufspüren,
	auffinden,
	Spur verfol-
	gen
description [dis'kripʃən]	– Beschreibung
wolf [wulf]	– Wolf
resigned [ri'zaind]	– resigniert
dog handler	– Hundeführer
[dɔg 'hændlə]	
irate [ai'reit]	– zornig,
	wütend
stung [stʌŋ]	– gereizt
well-groomed [gruːmd]	– gepflegt
paw [pɔː]	– Pfote
wallet ['wɔlit]	– Brieftasche
to sue [sjuː]	– verklagen

27. THE THREAT

threat [θret]	– Drohung
to groan [grəun]	– stöhnen
to stride, strode, strid-	– schreiten
den [straid]	
attitude ['ætitjuːd]	– Einstellung,
	Haltung
to snap [snæp]	– hier:
	jm. das Wort
	abschneiden
protection [prɔ'tekʃən]	– Schutz
trial ['traiəl]	– Prozeß,
	Gerichts-
	verfahren
to punish ['pʌniʃ]	– bestrafen

28. THE ANTIQUE RING

to shriek [ʃriːk]	– schreien
pale [peil]	– blaß
to gasp [gaːsp]	– keuchen
fake [feik]	– Fälschung

property ['prɔpəti]	– Eigentum,
	Besitz
to punish ['pʌniʃ]	– bestrafen

29. THE BURGLARY

to burgle ['bəːgl]	– einbrechen
valuable ['væljuəbl]	– wertvoll,
	kostbar
coin [kɔin]	– Münze
to scatter ['skætə]	– verstreuen
mess [mes]	– hier: Durch-
	einander,
	Unordnung
to circulate ['səːkjuleit]	– hier: in
	Umlauf setzen
description [dis'kripʃən]	– Beschreibung
to puzzle ['pʌzl]	– verwirren,
	vor ein Rätsel
	stellen
to solve [sɔlv]	– lösen

30. THE ELECTRIC DRILL

upstairs [ʌp'stɛəz]	– oben
electric drill	– elektrisches
[i'lektrik dril]	Bohrgerät
to mend [mend]	– ausbessern,
	reparieren
to prevent [pri'vent]	– hier:
	verhindern
to deny [di'nai]	– leugnen
to admit [əd'mit]	– zugeben,
	anerkennen
judge [dʒʌdʒ]	– Richter
would you mind	– würden Sie so
[maind]	freundlich
	sein
to sign [sain]	– hier: unter-
	schreiben
to escape [is'keip]	– flüchten,
	fliehen
honest ['ɔnist]	– ehrlich
to attempt [ə'tempt]	– versuchen
to persist in [pə'sist]	– beharren auf
to refuse [ri'fjuːz]	– ablehnen
to insist on [in'sist]	– bestehen auf

31. THE SECONDHAND CAR

| dilapidated | – verfallen, |
| [di'læpideitid] | baufällig |

150

exhaust [igˈzɔːst]	– Auspuff
obvious [ˈɔbviəs]	– offensichtlich, klar
bonnet [ˈbɔnit]	– Haube
to peer [piə]	– starren, spähen
compartment [kəmˈpaːtmənt]	– Fach, Abteil
mutter [mʌtə]	– murmeln
sparking plug [ˈspaːkiŋ ˈplʌg]	– Zündkerze
patch [pætʃ]	– Fleck
clumsy [ˈklʌmzi]	– ungeschickt, plump
fibreglass [ˈfaibəglaːs]	– Glaswolle
stern [stəːn]	– streng, hart
to wince [wins]	– (zusammen-)zucken
offence [əˈfens]	– Vergehen, Verstoß
tyre [taiə]	– Reifen
bodywork [ˈbɔdiwəːk]	– Karosserie
to weld [weld]	– zusammenschweißen
to reline [riˈlain]	– neu belegen (Bremsen)
to adjust [əˈdʒʌst]	– regulieren, abstimmen
to rewire [riˈwaiə]	– neu verkabeln, neue Leitung legen
to overhaul [ˈouvəhɔːl]	– überholen, überprüfen
to be in despair [disˈpɛə]	– verzweifelt sein
bargain [ˈbaːgin]	– vorteilhaftes Geschäft, günstiger Kauf

32. THE CROOK

crook [kruk]	– Gauner
plain [plein]	– einfach
van [væn]	– Lieferwagen
conspicuous [kənˈspikjuəs]	– auffallend, auffällig
to reveal [riˈviːl]	– enthüllen, aufdecken

simultaneous [siməlˈteinjəs]	– gleichzeitig
suspicious [səˈspiʃəs]	– verdächtig
menacing [ˈmenəsiŋ]	– drohend

33. THE LADDER

ladder [ˈlædə]	– Leiter
window cleaner [ˈwindəu ˈkliːnə]	– Fensterputzer
counter [ˈkauntə]	– Theke
wallet [ˈwɔlit]	– Brieftasche
to escape [isˈkeip]	– flüchten
to dump [dʌmp]	– wegwerfen, auskippen

34. THE COAT

convenient [kənˈviːnjənt]	– bequem
to regret [riˈgret]	– bedauern
alert [əˈləːt]	– hier: rege, munter
to slide, slid, slid [slaid, slid]	– gleiten
cash desk [ˈkæʃ ˈdesk]	– Kasse
to take charge [teik tʃaːdʒ]	– Verantwortung, Aufsicht übernehmen
to commit [kəˈmit]	– begehen, verüben
unaware [ˈʌnəˈwɛə]	– nicht wissend
to emerge [iˈməːdʒ]	– auftauchen, in Erscheinung treten
rack [ræk]	– Gestell, Gerüst, (Kleider-)Ständer
to snort [snɔːt]	– (wütend) schnauben

35. THE MARRIED MAN (1)

to investigate [inˈvestigeit]	– untersuchen, ermitteln
bigamy [ˈbigəmi]	– Bigamie
previous [ˈpriːvjəs]	– vorausgehend
belongings [biˈlɔŋiŋz]	– Habseligkeiten

indignant [in'dignənt]	– ungehalten, empört
to confirm [kən'fə:m]	– bekennen
to leap, leapt, leapt [li:p]	– springen
to share [ʃɛə]	– teilen
to burst into tears [bə:st]	– in Tränen ausbrechen

36. THE MARRIED MAN (2)

to keep watch [wɔtʃ]	– Wache halten, aufpassen
to give evidence ['evidəns]	– (als Zeuge) aussagen
yet again [jet]	– noch einmal, schon wieder
smugly [smʌgli]	– selbstzufrieden
court [kɔ:t]	– Gericht
witness ['witnis]	– Zeuge
valuable ['væljuəbl]	– wertvoll

37. THE SWINDLER

self-assured [self ə'ʃuəd]	– selbstsicher
to treat [tri:t]	– behandeln
to frown [fraun]	– die Stirn runzeln
Brazil [brə'zil]	– Brasilien

deposit [di'pɔzit]	– hier: Anzahlung
to pause [pɔ:z]	– innehalten
receipt [ri'si:t]	– Quittung
to fool [fu:l]	– hier: täuschen
to prove [pru:v]	– beweisen
to acquit [ə'kwit]	– entlasten, freisprechen
fraud [frɔ:d]	– Betrug
scrap [skræp]	– hier: Schrott

38. DECISIONS, DECISIONS!

gate [geit]	– Tor
steady ['stedi]	– sicher, fest, zuverlässig
neat [ni:t]	– hier: säuberlich, geschickt
confident ['kɔnfidənt]	– zuversichtlich, vertraulich
colt [kəult]	– Fohlen
mane [mein]	– Mähne
matted ['mætid]	– struppig
to avoid [ə'vɔid]	– vermeiden
groomed [gru:md]	– gepflegt, hier: aufgeputzt
huge [hju:dʒ]	– sehr groß
pile [pail]	– Haufen, Stoß
size [saiz]	– Größe
to make up one's mind	– sich entschließen

READING TEXTS

1. OPERATIONAL POLICE STRUCTURES

recommendation [rekəmen·deiʃən] – Empfehlung, Vorschlag

working party ['wə:kiŋ ·pa:ti] – Arbeitsausschuß, Arbeitsgruppe

rank [rænk] – Dienstgrad, Rang

evaluation [ivælju·eiʃən] – Bewertung, Beurteilung

to attach to [ə·tætʃ] – zuordnen

to be in charge [tʃa:dʒ] – leiten, verantwortlich sein

division [di·viʒən] – Abschnitt (Bezirk)

subdivision – Unterabschnitt

deputy ['depjuti] – Vertreter, Beauftragter

officer in charge of a relief [ri·li:f] – für die Wachablösung verantwortlicher Beamter

detached [di·tætʃt] – abgesondert, selbständig

resident constable ['rezidənt] – Einzelposten (ortsgebunden)

designate ['dezigneit] – bestimmen, ernennen

distribution [distri·bjuʃən] – Verteilung, Gliederung

2. THE ROLE OF THE CHIEF CONSTABLE

chief constable [tʃi:f ·kʌnstəbl] – höchster Dienstgrad der englischen Polizei (außer London)

section ['sekʃən] – Abschnitt

commissioner [kə·miʃnə] – höchster Dienstgrad der Londoner Polizei

to prosecute ['prəsikju:t] – strafrechtlich verfolgen, anklagen

accountable [ə·kauntəbl] – verantwortlich

delegated ['deligeitid] – übertragen sein

to be at s.o.'s discretion [dis·kreʃən] – im eigenen Ermessen von jm. stehen

police authority [pə·li:s ə·θəriti] – Polizeibehörde

to require s.o. to do sth. [ri·kwaiə] – von jm. verlangen etwas zu tun

to submit [səbmit] – vortragen, vorlegen

discharge of functions [dis·tʃa:dʒ] – hier: Amtsausübung, Erledigung der Amtspflichten

to refer [ri·fə:] – verweisen, zur Entscheidung übergeben

to provide for [prə·vaid] – vorsehen, bestimmen

to provide with – versehen mit, versorgen

county council [kaunti kaunsl] – Grafschaftsrat, (Behörde)

latter ['lætə] – letzterer

3. BASIC POLICE OBJECTIVES

objective [əb·dʒektiv] – Ziel, Zielvorstellung

to minimise ['minimaiz] – auf das Mindestmaß zurückführen

disaster [di·za:stə] – Katastrophe

to achieve [ə·tʃi:v] – erreichen

emphasis ['emfəsis] – Betonung, Nachdruck

to safeguard ['seifga:d] – schützen, sichern

maintenance ['meintinəns] – Erhaltung, Wartung

153

to supplement ['sʌplimənt] – ergänzen

involvement [in'vɔlvmənt] – Einbezogenheit, Beteiligung

beyond [bi'jɔnd] – darüber hinaus, jenseits

province ['prɔvins] – Aufgabenbereich, Wirkungskreis

to assume [ə'sju:m] – annehmen, auf sich nehmen

e.g. [i: dʒi] – zum Beispiel

to trace [treis] – aufspüren, auffinden

domestic dispute [də'mestik dis'pju:t] – Familienstreitigkeit

to confine [kən'fain] – beschränken

enforcement [in'fɔ:smənt] – Durchsetzung, Durchführung

4. FOOT-PATROLS

consideration [kənsidə'reiʃen] – Erwägung, Überlegung

value ['vælju:] – Wert

to obtain [əb'tein] – erlangen, sich verschaffen

distraction [dis'trækʃən] – Ablenkung

to focus on ['fəukəs] – *hier:* konzentrieren

prominent ['prɔminənt] – auffallend, berühmt

deterrent [di'terənt] – Abschreckung, Abschreckungsmittel

available [ə'veiləbl] – verfügbar

to solve [sɔlv] – auflösen, aufklären

provided [prə'vaidid] – vorausgesetzt

to equip [i'kwip] – ausrüsten

to tackle ['tækl] – anpacken, in Angriff nehmen

scope [skəup] – Spielraum

width [widθ] – Breite, Weite

tension ['tenʃən] – Spannung

to erupt [i'rʌpt] – ausbrechen

fatigued [fə'ti:gd] – ermüdet

contribution [kɔntri'bju:ʃən] – Beitrag

proviso [prə'vaizəu] – Vorbehalt

dormitory area ['dɔ:mitri 'ɛəriə] – außerhalb gelegenes Wohnviertel einer Großstadt

factory estate ['fæktəri is'teit] – Industriegebiet

dense [dens] – dicht

to put at risk [risk] – in Gefahr bringen

vulnerable ['vʌlnərəbl] – verwundbar

skirmish ['skə:miʃ] – Rauferei, Zusammenstoß

to preclude [pri'klu:d] – ausschließen

scheme [ski:m] – Schema, Entwurf, Plan

5. MOTOR CYCLES AND SCOOTERS

manpower ['mænpauə] – Arbeitskraft, (-kräfte)

labour-saving ['leibə 'seiviŋ] – arbeitssparend

device [di'vais] – Einrichtung

due to [dju:] – wegen

to quit [kwit] – verlassen, aufgeben

reluctant [ri'lʌktənt] – widerwillig, widerstrebend

allotted to [ə'lɔtid] – zugeteilt

disadvantage [dis'ədva:ntidʒ] – Nachteil

inclement [in'klemənt] – rauh, unfreundlich

to convey [kən'vei] – befördern, fortschaffen

bulky ['bʌlki] – sperrig

comparatively [kəm'pærətivli] – verhältnismäßig

6. PEDAL CYCLE

to increase [in'kri:s] – vergrößern, vermehren

to decrease [di:'kri:s] – verringern, abnehmen

optional ['ɔpʃənəl] – wahlfrei

moderate ['mɔdərit] – mittelmäßig, mäßig

little concern [litl kən'sə:n] – geringe Wichtigkeit

7. MOTOR CARS AND POLICE VANS

effort ['efət] – Anstrengung

to estimate ['estimeit] – schätzen

adverse ['ædvə:s] – ungünstig

reluctance [ri'lʌktəns] – Widerstreben, Abneigung

fuel consumption ['fjuəl kən'sʌmpʃen] – Brennstoffverbrauch

8. JOAN'S THE VILLAGE BOBBY

to reckon ['rekən] – errechnen, kalkulieren hier: der Meinung sein

Bwlchgwyn ['blətʃgwin] – Ort in Wales

to turn a cartwheel ['ka:twi:l] – ein Rad schlagen

gymnasium [dʒim'neizjəm] – Turnhalle

to be over the moon – außer sich sein

crossbred ['krɔsbred] – gekreuzt (biol.)

shipshape ['ʃipʃeip] – in tadelloser Ordnung

substation ['sʌbsteiʃən] – Polizeiposten

to cope [kəup] – fertig werden, gewachsen sein

lack [læk] – Mangel

annexe [ə'neks] – Nebengebäude

initial training [i'niʃəl] – hier: Grundausbildung

shift [ʃift] – Schicht

bemused [bi'mju:zd] – verwirrt

resourceful [ri'sɔ:sful] – einfallsreich, erfinderisch

to summon ['sʌmən] – (herbei)rufen, kommen lassen

funeral ['fju:nərəl] – Begräbnis

scattered ['skætəd] – verstreut

handcuffs ['hændkʌfs] – Handschellen

ditch [ditʃ] – Graben

barbed wire [ba:bd waiə] – Stacheldraht

prospect of ['prɔspekt] – Aussicht auf

stride [straid] – Schritt, Gang

to take sth. in one's stride – mit etw. spielend fertigwerden

9. SOCIAL VIOLENCE

social violence ['səuʃəl 'vaiələns] – soziale Gewalt, Gewaltäußerungen, Gewalttätigkeit

universal suffrage [juni'və:sl 'sʌfridʒ] – allgemeines Wahlrecht

Chartist ['tʃa:tist] – Mitglied der Chartistenbewegung (ca. 1840)

suffragette [sʌfrə'dʒet] – Frauenrechtlerin

to impose [im'pəuz] – auferlegen, aufbürden, aufdrängen

within the bounds [baundz] – im Bereich

threat [θret] – Drohung

sophistication [səfisti'keiʃən] – Ausgeklügeltheit, Verfeinerung, intellektuelle Einstellung

striking power ['straikiŋ] – Schlagkraft

to inspire [in'spaiə] – anfeuern, anregen

irrespective to [iris'pektiv] – ohne Rücksicht auf

hostage ['hɔstidʒ] – Geisel

155

to deal with [di:l]	– in Angriff nehmen, bekämpfen, sich befassen mit
clash [klæʃ]	– Konflikt, Kollision
reminiscent of [remiˈnisnt]	– erinnernd an
riot [ˈraiət]	– Aufruhr
impartiality [ˈimpa:ʃiˈæliti]	– Unparteilichkeit
asset [ˈæset]	– Vorteil
picket [ˈpikit]	– hier: Streikposten
intimidation [intimiˈdeiʃən]	– Einschüchterung
to subvert [sʌbˈvə:t]	– zerrütten, untergraben

10. POLICE DEVELOPMENTS

in terms of [tə:mz]	– in bezug auf, hinsichtlich
unprecedented [ʌnˈpresidəntid]	– beispiellos, noch nie dagewesen
training facilities [treiniŋ fəˈsiliti:z]	– Ausbildungsmöglichkeiten
lengthy [ˈleŋθi]	– sehr lang, ausführlich
contingency [kənˈtindʒənsi]	– unvorhergesehenes Ereignis
to participate [pa:tisipeit]	– teilnehmen
available [əˈveiləbl]	– verfügbar, vorhanden
flood [flʌd]	– Flut
key requirement [ki: riˈkwaiəmənt]	– wesentliche Voraussetzung
to improve [imˈpru:v]	– verbessern
demand [diˈma:nd]	– Forderung

11. POLICE AND DEMOCRACY

framework [ˈfreimwə:k]	– Gerüst, Gefüge, System

safeguard [ˈseifga:d]	– Schutz, Sicherstellung
plot [plɔt]	– Anschlag, hier: Handlung
challenge [ˈtʃælindʒ]	– Herausforderung
populace [ˈpɔpjuləs]	– breite Masse, breite Öffentlichkeit
countless [kauntlis]	– zahllos
outlaw [ˈautlɔ:]	– Verbrecher
to hire [ˈhaiə]	– mieten, jemanden anstellen
gunfighter [ˈgʌnfaitə]	– Gewehrschütze
to restore [riˈstɔ:]	– wiederherstellen
oppressive [əˈpresiv]	– drückend, unterdrückend
inhibition [inhiˈbiʃən]	– Verbot
to be constrained [kənˈstreind]	– hier: zur Mäßigkeit angehalten sein
to achieve [əˈtʃi:v]	– vollenden, ausführen
considerable [kənˈsidərebl]	– beträchtlich, erheblich
formidable [ˈfɔmidəbl]	– gewaltig, ungeheuer
array [əˈrei]	– Reihe, Menge, Aufgebot
to favour [ˈfeivə]	– begünstigen
to sacrifice [ˈsækrifais]	– opfern
unconvincing [ˈʌnkənˈvinsiŋ]	– nicht überzeugend
fallacious [fəˈleiʃəs]	– trügerisch, irreführend
assumption [əˈsʌmpʃən]	– Annahme
dispersal [disˈpə:səl]	– Zersplitterung, Zerstreuung
supremacy [sjuˈpreməsi]	– Souveränität, Überlegenheit
to prove [pru:v]	– sich erweisen, beweisen
impotent [ˈimpotənt]	– unfähig

12. TRAFFIC POLICING AND SELF-CONTROL

self-control [self kən·troul] – Selbstbeherrschung

law enforcement [lɔ: in·fɔ:sment] – Gesetzesvollzug

to epitomise [i·pitəmaiz] – darstellen, ausdrücken

to conclude [kən·klu:d] – zu dem Schluß kommen, folgern

to deprive [di·praiv] – berauben

livelihood [·laivlihud] – Lebensunterhalt, Auskommen

jail [dʒeil] – Gefängnis

to sneak [sni:k] – schleichen, *hier:* sich vordrängeln

to be liable to [·laiəbl] – wahrscheinlich sein

to assert [ə·sə:t] – behaupten, Anspruch geltend machen

to maroon [mə·ru:n] – aussetzen

to rely upon [ri·lai] – sich verlassen auf

pedestrian precinct [pri:siŋkt] – Fußgängerzone

to get snarled up [sna:ld] – in eine Stokkung geraten

diminution [dimi·nju:ʃən] – Verminderung

cop *(slang)* [kɔp] – Polizeibeamter

to harden [·ha:dn] – erhärten, verfestigen

futile [·fju:tail] – wirkungslos, sinnlos

vigorous [·vigərəs] – kraftvoll, energisch